Business
Advantage

Student's Book
Advanced
Martin Lisboa and Michael Handford

CAMBRIDGE
UNIVERSITY PRESS

CAMBRIDGE
UNIVERSITY PRESS

University Printing House, Cambridge CB2 8BS, United Kingdom

One Liberty Plaza, 20th Floor, New York, NY 10006, USA

477 Williamstown Road, Port Melbourne, VIC 3207, Australia

4843/24, 2nd Floor, Ansari Road, Daryaganj, Delhi – 110002, India

79 Anson Road, #06–04/06, Singapore 079906

Cambridge University Press is part of the University of Cambridge.

It furthers the University's mission by disseminating knowledge in the pursuit of education, learning and research at the highest international levels of excellence.

www.cambridge.org
Information on this title: www.cambridge.org/9780521181846

First published 2012
20 19 18 17 16 15 14 13 12 11 10 9 8 7

Printed in Dubai by Oriental Press

A catalogue record for this publication is available from the British Library

ISBN 978-0-521-18184-6 Student's Book with DVD
ISBN 978-0-521-17932-4 Teacher's Book
ISBN 978-1-107-63783-2 Personal Study Book with Audio CD
ISBN 978-1-107-66634-4 Audio CDs

Map of the course

Topic: International marketing	Lesson	Focus	Language	Input: Reading / Listening	Output: Speaking / Writing
Unit 1: Market entry strategies	1.1 Theory	An overview of market entry strategies	Market entry terms and concepts	Interview with Dr Dennis De, ESB Business School / *An Introduction to International Marketing* by Keith Lewis and Matthew Housden, University of Greenwich	Select an appropriate market entry strategy for a private university
	1.2 Practice / Case study	Entering the global market	Adding emphasis to explanations	*Quintessentially Group* Interview with Paul Drummond, Co-founder and Group Commercial Director	Select a franchise partner in a new country market
	1.3 Skills	Brainstorming	Strategies for moving discussions forward	Recording of a management training session on brainstorming	Brainstorm a new brand slogan
Unit 2: Standardisation and differentiation	2.1 Theory	Different approaches to international marketing	Word formations and word partnerships	Two perspectives on international marketing – Dr Marieke de Mooij, University of Navarra and Dr Jim Blythe, University of Glamorgan	Adapt advertisements to fit different cultures
	2.2 Practice / Case study	Standardisation and differentiation of a product in different markets	Language to describe brands, products and markets	*Piaggio Vietnam* interview with Costantino Sambuy, CEO	Decide where to position a brand in a specific market
	2.3 Skills	Time management	The language of time management	Extract of a lecture by Randy Pausch, Virginia University / meeting extract to discuss time management at an IT company	Advise an employee on better time management
Writing 1	Writing notes for presentation slides	Create effective notes for presentations	Language for preparing presentation slides	Presentation materials from Eye to Eye Television	Prepare and deliver a welcome presentation

▶◀ **Watch Sequence 1 on the DVD to find out more about International marketing.**

Topic: Competition and entrepreneurship	Lesson	Focus	Language	Input: Reading/Listening	Output: Speaking/Writing
Unit 3: Competition within industries	3.1 Theory	Porter's Five Forces Theory of Competition	Different ways of making comparisons	Interview with Dr Alex Muresan, London Metropolitan University	Analyse and present an industry's competitive forces
	3.2 Practice / Case study	Competition within an industry	Noun phrases	*The UK budget hotel industry* article from *Daily Mail*	Present a hotel chain to potential investors
	3.3 Skills	Making a sales pitch	Persuasive language	Extract from a sales presentation by *Bizantra*	Make a persuasive e-presentation of a product or service
Unit 4: Entrepreneurship	4.1 Theory	Ways of fostering entrepreneurship	Language for giving informal advice	Interview with Dr Shai Vyakarnam, Cambridge Judge Business School, University of Cambridge	Propose a project to foster entrepreneurship in schools
	4.2 Practice / Case study	Entrepreneurship in action	Quantifying data	*Jack Ma (Alibaba)* Extract from *The Inside Story Behind Jack Ma and the Creation of the World's Biggest Online Marketplace*	Explore ideas for starting a business in China
	4.3 Skills	Collaborative and aggressive negotiation strategies	Negotiating language	Extract from a negotiation between a manufacturer and a supplier	Negotiate on price
Writing 2	Business plan and executive summary	The structure of a business plan	Key features of an executive summary	Advice on writing a business plan from *Royal Bank of Canada*	Write an outline business plan

▶◀ **Watch Sequence 2 on the DVD to find out more about Competition and entrepreneurship.**

Topic: Management and leadership	Lesson	Focus	Language	Input: Reading/Listening	Output: Speaking/Writing
Unit 5: Crisis management	5.1 Theory	Dealing with crisis events	Comparison of strategy and tactics	Extract from *The Black Swan – The Impact of the Highly Improbable* by Dr Nassim Nicholas Taleb	Decide tactics to deal with crisis events
	5.2 Practice / Case study	Successfully dealing with a crisis	Financial terms	*Ceramic Fuel Cells Ltd* Interview with Brendan Dow, Managing Director	Prepare for 'What if … ?' scenarios
	5.3 Skills	Dealing with conflict	Conflictual idioms and metaphors	Extract from a meeting between a restaurant manager and drinks supplier	Deal with a conflictual situation
Unit 6: Leadership	6.1 Theory	Leadership styles and qualities	Describing leadership styles and behaviour	Extract from 'Leadership that gets results' by Daniel Goleman in *Havard Business Review*	Choose a leader to fit a specific type of organisation
	6.2 Practice / Case study	A business leader	Understanding proverbs	Interview with Nikki King, UK Businesswoman of the Year	Advising an organisation on leadership
	6.3 Skills	Motivating staff	Transactional and transformational language	Extract from a team-building meeting in a hotel	Motivate a staff member
Writing 3	Write effective emails	Email exchanges	Features of effective emails	Emails from a chain of correspondence amongst colleagues	Write a fast email exchange between colleagues

▶◀ **Watch Sequence 3 on the DVD to find out more about Management and leadership.**

Topic: Globalisation	Lesson	Focus	Language	Input: Reading/Listening	Output: Speaking/Writing
Unit 7: International communication	7.1 Theory	Culture in international business	Key intercultural words and concepts	Interview with Dr Fons Trompenaars, President of Trompenaars Hampden-Turner	Explore and present a work culture
	7.2 Practice / Case study	Internationalising a company	Linking ideas and information	*Rakuten* an article on their English language policy from *The Japan Times*	Develop an English language policy for an international company
	7.3 Skills	Conducting successful intercultural communication	Collaborative turn-taking	Extracts from interviews with business experts	Make recommendations to improve communication in an international company
Unit 8: International outsourcing	8.1 Theory	Avoiding outsourcing pitfalls	Outsourcing language	Extract from a journal article by Jérôme Barthélemy, ESSEC Business School	Discuss cases of extreme outsourcing
	8.2 Practice / Case study	Offshore outsourcing	Modifiers and intensifiers	*Business Processing Association Philippines* Interview with Gigi Virata, Senior Executive Director	Resolve misunderstandings between client and outsourcing provider
	8.3 Skills	Dealing with Q&A	Inviting and replying to questions	The Q&A session from an annual shareholder meeting	Deal with a Q&A session discussing staff redundancies
Writing 4	Follow-up emails	Responding to emails	Reminding, explaining and requesting	Email from a sales company in USA to a client in China	Write an email to a potential client

▶◀ **Watch Sequence 4 on the DVD to find out more about Globalisation.**

Topic: Design, technology and innovation	Lesson	Focus	Language	Input: Reading/Listening	Output: Speaking/Writing
Unit 9: Affordable innovation	9.1 Theory	Affordable innovation through reverse innovation	Concepts of innovation	Article *Made in India for the World* from *Business Today, India*	Debate low-cost innovation solutions
	9.2 Practice / case study reverse	Low-cost reverse innovation in practice	Word partnerships	*GE Healthcare* interview with Professor Vijay Govindarajan, Chief Innovations Officer	Develop a reverse innovation marketing strategy
	9.3 Skills	Dealing with criticism	Direct, indirect, negative and constructive criticism	Extract from a marketing meeting	Make and take criticism
Unit 10: Design and invention	10.1 Theory	Design in business	Noun–noun word partnerships	Interview with Dr Clare Brass, Royal College of Art	Design a solution to an everyday problem
	10.2 Practice / Case study	A design-led company	Multiple adjectives / Making analogies	*Dyson* An article about Dyson and an extract from an interview with Sir James Dyson, founder	Explain unusual inventions to potential investors
	10.3 Skills	Communicating negative information in a positive light	Understand euphemisms	Extracts of a presentation given by the Sales Director of a large telecommunications company to managers	Communicate negative information and bad news in a positive way
Writing 5	Writing for meetings	Notes, minutes and agenda	Structure and style in meeting minutes	Extracts from and agenda for a meeting at a large Management Consultancy	Produce an agenda, notes and minutes of an issue affecting the workforce

▶◀ **Watch Sequence 5 on the DVD to find out more about Design, technology and innovation.**

Topic: Trade, finance and the economy	Lesson	Focus	Language	Input: Reading / Listening	Output: Speaking / Writing
Unit 11: The economic environment	11.1 Theory	Government influence on the economic environment	Word partnerships and verb patterns	Interview with Tatiana Damjanovic, University of Exeter	Assess impact of government and central bank action on a family household
	11.2 Practice / Case study	Managing economic and financial risk	Economic and financial terms and phrases	*Unilever* Extract from company annual report	Advise a company on managing financial risk
	11.3 Skills	Presenting charts and statistics	Language for structuring and describing	Extracts from a presentation on *Driving International Success: Reaching Auto Consumers Globally* by Josh Crandall, President of Netpop Research	Represent data on a chart and present it on a slide
Unit 12: International trade	12.1 Theory	Free trade or protectionism?	Inversion	Extracts from *Making Globalization Work* by Joseph Stiglitz	Debate arguments for and against free trade
	12.2 Practice / Case study	The impact of signing a free trade agreement	Terms of economic convergence and divergence	*NAFTA Office of Mexico in Canada* Interview with Carlos Piñera, Chief Representative	Look at reasons for and against joining a free trade association from business and government perspectives
	12.3 Skills	Managing meetings	Language for negotiating problems	Extracts from a meeting at a business training provider	Overcome problems in meetings
Writing 6	Reporting statistical information	Describing graphs with financial and economic data	Trends, developments and changes	Financial information on leading oil companies	Write a report

▶◀ **Watch Sequence 6 on the DVD to find out more about Trade, finance and the economy.**

Topic: 21st-century enterprise	Lesson	Focus	Language	Input: Reading / Listening	Output: Speaking / Writing
Unit 13: Sustainable development	13.1 Theory	The triple bottom line	Topic vocabulary	Extracts from *The Triple Bottom Line: What Is It and How Does It Work?* by Dr Timothy F. Slaper and Tanya J. Hall	Use the triple bottom line to discuss impacts on stakeholders
	13.2 Practice / Case study	The sustainable city	Contrasting language	*Masdar City* promotional presentation	Develop a sustainable city
	13.3 Skills	Problem-solving	Suggestions and advice	Extracts from a discussion at a pharmaceutical company	Discuss solutions to problems in a meeting
Unit 14: Social enterprise	14.1 Theory	Perspectives on social enterprise	Word partnerships	Interviews with Professor Jane Wei-Skillern, Stanford Graduate Business School and Dr Helen Haugh, Cambridge Judge Business School, University of Cambridge	Discuss funding for a social enterprise in crisis
	14.2 Practice / Case study	A social enterprise in action	Referencing	*Trashy Bags* Extracts from company website	Compete for a work placement opportunity
	14.3 Skills	Conference calls	Managing a conference call and interrupting language	A conference call between employees of *RESNA*	Participate in a conference call to discuss branding
Writing 7	Writing a covering letter for a CV	Job applications	Error correction	Career advice from a job recruitment agency	Write a CV covering letter

▶◀ **Watch Sequence 7 on the DVD to find out more about 21st-century enterprise.**

Authors' thanks

We are enormously grateful to all those people who contributed, supported and put up with us during the writing process. Particular thanks go to all the team at Cambridge University Press. To our editor Neil Holloway, who has played several roles in the project – a clear-minded editor, a motivating guide, a critical reader, and a solid supporter and helper. To Chris Capper, the publisher, for being a firm guiding hand who led the project with skill and diplomacy. To Lyn Strutt for copy-editing with great skill, enthusiasm and a keen eye for detail. To Laurence Koster for a great job with the DVD. To Chris Doggett and Kay George for helping to track down all the permissions that have retained the book's authenticity.

Our thanks go to all the interviewees, who kindly gave us their time and valued expertise: Dr Dennis De, Paul Drummond, Costantino Sambuy, Andrew Guy, Dr Alex Muresan, Dr Shai Vyakarnam, Brendan Dow, Nikki King, David Prasher, Dr Fons Trompenaars, Professor Hiro Tanaka, Charlie Peppiatt, Tim Rabone, Gigi Virata, Professor Vijay Govindarajan, Dr Clare Brass, Sir James Dyson, Dr Tatiana Damjanovic, Carlos Piñera, Professor Jane Wei-Skillern, Dr Helen Haugh.

We would like to thank our students, colleagues, friends and family, who have helped so much to make this book what it is.

Martin: Thanks to my wife Manuela and my children Max and Nico for their good sense of humour and understanding of life outside the world of *Business Advantage*. Thanks are also very much in order to the numerous students, colleagues and friends in business and academia whose ideas and suggestions have added real value to the material.

Michael: I owe a debt of gratitude to Martin, my co-author, and to Neil Holloway and Chris Capper, for their considerable support and understanding. Also, thanks to my wife Mayu and daughters Maya and Julia for keeping me going, and to my students and teachers for educating me.

Introduction

What is *Business Advantage* and how can it help you?

Welcome to *Business Advantage* Advanced. *Business Advantage* gives you the theory, practice and skills that will lead you to success in international business.

Business Advantage Advanced is the third book in the *Business Advantage* series. It is aimed at students who wish to progress through the C1–C2 level.

How is the course organised?

There are 14 units in each book. The unit topics at the Advanced level have been chosen to provide you with key themes of business taught on a general management training course or on an academic Business Studies course. Each unit is divided into four lessons.

- **Theory**
  Presented by professors and lecturers from business schools and universities – you will gain new understanding of key business principles and ideas.

- **Practice**
  A case study based on texts and interviews with managers in *real* companies – you will learn how business theory is applied in practice in the real world.

- **Skills**
  Based on *real* recorded communications in companies – you will understand how business people *really* speak to help you perform successfully at work.

- **Writing**
  Based on authentic material which will enable you to produce a variety of effective written business communications (every two units).

What is included in each lesson?

Introduction

You are introduced to the main content in a user-friendly format. We use your personal experiences, visual images and quizzes to prepare you carefully.

Language focus

To improve and broaden your vocabulary and grammatical range. The language syllabus covers the main tenses and grammatical structures appropriate to your level plus key vocabulary and phrases. The language presented is drawn extensively from research and actual examples of English used in business taken from the Cambridge English Corpus 👁 – one of the world's largest databases of authentic written and spoken language. You can be confident that the language presented is real language used in business today.

Reading or Listening

Introduces and develops theories, topics and ideas about business that are useful in both English and your own language. You also have the chance to improve your speaking skills through discussion questions at the end of each section.

Output

Each lesson builds to a final Output section. This is usually a group task where you have to *use* the language and ideas presented to solve a problem or deal with a business dilemma or issue.

Critical analysis and Intercultural analysis

Every unit also includes at least one Critical analysis and Intercultural analysis section. Critical analysis will help you develop questioning skills that are necessary in the academic and business world. Intercultural analysis will help you develop an understanding of your own culture and other cultures – a vital skill in today's business world.

Transferable skill

You will also find a Transferable skill section in each unit which will provide you with some very useful tools, such as speed-reading techniques, that will improve the way you learn and the way you work.

What is on the DVD?

The DVD in the Student's Book contains video case studies to watch after every two units. You can use the DVD for extra listening practice and to find out more about the business topics in *Business Advantage*. There are documentaries filmed at companies as well as round-table discussions filmed with MBA students from the Cambridge Judge Business School, University of Cambridge. When you see ▶◀ in your Student's Book, ask your teacher about watching the DVD sequence in class, or watch it at home on your computer or TV.

The video case studies are accompanied by worksheets available on the *Business Advantage* website: **www.cambridge.org/elt/businessadvantage**

What is in the Personal Study Book?

The Personal Study Book gives you extra practice of the grammar, vocabulary and skills you have covered in the Student's Book. There are also additional reading activities focusing on inspirational business leaders and thinkers, together with further case studies on a variety of organisations.

Where can I find more activities?

Ask your teacher about the Professional English Online website for extra activities to do in class: **www.cambridge.org/elt/pro**

Martin Lisboa is a teacher, presenter and author. His interests span EAP, Business ELT, Business Studies and doing business. He has an MBA from the OU Business School and has taught in Mexico, the UK and Italy. Martin set up his own executive language school in London, and was Senior Lecturer at London Metropolitan University and Assistant Director (Marketing) at the British Council, Milan.

Michael Handford PhD (Nottingham) works at the University of Tokyo, where he is professor of the Institute for Innovation in International Engineering Education. He is the author of *The Language of Business Meetings* (Cambridge University Press), and has worked as a communication consultant with several multinational companies.

1 Market entry strategies

1.1 Theory: An overview of market entry strategies

Learning outcomes
- Understand how companies enter new geographical markets.
- Learn terms and concepts connected to market entry strategies.
- Select an appropriate market entry strategy for a management education institution.

Introduction

1 Ford cars are produced in many countries, but the 'nationality' of the company is American. Ask other students what products they use, and complete the table on the right.

2 Discuss the following questions about products you use that are <u>not</u> produced by local companies in your country.

1 How do you think these foreign companies get their products into the hands of consumers in your country?

2 What are some of the risks and opportunities facing companies when they enter a new market?

	Brand and / or model name	Nationality of company
computer		
mobile phone		
car/motorbike		
favourite clothes brand		
favourite drink		
favourite food		

Business view

Dr Dennis De is Professor of Economics and Entrepreneurship at ESB Business School, Reutlingen University, Germany.

Listening: Defining different types of market entry strategies

 1.02

1 You are going to hear Dr Dennis De describe six different market entry strategies. Before you listen, try to match the short summary definitions (a–f) to the strategies in the table below.

1	Indirect exporting	a	This involves finding a corporate partner in the target market you are exporting to. It could be a distributor or another company in the same field that doesn't manufacture your product.
2	Direct exporting	b	This involves entering a new country market by buying an existing company within that market together with a list of existing customers.
3	Acquisition	c	This involves two companies setting up a third company together that they jointly own.
4	Greenfield development	d	This is where one party grants to another party the right to distribute goods or services using their brand and system in exchange for a fee.
5	Joint venture	e	This involves using export agents or export houses based in the exporter's home country. This means the exporting company has no direct contact with people based in the countries they are exporting to.
6	Franchising	f	With this strategy, the company sets up new production facilities abroad where they can design everything afresh according to their own plans.

2 Listen to the descriptions and check your answers.

3 Listen again and take notes of the specific advantages and disadvantages mentioned for these six entry strategies.

Critical analysis

Why might a company entering a new market want to set up a joint venture?

Language focus: Market entry terms and concepts

1 Complete the following descriptions of market entry strategies and concepts using terms from the box.

risk exposure   overseas production   exit strategy   control
profit opportunity   commitment   electronic distribution

Market entry strategies

1 _____ – refers to an online market entry strategy for information-based products in digital formats such as e-books and online education training courses. These are sold to customers directly through the company's own website or through a third-party site such as Amazon.

2 _____ – involves setting up manufacturing or service delivery centres abroad. It is a general market entry strategy that can include a number of different strategies.

Market entry concepts

3 _____ – refers to the level of potential danger the company is opening itself up to, by adopting this particular market entry strategy.

4 _____ – refers to a type of reserve plan or contract clause that enables companies to terminate their operations and get out of the market as quickly as possible with the minimum damage in case of difficult circumstances.

5 _____ – refers to the company seeing a chance to gain extra revenues by entering a new market.

6 _____ – refers to the company's ability to determine things such as how their product or service is sold, the price it sells for, the customer service provided as a result of adopting a particular market entry strategy.

7 _____ – refers to the time, cost and effort required to manage the international aspect of your business as a result of adopting a particular market entry strategy.

2 Which of the specific entry strategies mentioned here and in the Listening can involve companies in overseas production?

Reading: Entry strategy overview

1 Read the extract on page 12 from *An Introduction to International Marketing* by Keith Lewis and Matthew Housden from the University of Greenwich, London. Are the following statements true or false?

1 Companies need to be close to their international customers.

2 Companies should first start with a market entry strategy that involves minimal commitment and risk and then progress to other strategies.

3 Smaller companies have similar entry strategy choices to larger companies.

4 A global perspective is equally important for both small and large companies.

5 All entry strategies have different levels of risk and give the company different levels of control over that risk.

6 It is generally easy and painless to exit a market that companies have entered.

7 Companies need to focus above all on controlling their exposure to risk.

8 Before deciding on which entry strategy to adopt, companies need to ask themselves a set of questions.

2 Do you disagree with the authors on any of their points? Try to find at least one point of difference.

International marketing is about the relationship between an organisation and its overseas customers. Essentially it revolves round the question 'How close do I need to be to my customer in order to succeed?'

There are two broad options. We can make the product at home and transport it to our target market(s), or we can make the product overseas in the target market or the country of our choice. The first is described as exporting and the second as overseas production. Exporting can be either direct or indirect; in the latter case there is no direct contact between the exporter and the customers in the overseas market. Overseas production can be either with or without direct investment.

There is no sequential process or requirement to start with export and move to overseas production and foreign direct investment. Clearly, for the smaller company the resources available will preclude some options. However, a smaller company can gain a global presence quite quickly through the development of franchise agreements or through electronic distribution in various digital formats of, say, information-based products. In today's virtual reality marketplace, smaller companies have access to global markets through a wide variety of channels – an option previously available only to major corporations. The global imperative is therefore as much a concern for smaller companies as it is for larger players.

Each entry strategy involves a greater or lesser degree of risk and provides the marketeer with greater or lesser degree of control over this risk. In the international marketing battlefield, the choice of market entry strategy:

- sets out the rules and scope of the terms of engagement with the competition
- confirms the extent and the seriousness of commitment to the local market
- once committed to is often hard to change without substantial risk and often incurs financial penalties
- is therefore always associated with an equally well-considered exit strategy.

It is the ability of the international marketeer to configure the need for profit with exposure to risk through strategic control that will determine success or failure. The company's entry analysis must focus on the answers to the following questions:

– What level of profit is available in the chosen market?
– Over what timescale?
– What assets do we require (capital and labour)?
– What are the affordable financial commitments?

Source: *An Introduction to International Marketing* by Keith Lewis and Matthew Housden

Output: Select an appropriate market entry strategy

You work for a management school in a private university in Spain which provides a whole range of management education and training courses from short strategy development courses tailor-made for individual company needs, to full-time one-year postgraduate MBA courses for individual managers.

You want to grow the business by attracting more international executives and become a truly international business school. At present only 10% of your students come from outside Spain. International executives represent a potentially highly profitable and fast-growing sector of the management education market. Failure to internationalise will mean losing your core market as more and more Spanish managers decide to enrol elsewhere in order to experience an international study environment.

Stage 1
Divide into small groups. Each group is going to discuss two possible market entry strategies.

Group A look at page 137.
Group B look at page 141.
Group C look at page 145.

Stage 2
Re-form into new groups that consist of members of Groups A, B and C. Listen to each other's summary descriptions of the advantages and disadvantages of the entry strategies discussed. Ask questions and come to a consensus agreement on the best market entry strategy to meet your objectives.

1.2 Practice: Entering the global market

Learning outcomes

- Understand how a luxury lifestyle company expands internationally.
- Emphasise points in explanations.
- Select a local franchise partner to open a new country office.

Profile: Quintessentially

Quintessentially is an international luxury lifestyle company, established in London in December 2000. It operates as a multi-faceted club that provides a worldwide concierge service to members 24 hours a day, 365 days a year, via telephone, text or online, wherever they are in the world. Its services range from advice and assistance on dinner bookings, theatre tickets and access to inaccessible events and film premieres, to more unique things like fully managing real estate portfolios, bespoke shopping, luxury travel, private aviation and art investments. It has expanded quickly and now has offices in over 60 cities worldwide, ranging from established country markets in Europe, North America and Asia, to new emerging markets such as Mozambique, Lebanon, Ukraine and Saudi Arabia. Annual membership fees start at £1,000 for general membership and go upwards of £24,000 for global elite membership.

Introduction

1 Read the dictionary definition of 'concierge' from the *Cambridge Advanced Learner's Dictionary* and answer the question below.

> **concierge** /ˌkɒnsiˈeəʒ/ *noun* someone who is employed in a hotel to help guests arrange things

What type of services do you think guests might require of a concierge in a luxury hotel?

2 Read the profile of Quintessentially and discuss the similarities and differences between this company and a concierge service in a luxury hotel. If you could use the services of one or the other, which would you choose? Why?

Business view

Paul Drummond is Co-founder and Group Commercial Director of Quintessentially Group.

Listening 1: Quintessentially client profile

🔵 1.03

1 Read the membership profile details below and then listen to the first part of the interview with Paul Drummond and complete the information.

1 Gender balance: _____

2 Age range: _____

3 Typical occupations: _____

4 Lifestyle: _____

5 Example of unusual request: _____
_____

Intercultural analysis

To what extent do you think the tastes, interests and aspirations of the world's rich elite is standardised across all cultures? What might this mean in practice for businesses such as Quintessentially?

Listening 2: Characteristics of new country markets and local partners

🔘 1.04

1 Read the notes on the next part of the interview and predict the answers.

When Quintessentially considers opening an office in a new international market, it is looking to see that there is a good number of 1 _____ who could potentially join the club as members. The market or area itself would need to have a 2 _____ , nightclubs and events parties.

Generally, Quintessentially head office is approached through its 3 _____ . When they go out and meet a potential local partner, first impressions are 4 _____ . If first impressions aren't positive, then they need to 5 _____ .

The company assumes potential partners are well connected, sophisticated and 6 _____ within their own country. The main aim is to find people who are 7 _____ , have lots of energy and are driven to succeed. The people they try to avoid are people who are attracted to the brand for 8 _____ .

2 Listen to the second part of the interview and complete the notes.

3 Discuss the following questions.

1 Someone who has over $1 million in liquid assets (cash or investments that can be quickly and easily converted into cash) is commonly referred to as a high net worth individual. Why would this target be more attractive to luxury lifestyle companies than individuals who are simply asset rich (holding property and long-term investments)?

2 Do you think the characteristics of your city or region would be an attractive market for Quintessentially to establish an office in? Why/Why not?

Listening 3: Quintessentially's market entry strategy

🔘 1.05

1 Before you listen to the final part of the interview, look at the diagrams in exercise 2, which represent organisational structures for two different international companies. How do you think these companies organise their international operations differently?

2 Listen to the final part of the interview and answer the questions.

1 What is the company's preferred entry strategy model in new international markets?

2 Which of the diagrams below best represents the company's international operations?

3 What two reasons are given to justify the choice of preferred entry strategy?

4 Why is control a key factor for the company in managing its international operations?

Diagram A

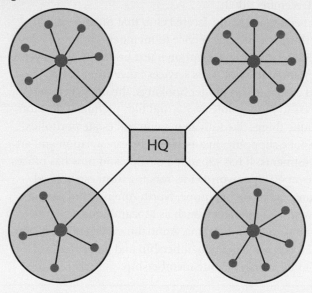

Diagram B

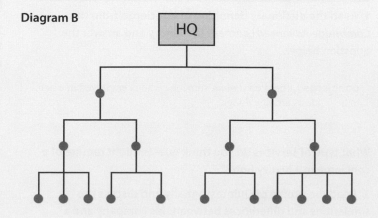

1.05

Using diagrams to take notes is both an efficient way to record information and a highly effective way to recall that information and understand the relationships between the various component parts.

1 Listen again to Listening 3. Label the correct diagram in exercise 2 with the names of the four regional markets and four 'hub cities' that represent the company's international operations.

2 Discuss and answer the following questions.

1 Which part of the diagram represents the franchise branches and which part the offices wholly owned by Quintessentially? Write this information on your diagram and then discuss what the relationship is between the two.

2 This organisational structure is referred to as a 'hub and spokes' structure. Why?

Language focus: Adding emphasis to explanations

A common way to emphasise key points of an explanation or argument in speech is to place the important information in the second part of the sentence.

1 Look at the examples below taken from the interview with Paul Drummond and discuss how they are constructed.

The key determining factor is that members travel a lot.

What I am always looking for is people who are entrepreneurial.

The first thing I want to say is that the majority of what we do is very practical.

What we don't really want are people who are attracted by the brand for the brand's sake.

2 Common introductory phrases to add emphasis using this type of construction include: 'The point is …', 'What we need to do is …', 'The main benefit is …'. Can you think of any similar phrases?

3 The sentences below lack 'punch'. Reformulate them into similar constructions to the ones listed above.

1 Joint ventures often fail.

2 The franchise model allows Quintessentially to standardise quality.

4 Complete the following sentences in your own words to add emphasis to the points you want to make.

1 The aim of a first business meeting with a prospective new partner is …

2 What international companies really need to focus on is …

3 The good thing about using local people to run local office operations is …

4 The best way for Quintessentially to attract new international members is …

5 The biggest risk Quintessentially faces when entering a new country market is …

Compare your sentences with a partner by reading them out aloud and discuss to what extent you agree with each other's views.

Output: Selecting a franchise partner in a new country market

As part of the interview process for new International Business Managers at Quintessentially, candidates are asked to take part in a team task to analyse and select the most attractive partner to do business with in a new country. You should choose which person in which country you would most like to do business with. The choices are Angola, Serbia or Pakistan.

Stage 1

Form small groups and turn to page 137 to view details of the three potential partners and their country profiles. Study the profiles of the three country markets and teams and select one you will sign a contract with. Make sure to fully discuss why you are making this choice and resolve any disagreements within the group.

Stage 2

Complete the following bullet points as a summary of your reasons for having made your particular choice of country/partner and report this information to another group. Be prepared to ask and answer any questions from the other groups to support your arguments. Come to a consensus agreement on which country to open the new office in.

Summary of reasons to support your decision:

- The main reason why we chose this local partner was …
- What we were looking for was someone …
- What we liked about the country market was …
- The main problems with the other local partners were ….

1.3 Skills: Brainstorming

Learning outcomes
- Understand key principles for running brainstorming sessions.
- Use fluent pronunciation features to keep discussions moving.
- Use brainstorming techniques to create a brand slogan.

Introduction

1 Brainstorming is usually done in groups and is a creative approach to problem-solving using a variety of techniques in a relaxed, informal and fun environment. Read the following stages of a brainstorming session and put them in the correct order.

1 Select the most promising ideas
2 Clearly present or explore the problem
3 Plan how to implement ideas
4 Do an icebreaker (optional depending on group)
5 Use lateral-thinking techniques to generate ideas

2 An 'icebreaker' is generally a short 5–10 minute activity. It can have many purposes including energising the group and helping people get to know each other. In small groups, take one of these three everyday objects – a pen, a key or a coin – and place it on the table in front of you. Now brainstorm as many uses of this object as possible in two minutes. The winning team is the one that generates the most uses for this object.

Listening 1: Principles of running a classic brainstorming session

 1.06

Listen to a training manager teaching other managers in a company how to run brainstorming sessions in their work teams. Answer the questions below.

1 Which of the following guidelines does the manager mention for running a brainstorming session?

1 You need a facilitator who clearly presents the problem.
2 Get contributions from everyone present.
3 Keep atmosphere fun, lively and informal.
4 You need a 'scribe' to record people's ideas.
5 You need a whiteboard or flipchart and marker pens.
6 Build on other people's ideas.
7 No premature evaluation (no prejudging or criticising people's ideas).
8 'Anything goes' approach (all ideas accepted).
9 Encourage unusual or 'crazy' ideas.
10 Quantity breeds quality (the more ideas, the better).
11 Set a time limit.
12 If possible, run the session away from the office.

2 Discuss the following questions.

1 The manager uses a sporting metaphor from the world of wrestling, 'no holds barred', which means without restrictions or rules. Which guideline does this refer to?
2 The manager mentions that after the initial brainstorming phase, there is a 'selective phase'. What do you think people do in this phase?
3 Which of these brainstorming guidelines did you follow when you did your icebreaker mini-brainstorming session?

Listening 2: A problematic brainstorming session

 1.07

1 Listen to an office manager setting up a staff brainstorming session for travel consultants working for a tour operator. What is the aim of this session?

2 Listen again. What is wrong with the way this brainstorming session is being set up? Discuss with a partner and look at the audio script below if necessary.

Audio script

 1.07

Manager: … that's the situation. Erm, what I'd like to do is now if maybe … if you can kind of work in groups or perhaps two or three of you on the … on the flipchart. List down reasons why you think that we need to be consistent with the way we deal with customer enquiries. Anything that goes through your head, such as the need to follow a company standard. Also, remember the customer feedback was that we are inconsistent in answering calls. That was particularly …

Language focus: Using fluent pronunciation features to move discussions forward

🔘 1.08

1 Listen to these typical expressions used to keep discussions moving in brainstorming sessions. Notice how fluent speakers tend to link sounds together. Mark the links between the words. The first one has been done as an example.

1 Anyone else got anything to add here?

2 Mandy, what do you think about that?

3 That's a great idea!

4 What about building on Paul's idea to ...

2 Practise saying the expressions with clear linking. Which type of words should be linked together when spoken?

3 Fast talkers may miss sounds out altogether – for instance, 'tend to' may sound like 'tento'; or they may blur sounds – 'want to' can sound like 'wanna'. The following typical phrases used in brainstorming sessions are written as if spoken. Say them aloud and then write the standard spelling for each one.

1 weagonnastartbylookinat ...
2 howabougoingwithiansideato ...
3 letsgowithisideaov ...
4 mabeweshudgowidavzideaov ...

4 Listen to the phrases spoken aloud and then practise saying them.

🔘 1.09

5 Being aware of the pronunciation features presented here can really help your listening ability. Listen to the following company slogans said at speed, and match them with the company.

🔘 1.10

6 Listen again and write the slogans in full. Then reformulate them as if they were spoken, using the model shown in question 3 above. Make sure to account for missed sounds and blurred sounds. When you have finished, practise saying them at speed.

Critical analysis

What kind of brainstorming and research work do you think advertising agencies did to create the slogans above? How good do you think these slogans are?

Output: Brainstorming a new brand slogan

You are going to take part in a brainstorming session to create a new slogan for a company or product brand you know well.

Stage 1
As a class, choose a brand that everyone in the class is familiar with – a major supermarket brand, a soft drink brand, etc.

Stage 2: The 'anything goes' brainstorming phase
Get into two groups. Each group should choose a facilitator to lead this brainstorming session. The facilitator for each group should read the instructions at the back of the book and then conduct the brainstorming session for their group.

Group A facilitator look at page 137.
Group B facilitator look at page 142.

Whilst the facilitators are preparing, the other team members should review the language and content from this lesson, to be ready to use it during the brainstorming session.

Stage 3: The selective phase
Compare your results (and the process you used to get them) with another group and work together to create a single brand advertising slogan. If there is time, discuss what you could include in a 30-second TV commercial based around this slogan – the sounds, images and text.

Nike (sportswear)

McDonald's (fast food)

L'Oréal (cosmetics)

2 Standardisation and differentiation

2.1 Theory: Different approaches to international marketing

Learning outcomes
- Understand why companies standardise and differentiate their marketing strategy.
- Learn word formations and terms of international marketing.
- Propose adaptations of promotions for different country markets.

Introduction

1 Look at these international marketing blunders and think about why the promotions and products failed.

1 An Italian biscuit maker showed kids eating biscuits for breakfast. Parents in the USA were not impressed.
2 A Japanese manufacturer exported top-opening washing machines to the UK. They didn't sell.
3 Mexican consumers were amused by this slogan for a pen from the USA: 'It won't leak in your pocket and embarrass you.'
4 A North American airline introducing flights from Hong Kong upset its first passengers by giving them white carnations.

2 What are the general 'lessons' that companies can learn from these blunders when marketing products internationally?

Language focus 1: International marketing terminology

The following marketing and international marketing terms occur in the Reading texts. Match the terms to the definitions.

1 differentiation	**a** Costs of going into a new market. For example, in an international context, firms will have costs associated with the adaptation of their products/services to enter new country markets.
2 economies of scale	**b** Examples include opportunities and threats coming from a socio-cultural, legal, economic, political or technological source.
3 segmentation	**c** Strategic decision involving where to place your product or service in the marketplace. McDonald's might be fast food in the USA, but in an emerging market like India the emphasis is on creating a restaurant experience for middle-class families.
4 cultural sensitivity	**d** Dividing a market into different parts. Each part of the market consists of a group of customers with similar needs and wants.
5 market positioning	**e** Cultural values and generally accepted behaviour.
6 (market) entry costs	**f** Responsiveness to cultural diversity.
7 (business) environmental factors	**g** The process of customising or adapting aspects of your business (prices, product features, promotion, etc.) to the needs and requirements of a local market. It's the opposite of standardisation.
8 cultural norms	**h** Benefits of lower unit costs as a result of producing higher volumes of a given product.

Business view

Dr Marieke de Mooij is author of *Global Marketing and Advertising: Understanding Cultural Paradoxes*, and visiting professor at European University Viadrina, Germany and the University of Navarra, Spain.

Dr Jim Blythe is author of *Principles & Practice of Marketing*, and Reader in Marketing at the University of Glamorgan, UK.

Reading: Two perspectives on international marketing strategies

Skim reading the text by 'passing your eyes over the text' allows you to get a quick general understanding of what the text is about, without being concerned with any specific details. When skim reading it is <u>not</u> necessary to read or understand every word.

1 Skim read Text A on this page and Text B on page 20 with a time limit of four minutes and then choose the correct letter (A or B) to complete the descriptions of the author's position.

1 In Text _____, the author strongly believes that taking a standardised approach to business across different international markets is the wrong strategy to follow.
2 In Text _____, the author outlines how companies can take a standardised approach to international business, or adapt and differentiate their strategy to the needs of local markets, depending on the nature of the product and promotion.

2 Student A should read Text A and answer the questions on this page. Student B should read Text B and answer the questions on page 20. When you have finished, check your answers with another student who has read the same text as you.

1 What two aspects of a company's strategy can change depending on the country market it is operating in?
2 What is unusual about McDonald's India compared to McDonald's elsewhere?
3 What two types of broad strategy can firms follow across different country markets?
4 Which companies have more chance of success by taking a standardised approach to strategy across different country markets?
5 How common is it for firms to completely standardise their advertising across different country markets?

3 After reading, cover your text and exchange information with somebody who has read the other text. Which text do you agree with most? Why?

Text A

International Marketing – Global Strategy

Strategy is about developing competitive capabilities and finding a competitive position within the marketplace. In international markets, the competitive capabilities that the firm has in one country may not be the same as those it has in another country: equally, the competitive position a firm adopts in one country may be different from that held in another. For example, McDonald's is regarded as a standard fast-food brand in its native USA, but in India and other emerging markets it is marketed as a premium brand. Interestingly, India is one of the only countries in the world where McDonald's doesn't sell hamburgers, Big Macs or any other beef products. Being a predominantly Hindu country where the cow is sacred, this would offend cultural sensitivities.

Firms wishing to enter a given overseas market will need to consider the same environmental factors as they would consider periodically within their home markets, but a key issue in global marketing is the degree to which the company is prepared to standardise its products and marketing approach.

Firms might decide on a globalisation strategy by which the company's products, attitudes, brands and promotion are standardised throughout the world, with global segments being identified, or conversely might decide on a differentiation strategy whereby the company adapts its thinking (and marketing) to each new market. The companies which are most likely to seek a globalisation policy are those whose products are not culturally specific, and whose promotions can be readily understood throughout the world.

Research shows that relatively few companies standardise their advertising. Of 38 multinational companies surveyed, 26 said that they used standard advertising, but only 4 of these were completely standardised. The others varied from limited standardisation (perhaps only the corporate logo remaining the same) through limited standardisation of key elements (such as packaging), through to standard methodologies and approaches with minor adaptations.

Source: *Principles & Practice of Marketing* by Jim Blythe

Global Marketing – Tailoring Your Strategy to Fit the Culture

When it comes to global communications and advertising, multinational companies want to opt for a standardised approach because of the obvious benefits of economies of scale. However, what they gain by economies of scale, they lose in effectiveness. For a long time, international advertising strategists believed that emotional or feelings-based appeals would travel better than thinking-based appeals, because of the assumed universality of human values such as love and happiness. Analysis of advertisements in international media such as Newsweek, Business Week and CNN shows that this is the approach that has been taken by U.S. companies in particular. In reality, however, the messages being communicated are less universal than is commonly assumed, more a reflection of the home country's own value system. As with a company's identity and its brand strategies, advertising must also communicate values that match those of the receiver rather than the culture of the producer. Advertising is most effective when it succeeds in reflecting the culture of the consumer it is trying to reach.

A communications and advertising strategy that is defined according to each and every distinct market may make Western marketers nervous, but in the end, it earns money by being more effective than taking a one-size-fits-all approach. If you want to reach consumers in different parts of the world, my advice is always the same: Speak to them in a way they understand, that fits their communication style. The new paradigm is cultural segmentation: defining markets based on their cultural specifics, and then developing culture-fit strategies. A strong corporate identity needs to go hand in hand with cultural sensitivity. Instead of being 'consistent', companies should be pragmatic and adapt to the cultural mind sets of consumers. This is the future of global strategy.

Source: Marieke de Mooij, *IESE Insight* magazine, IESE Business School, Barcelona

1 Why do multinational companies want to standardise their marketing approach across different country markets?

2 Why do international advertising experts use messages based on emotions and feelings?

3 According to the author, how universal are feelings and emotions such as love and happiness?

4 According to the author, how can companies best communicate their message in international markets?

5 What marketing strategy does the author propose for international companies?

1 Complete the gaps in the table below with the correct form of the word.

Noun	Verb	Adjective
standardisation/ standard	a _____	b _____ / _____
differentiation	c _____	d _____ / _____
adaptation	e _____	f _____
environment		g _____
globalisation	h _____	i _____
segmentation/ segment	j _____	k _____
minimum	l _____	m _____

2 Choose words from the table above to form common word partnerships with all the words to their left or right.

1 _____ : products   global pricing   approach   promotion

2 _____ : entry costs   differentiation   risk   tax

3 _____ : economy   market segments   strategy

4 competitive   economic   political   socio-cultural   : _____

5 customer   market   demographic   geographic   : _____

6 product   local   brand   : _____

3 Complete the following sentences with your own words and at least one word partnership from exercise 2 above.

1 The key to international marketing success lies in …

2 As people travel more and cultures converge together, …

3 The big question that faces international business today is …

4 When first entering into a country market, companies need to …

5 If regional trading blocks …

You are going to analyse advertisements for products and services from the UK and the USA and decide how appropriate they are for your own country markets. What might need adapting?

Stage 1
Work in two groups.

Group A look at page 138 and discuss your advertisement.
Group B look at page 142 and discuss your advertisement.

Stage 2
You are going to design a new advertisement for the product/ service that you have discussed. Try to design a completely new advertisement for your product/service, to be used in your country or a country you know well.

Stage 3
Give a presentation of your new advertisement to the other group. Explain the changes and why you have made them.

2.2 Practice: Piaggio Vietnam

Learning outcomes

- Understand how a European company markets its products in an emerging market in Asia.
- Describe a company's products, brands and markets.
- Make decisions to position a new brand in an emerging market.

Profile: The Piaggio Group

The group was formed in 1884. It is based near Pisa in Italy and is one of the world's biggest manufacturers of two-wheeled motor vehicles. Their most famous brand is the Vespa, which is the classic Italian scooter. It has been produced for over 60 years. The company is also very well-known for selling small light commercial vehicles. They have manufacturing operations in a number of different countries including India, Vietnam, Spain and Italy.

Profile: Piaggio Vietnam

Piaggio Vietnam was established in 2007 when the company started building a new plant for the production of two-wheeled vehicles. The plant has the capacity to produce 100,000 vehicles per year. Production has started with the Vespa. At the beginning of 2010 the company started exporting to neighbouring countries in South East Asia. In Vietnam, 70% of sales of the Vespa are to women, while in Europe 80% of sales are to men. Asia is by far the biggest market in the world for two-wheeler vehicles.

Introduction

1 Read the profiles of the company and look at the photos of the Vespa. Discuss how you think the Vespa that is designed and built in Vietnam for the Vietnamese and South East Asian market might compare to the Vespa designed and built in Italy for the Italian and European market. Think in terms of brand strategy, product features, promotion and pricing.

2 What emotions, feelings and associations do you connect with Italy and Italians? How might Piaggio emphasise its Italian 'nationality' in its advertising in Vietnam?

Language focus 1: Describing brands and products

1 You are going to hear an interview with the CEO of Piaggio Vietnam. The underlined words in the following sentences are taken from the interview. Choose the best word or phrase in italics to complete the definitions of the underlined words.

1 Heritage refers to features from the past of a country (such as its buildings or traditions) that have *historical importance / disappeared*. Used in a business context you can talk about the heritage of a company or brand.

2 DNA is the chemical in our cells that carries genetic information. It is often compared to a code that determines our fundamental *desires / identity*. It is used in a business context too when we talk about the DNA of a company.

3 Icons are classic objects (or people) that are *unrepresentative / representative* of a wider group. A red Ferrari, the leaning tower of Pisa and the Colosseum are all considered classic Italian icons.

4 In simplistic terms, <u>ergonomics</u> is the science of designing things to be *comfortable and efficient / original and beautiful* for people.

5 A <u>workhorse</u> is a *functional / stylish* machine that you can depend on for hard everyday use.

6 <u>Positioning</u> in a business context is about where you locate your *brands and products / offices and factories* in the marketplace in relation to the competition and your own business strategy.

2 Think about how some of these words might refer to Piaggio and the Vespa brand.

Example: *Piaggio's Italian heritage is probably used a lot in its advertising and promotions in Vietnam.*

Business view

Costantino Sambuy is Chief Executive Officer, Piaggio Vietnam and Executive Vice-President of the company's Two-Wheeler Division, Asia.

Listening 1: Brand strategy

 1.11

1 Listen to Costantino Sambuy talk about Piaggio's marketing strategy for Vietnam and answer the questions.

1 How are the Vespa brand values connected with Italy?

2 How is the Vespa brand positioned in Vietnam compared to Western markets?

3 What will happen in the second phase of their penetration of the Vietnamese market?

4 How will the Piaggio brand's price compare to the local market?

5 What segment of the Vietnamese market will the Piaggio brand be targeted at?

6 Why won't Piaggio produce low-cost scooters for the mass market?

2 How do Costantino Sambuy's views differ from your own ideas about the company and the Vespa brand?

Listening 2: Promotion strategy

1.12

1 The second part of the interview contrasts the company's strategy in Vietnam with that in Italy and Europe. Listen and take notes to complete the table.

	Vietnam compared to Europe
Promotion	
Dealer network	
Celebrities	

2 Listen again to add more information to the table.

Listening 3: Product strategy

1.13

Listen to the final part of the interview. Are the following statements true or false?

1 The Vespas in Vietnam and Italy are very similar.

2 They have modified the height of the seat and the height of the handlebars.

3 Customers in Italy and Vietnam use the product in the same way.

4 The new bright pink colour added to the Vespa range was really appreciated in Vietnam.

5 Piaggio's innovative local adaptations are well received by the local market.

Critical analysis

1 Costantino Sambuy says that 'Vespa has always positioned itself strongly in the cinema business, starting with *Roman Holiday*'. What are the advantages for Piaggio of having the Vespa featured in movies such as this?

2 Featuring products in movies is a recognised promotion channel for companies known as 'product placement'. Can you think of any examples of this in films that you have seen? What were the benefits to the company in each specific case?

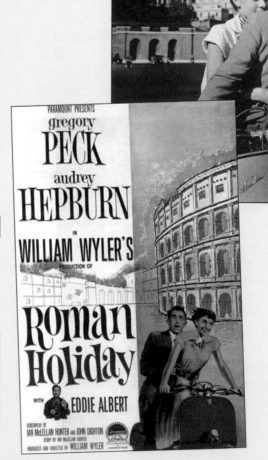

Language focus 2: Describing products, brands and markets

There are three common ways to describe products, brands and markets: adjective/noun combinations ('luxury market'), noun/noun combinations ('brand image') and compound adjectives that link two words together ('high-quality product').

1 In the table below, which word in the first column does **not** make a word partnership with the word in the same row in the second column?

Adjective	Noun
1 core mass local branded emerging domestic	market
2 premium mass own leading	brand
3 standardised branded emerging core unique	product

Noun	Noun
4 home target niche consumer competition export	market
5 designer car consumer competitor innovation	brand
6 competitor niche retailer lifestyle	product

2 There are a number of types of compound adjectives that are commonly used in business. Look at the following lists and write one example from each of the four lists to comment on the products and brands in your country or region.

Example: The top-end market for cars in the UK is dominated by Mercedes, BMW, Audi and Jaguar.

- high/low + noun: low-quality product high-tech industry high-profile client low-cost airline
- fast/fastest + *ing*: fast-changing markets fastest-growing segment fast-moving industry
- top/long/medium + noun: top-end market long-term strategy top-range model medium-income countries top-selling brand
- well/premium + past participle: well-known brand well-designed product premium-priced product

Compare your written comments with a partner and ask and answer any additional questions to find out more about the products, brands and markets.

3 Complete the following sentences using an appropriate word partnership from the box.

niche market premium-priced fastest-growing segments
core product well-known brand

1 After establishing its search engine as its _____, Google has added products like mobile phone apps to its portfolio.

2 Organic farming is a way for small farmers to find a _____ for their crops.

3 Adidas products are _____ but not as expensive as other leading brands.

4 Women entrepreneurs represent one of the _____ of the small-business economy.

5 Many people prefer to buy a _____ rather than the supermarket own brand.

Transferable skill: Using repetition for persuasive effect

An effective way of influencing your audience is through repetition. This is especially relevant when making a business case or giving a presentation.

1 Listen to three examples from the interview and practise saying them aloud. Notice the slight pauses between each repetition and try to reproduce this.

🔊 1.14

1 Our values are linked with heritage, with design, with Italy, with glamour.

2 So we make it, in this case, much more glamorous, much more fashionable than it is in Italy.

3 From a product standpoint it is the same, the engine is the same, the suspension is the same because the customer usage of the product is the same.

2 Make a case for the introduction of the Piaggio brand in Vietnam. Write a sentence (using repetition) on each of the following points and then practise saying them aloud in small groups. Who makes the most compelling argument in the most persuasive way?

a How the Piaggio scooter will be better than the competition (quality and service differences)

b How the Piaggio brand will differ from the Vespa brand (target market, image and price differences)

Output: Brand positioning

The new Piaggio brand will be launched in the Vietnamese market next year. The scooter will be built in Piaggio's Vietnam plant. The Senior Management of Piaggio Vietnam have requested a report from two groups of international management consultants on how it should be marketed.

Stage 1

Divide into small groups and turn to the back of the book to read a summary of your group's research findings and prepare your presentation.

Group A look at page 138.
Group B look at page 142.

Stage 2

As a class, choose two groups (one Group A and one Group B) to make the presentation to the class. The class should adopt the role of the Senior Management Team of Piaggio Vietnam. Listen to the presentations, ask questions at the end, and then decide which strategy to adopt.

2.3 Skills: Managing time

Learning outcomes

- Learn techniques for time management.
- Use collocations to discuss time management.
- Negotiate priorities.

Introduction

1 Read the dictionary definition of 'procrastinate' from the *Cambridge Advanced Learner's Dictionary* and answer the question below.

> **procrastinate** /prəʊˈkræstɪneɪt/ *verb* to keep delaying something that must be done, often because it is unpleasant or boring

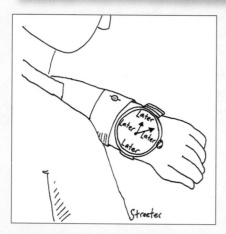

What kinds of things do you procrastinate about?

2 Look at the matrix below, which is a standard tool for categorising tasks. Complete the table with the following:

build relationships
deal with pressing problems
respond to needless interruptions
prepare for meetings
take time out to relax

surf the net
creative thinking
deal with boss's bad moods
deal with crises
chat with colleagues

	urgent	**not urgent**
important		
not important		

3 Think of some activities that you do regularly, and add them to the table. Try to think of at least one for each of the four boxes.

4 How would the matrix of a good time manager look, compared to that of a bad time manager?

5 Do you think using this matrix could help your time management? Why/Why not?

Language focus: Time management language

1 Complete the collocations about time management by matching the first part (1–10) with the second part (a–j).

1	to fail	**a**	from procrastination
2	to suffer	**b**	your goals
3	to catch	**c**	a 'to-do' list
4	to make	**d**	a desirable outcome
5	to stick	**e**	the most important task
6	to decide	**f**	to keep track of time
7	to miss	**g**	up on your work
8	to visualise	**h**	a deadline
9	to prioritise	**i**	to the schedule
10	to achieve	**j**	on objectives

2 Which of the above are bad for time management?

3 Think of someone you know who procrastinates a lot. Using some of the phrases from exercise 1, what advice could you give him/her?

4 A common proverb used about time management is 'He who fails to plan, plans to fail.' What does it mean? Do you agree? When might it be inappropriate to plan?

Business view

Randy Pausch (1960–2008) was a professor of computer science and human–computer interaction at Carnegie Mellon University.

Listening 1: Lecture on time management

1.15

1 You are going to listen to a lecture Randy Pausch gave at Virginia University on how people can manage their time effectively. Before you listen, try to predict what he might say about these topics.

- Goals, priorities and planning
- Experience
- Planning
- 'to-do' lists

2 Listen and make notes on what he says about these topics.

3 In small groups, compare your notes. Then discuss whether any pieces of advice seem particularly useful for you, in your study or work.

Intercultural analysis

1 How punctual are people in your culture expected to be? Are you typical of your culture?

2 What problems could occur when somebody from a punctual culture has a meeting with someone from a more relaxed culture?

Listening 2: IT company team meeting

1.16

Listen to an extract of a meeting in an IT company. The team leader, Jennifer, is talking to her technical team about managing their time and setting deadlines. Are the following statements true or false?

1 Jennifer does not have time management issues.

2 At least one member of the team wants stricter guidance.

3 The team agrees that they need to set deadlines, but be flexible with them.

Critical analysis

1 According to Randy Pausch, it is better to set goals and deadlines first, but be ready to change them. Do you think the technical team follow this approach?

2 In your opinion, is the team leader a strict manager? Do you think her approach would be suitable if you / your colleagues / your classmates had time management issues and were in her team? Why/Why not?

Output: Advising an employee on better time management

Hannah Barnes is a sales executive for a travel company. Her manager is concerned about her time management. She has a poor success rate with cold-calling potential clients and the database which she is supposed to update weekly is not being done. She works part-time from 8am to 1pm five days a week. Below is a list of her duties and the chart shows how she spends her day, split up into hours. She doesn't like cold-calling clients and feels she lacks the skills to update the IT system.

Main duties	Other duties
■ cold-calling potential clients ■ booking trips for clients who visit the agency ■ following up potential clients who have expressed an interest	■ updating the department database weekly ■ arranging matches for the department football team

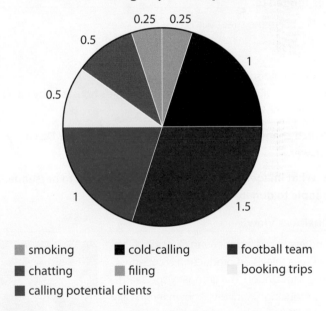

Hannah's working day (time spent in hours)

- ■ smoking
- ■ cold-calling
- ■ football team
- ■ chatting
- ■ filing
- □ booking trips
- ■ calling potential clients

Stage 1

Work in small groups and discuss how a manager could help Hannah become a more productive worker. Consider her use of time and the way she prioritises her tasks.

Stage 2

Work in pairs and role play a meeting between Hannah and her manager about the changes she needs to make and how you can work together to improve her performance.

Stage 3

Report back to the group on what you decided.

▶◀ **Watch Sequence 1 on the DVD to find out more about International marketing.**

Writing 1: Writing notes for presentations

Learning outcomes
- Write notes to accompany presentation slides.
- Create slides with bullet points and write notes to expand them.
- Give timed presentations from notes and slides.

Introduction

1 Charities are independent organisations that help people in need – there are charities that help the poor, help the homeless, help the aged, help fund medical research, etc. Many of these are multi-million dollar organisations. What are the biggest charities in your country and what do they do?

2 As independent organisations, charities are not reliant on government for funding. Look at the following ways charities can raise money and tick the ones you have personally seen or responded to.

- People in the street with collection boxes
- TV adverts
- Online adverts
- Corporate sponsorship
- Direct mail (letters sent by post to people's houses or by email to their inboxes)

Which channel do you think is the most effective? Discuss your answer.

3 What images and messages do charities use to persuade people to donate money to them?

Business view

Andrew Guy is founder and Director of Eye to Eye, a television production company based in London. The company specialises in producing TV adverts, known technically as DRTV (Direct Response Television), for the charity sector.

Language focus: Preparing slide presentation notes

🔘 1.17

Presentation software, such as PowerPoint, has a function that allows you to write notes for each slide in your presentation. These are helpful to refer to, before or during the presentation (especially for more inexperienced presenters or people unfamiliar with the content).

1 The following slides and notes are from a presentation that Andrew Guy gives to prospective clients, to explain how DRTV works. In pairs, look at the notes to the opening two slides and practise presenting these slides to each other.

Slide 1 – 15 secs
- Thank you for inviting me …
- Aim of talk – creating TV advert

> ### Creating DRTV
> Presentation 28th April 20 __

Slide 2 – 30 secs
- 2 key parts to DRTV: emotion + reason
- Emotion – get people connected to subject / get them to care = they donate money
- First emotion, then give them reasons

> ### Principles of DRTV
> It's all about reason and emotion

2 Now listen to Andrew Guy's presentation. How different was it to your practice presentation? How useful were the notes?

3 Which of the following guidelines below have been used to write the notes for the slides above?

Guidelines – Writing presentation notes

1 Include timings.
2 Highlight any words you need to emphasise.
3 Write mostly in note form, not full sentences.
4 Use abbreviations.
5 Use symbols and acronyms.
6 Write the first few words of the slide introduction.
7 Write key phrases/words and omit small words.
8 Use bullet points.
9 Write instructions to yourself.
10 Put the notes in the order you say the information.

Writing skill: Creating bullet points on slides and adding notes

When you create information slides with bullet points on them, you need far fewer notes as you can place the key information on the slide itself. The preparation notes you make are therefore confined to any extra information you might want to add in order to expand the bullet points on the slide.

1 Read the sentences below that form the basic content of the next two slides of the presentation and transform them into summary bullet points. Use words taken from the sentence and do not exceed the maximum number of words indicated. Write your answers on the slide templates provided – the first bullet has been done for you as an example.

Slide 3

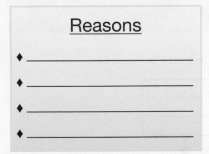

Reasons

♦ Simple, compelling proposition

♦ _____

♦ _____

♦ _____

1 You need to give people a simple, compelling proposition. (3 words)
2 There has to be a reason for people to respond now. (4 words)
3 You need to use persuasive, engaging words. (3 words)
4 Be very wary of using ideas that are too clever and demanding, as they rarely work. (5 words)

Slide 4

Reasons

♦ _____

♦ _____

♦ _____

♦ _____

1 The length of the advert is absolutely critical. (4 words)
2 You should include lots of captions and voice-over in your advert. (6 words)
3 You need to show the needs of the people your charity is helping and the solutions your organisation is providing. (4 words)
4 Most important of all, make it clear you need a response from the beginning of the advert. (8 words)

2 Now listen to the presentation of these two slides. Circle the three bullet points that are more fully expanded.

🔊 **1.18**

Slide 3: 1st / 2nd / 3rd / 4th bullet point
Slide 4: 1st / 2nd / 3rd / 4th bullet point

3 In order to remind yourself what to say during the presentation of these slides at a future date, write a summary note for each of the three expanded bullet points. Look at the audio script on pages 149–150 to help you. Each summary note should have a maximum of five words.

Critical analysis

There are three broad ways of creating presentation slides:
- Text-only slides (like the ones presented here)
- Image-only slides
- Combination of image and text on slides

What are the advantages and disadvantages of each?

Output: Prepare and deliver a welcome presentation

You are going to prepare the first part of a welcome presentation. Choose <u>one</u> of the two option choices below.

1 A welcome presentation to new recruits coming to work for the first time in your organisation or department.
2 A welcome presentation to new students starting their studies at your university or college for the first time.

Stage 1
In small groups discuss what information you want to communicate to these new recruits/students in a short presentation and then prepare the first four slides of this presentation.

Slide 1 – Welcome slide
Slides 2, 3, 4 – Information slides

The slides you create should be varied in format. Make sure your presentation includes both slides with one simple message, or one simple message and a title (similar to Slide 2 on page 26) <u>and</u> slides with bullet points and a title (similar to Slides 3 and 4 on this page). When writing slides with bullet points, include a maximum of four bullets on a slide and note the style of writing bullet points is <u>not</u> in full sentence form. Include images on any slides you think need them.

Stage 2
Using the guidelines, write notes for each of the four slides. Don't forget to include timings – a maximum of three minutes in total.

Stage 3
Pass your slides and notes to another group. Take a few minutes to study the new slides and notes you receive. Highlight any words you feel should be stressed and practise giving the presentation in your group. When you are ready, give the presentation to the other group. After both groups have given their presentation, discuss how easy/difficult the task was and how effective the slides and notes were. Could they be improved at all?

3 Competition within industries

3.1 Theory: Five Forces Theory of Competition

Learning outcomes

- Understand the basic principles of the Five Forces Theory of Competition.
- Use comparisons and language phrases with prepositions to discuss competition.
- Analyse competitive forces in a specific industry and report conclusions.

Introduction

1 How competitive is your environment? Discuss one of the following situations:

– the difficulty of getting a good job in your industry sector (or one you would like to enter)
– the difficulty of getting into a top university (or one you would like to enter)

2 What can you do in the above competitive scenarios to increase your chances of success?

Business view

Dr Alex Muresan is Senior Lecturer in Marketing at London Metropolitan University.

Listening 1: General description of the 'Five Forces' diagram

 1.19

1 You are going to hear Alex Muresan explaining Michael Porter's Five Forces Theory of Competition. Listen to the first part of the interview and complete the gaps in the diagram.

2 Answer the questions.

1 What is the difference between horizontal competition and vertical competition in the supply chain?
2 Which of the forces are categorised as horizontal competition and which as vertical? Mark each one as H or V on the diagram.
3 What should firms do when any of these forces change?

The Five Forces That Shape Industry Competition

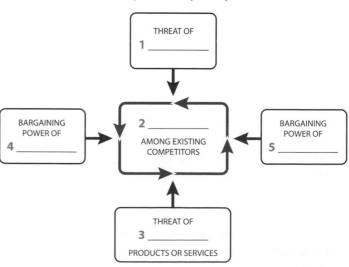

Adapted from *Competitive Strategy: Techniques for Analyzing Industries and Competitors* by Michael Porter

Transferable skill: Using a diagram to express ideas

Look at the diagram below of a supply chain for a coffee brand. The vertical line shows vertical competition – all the suppliers from the source supplier (the coffee bean farmer) to the end-user (the coffee drinker). Horizontal competition – competition on the same level – is shown on the horizontal line, i.e. the names of the direct competitors to the brand. Draw a similar supply chain diagram for one of the following branded products.

- a T-shirt from a branded clothes shop
- a brand of mineral water
- a sports shoes brand
- a book from a bookshop chain

Coffee bean farmer (source supplier)

Local coffee bean wholesaler

Local coffee bean buyer (exporter)

Coffee roasters / brands

Lilly Caffè   Moka Caffè   Trio Caffè

Supermarket retailer / coffee bar

Intermediate consumer – coffee buyer

Coffee drinker (end-user consumer)

Listening 2: Analysis of competitive rivalry

 1.20

1 Look at the table below, which gives examples of six factors that influence competitive rivalry between companies within the same industry sector. Try to complete the explanations using the words 'more' or 'less'.

Factor influencing competitive rivalry	Explanation
Concentration of the industry	1 The more competitors of equal size in the market, the _____ intense the rivalry is.
Rate of market growth	2 The faster the market growth rate in an industry sector, the _____ intense the rivalry is.
Structure of costs	3 The higher the fixed costs* in an industry, the _____ intense rivalry is.
Degree of differentiation	4 The higher the level of brand awareness amongst customers, the _____ intense the rivalry is. 5 The more customers perceive products in an industry sector to be very similar, the _____ intense the rivalry is.
Switching costs	6 The higher the costs for customers to move from one product to another in an industry sector, the _____ intense the rivalry is.
Exit barriers	7 The higher the barriers to leaving an industry sector market, the _____ intense the rivalry is.

* *fixed costs* = costs that are <u>not</u> linked to production or sales. For example, an airline would pay the same amount of money to lease its aircraft if it flew one person or 10,000 people in a month.

2 Listen to the second part of the interview with Dr Alex Mureson and check your answers.

3 Listen again and complete the following sentences so that they provide reasons for the six factors listed in exercise 1.

1 Companies that are equal in size will have more intense rivalry because …
2 In low-growth markets, companies compete for …
3 Companies with high fixed costs will cut prices to …
4 When customers see no difference between competing products, they …
5 Switching costs are high when the customer has invested …
6 Companies won't exit a market quickly or easily if …

4 Discuss which of the six factors has the biggest influence on competitive rivalry in an industry that you know well.

Language focus 1: Changing comparisons

1 What do you notice about the differences in language structure and meaning between the two examples given below?

- Competitive rivalry in an industry sector is more intense when there are more competitors operating in the sector.
- The more competitors there are in the industry sector, the more intense the competitive rivalry there is.

2 Complete the following sentences regarding how you think competition will change in relation to the other forces within Porter's Five Forces theory. The first one has been done for you.

Example: The more unique the service that suppliers provide in an industry sector, the more power the suppliers will have and consequently the more competitive the industry will be.

1 Supplier power: The more unique the service that suppliers provide in an industry sector, …
2 Buyer power: The less sensitive buyers are to the price of products in an industry sector, …
3 New entrants: The less specialist knowledge or technological expertise needed to enter an industry sector, …
4 Threat of substitutes: The better the performance of a potential substitute product for an industry sector, …

Language focus 2: Phrases of competition with dependent prepositions

1 Prepositions commonly occur after certain adjectives, verbs or nouns. Look at the following examples, which come from the interview with Dr Alex Muresan, and complete them with the correct prepositions.

1 [Horizontal competition] is those people who compete _____ the same level _____ you.
2 For most industries, the intensity _____ competitive rivalry is the major determinant _____ competitiveness.
3 The pressure _____ companies to compete will be higher.
4 The state _____ competition _____ an industry depends _____ five basic competitive forces.
5 Switching costs are high [when] the product is specialised and the customer has invested a lot _____ resources _____ learning how to use [the product].

2 What other dependent prepositions can you see in the diagram in Listening 1?

3 How high are the switching costs for you personally to change your computer operating system? Explain your answer.

Output: Analysis and presentation of an industry's competitive forces

You are going to analyse competition in an industry sector and present your conclusions.

Stage 1: Selecting an industry and identifying the competition
As a class, select an industry sector that you know well (for example: budget airlines, the soft drinks business, tablet computers, fast-food restaurants, computer operating systems). Decide on a specific geographical market focus and list the names of the main competitors within the sector in this market.

Stage 2: Analysing competitive forces
In small groups you are going to discuss some of the five competitive forces that shape competition in the industry / market sector you selected in Stage 1. Divide into groups.

Group A look at page 138 and discuss rivalry among competitors.
Group B look at page 142 and discuss supplier power and the threat of new entrants.
Group C look at the information below and discuss buyer power and the threat of substitutes.

Group C

In your group, discuss buyer power and the threat of substitutes for the industry you have chosen. Your discussion should cover the following bullet points – **for each point, you need to ask each other how the answers to the questions below affect competition within this industry**.

Threat of substitutes
- What are they? How big is the threat?
- What threats of substitute products/services could there be in the future?
- How easy is it for present industry competitors to exit their industry and move into new substitute industries? Has there been much evidence of this with the present industry competitors?

Buyer power
- Who are the different customer groups for this industry? Are all the customer groups the same size? Are there one or two important customer groups, such as particular groups of business customers?
- How closely are customers tied to the companies' products? How high are the switching costs for them to move to another competitor? How sensitive are they to price?

Stage 3: Combining analysis of all five industry competitive forces
Reform into new groups containing members of Groups A, B and C from Stage 2. Share the key points of your previous discussions and create a 'Five Forces' diagram showing the main points you agree on. If there is time, present your analysis to another group and compare your diagrams.

3.2 Practice: The UK budget hotel industry

Learning outcomes

- Understand how budget hotels can succeed in the hotel market.
- Use noun phrases to communicate content.
- Persuade others of your competitive advantage.

Profile: UK budget hotels

The UK is the world's sixth most visited tourist destination, attracting around 30,000,000 visitors every year. Each of the UK's 49,000,000 adult population spends on average just under a week at hotels in the UK for tourism purposes. Increasingly, large budget hotel companies are accounting for a considerable part of the market, and two chains – Travelodge and Premier Inn – make up 60% of the budget market. The budget hotel sector is predicted to double in size over the next two decades. Budget hotels may lack some of the features of other hotels, such as minibars, room service and restaurants.

Introduction

1 When choosing a hotel, which factors are the most important for you? For example, price / location / recommendation / level of service / food?

2 Look at the profile and think of as many differences as you can between budget hotels and luxury hotels. Consider cost / service / room / refreshments / the experience / location / booking process, etc.

Language focus 1: Effectively conveying information with noun phrases

A noun phrase is a group of words in a sentence which together behave as a noun – for example, 'the UK's budget hotels'. Noun phrases are able to communicate a lot of information in a small space, and are therefore very useful when writing.

1 Put each group of words in order to make a noun phrase.

1 airlines the no-frills
2 has recession businesses one the thing taught
3 decisions beneficiary of any a major
4 the coming predictions about confident year
5 chains UK the hotel budget
6 for value money conspicuous

2 Put the noun phrases from exercise 1 into the paragraph below.

a _____ is that companies offering b _____ will continue to thrive. c _____ are making d _____ . And, not surprisingly perhaps, e _____ also expect to be f _____ by British tourists to abandon foreign holidays for British breaks.

3 The above paragraph is the beginning of the newspaper article on page 32. Read the whole paragraph again. What is the main idea? Give the paragraph a title, using a noun phrase.

Skimming means quickly looking over a piece of writing without reading every word, whereas scanning means looking for specific information.

1 Should you use skimming, scanning or neither in the following situations?

1 You have a meeting starting five minutes from now, and need to read the report which will be discussed.
2 You need to quickly check to see if a long academic journal article is relevant for your research.
3 You need to gain a thorough understanding of a difficult report.
4 You need to tell your boss the price of an item in a report.
5 You are in a time-pressured exam which involves reading long texts.

2 Which reading technique, skimming or scanning, is most appropriate for answering the following questions about a text?

1 Who wrote the piece?
2 What is the style of the writing (e.g. a report)?
3 What is the overall topic of the piece?
4 Is the piece set in a particular location?

Look at the newspaper article below and answer questions 1–4 above as quickly as you can, using skimming and scanning.

3 What is the key benefit of using skimming and scanning, and what is a possible danger?

Reading: Newspaper article on budget hotels

1 Skim the article. Is the general tone:

a promotional?
b descriptive?
c critical?

Check out the UK's budget hotels

By Frank Barrett

One thing the recession has taught businesses is that companies offering conspicuous value for money will continue to thrive. The no-frills airlines are making confident predictions about the coming year. And, not surprisingly perhaps, the UK budget hotel chains also expect to be a major beneficiary of any decisions by British tourists to abandon foreign holidays for British breaks.

Actually, the budget chains have wisely shadowed the business model of airlines such as easyJet and Ryanair – not only following the shift to a 'no-frills' style, but imitating the online model of inviting people to book early for even better rates (according to Travelodge, more than 85 percent of its bookings are now made online).

This month the UK's largest budget hotel chain, Premier Inn, took the airline approach one step further by launching a trial of self check-in at five hotels across the UK. The company says the new technology can reduce check-in time to less than a minute for guests.

The self check-in automated 'pods' have already been successfully trialled at the London King's Cross Premier Inn. They have now been rolled out to four other locations – Birmingham NEC, Luton Airport, Manchester City Centre GMEX and Sheffield City Centre St Mary's Gate.

Premier Inn's main rival Travelodge's latest marketing idea has been inspired by the supermarket wars in monitoring the rates of rival chains and cutting where appropriate.

It has launched what it describes as the hotel industry's biggest-ever price-cutting campaign with the aim of attracting extra domestic holidaymakers this year.

The company says the growing recession has encouraged more British travellers to holiday at home, so the budget hotel company has introduced a 'price check' programme to highlight the massive savings to be made if consumers shop around.

Travelodge has teamed up with an independent price-monitoring company to check more than 1,300 hotel rates every day. The budget chain's desire to be the undisputed champions of price will mean investing £13 million in price cuts this year. As well as its 'price check' programme, Travelodge will maintain its successful £9 and £19 sales throughout the year and sell two-and-a-half-million rooms at less than £30.

Despite the UK's worsening economic conditions, Travelodge is maintaining its major growth programme, with another 36 hotel openings in 2009. New sites in resorts such as Bournemouth, Scarborough and Blackpool indicate the chain's belief that the British seaside is likely to enjoy a revival this summer.

With Premier and Travelodge both confident of growth – currently the two chains account for about 60 percent of the budget hotel market – smaller rivals will have to work hard to compete. From the point of view of the traveller, the ferocious competition can only mean ever more attractive prices and a continuing drive to improve hotel comfort and service.

The success of the budget chains is also having an impact on other hotel sectors. In the past few years there has been an obvious growth in the number of smaller, affordable boutique hotels that offer an attractively furnished hotel room at a keen price.

In the budget hotel war, it seems everyone's a winner.

Source: *Daily Mail*

2 Skim the article, and choose the answer below which best describes how it is structured.

1 The article is divided into separate sections on budget airlines, budget hotels and supermarkets.
2 The first section compares budget hotels to budget airlines, while the second section compares budget hotels to supermarkets.
3 The first section talks mainly about one budget hotel chain, while the second section talks mainly about another budget hotel chain.

3 Scan the article, and fill in the table below with either Yes, No or Not stated.

	cheap airlines	budget hotels	supermarkets
'no frills' style	Yes	Yes	Not stated
invite early booking			
self check-in			
monitor prices of rival chains			
offer budget and luxury ranges			
conduct price-cutting			
offer a 'price check' programme			

4 Reread the article and discuss any extra information that you found when you weren't skimming and scanning.

Language focus 2: Recognising persuasive language

According to the philosopher Aristotle, the ability to stir emotions is one of the most powerful persuasive techniques in communication.

1 Look at these sentences about budget hotels (some are taken from the newspaper article). Which of the sentences use emotional language?

1 In the budget hotel war, it seems everyone's a winner.
2 They love the value we offer, our clean and comfortable rooms and the warm welcome they receive from our team members.
3 The company says the new technology can reduce check-in time.
4 The ferocious competition can only mean ever more attractive prices.

2 Underline the emotional language in the sentences.

3 Look at the slogans of famous companies and products below.

1 Can you match the slogan (1–4) to the type of company or product (a–d)?
2 What feelings and emotions is each company trying to appeal to?

1 Catch our smile	a hotel chain
2 Motion and emotion	b airline
3 Save today, save tomorrow	c car manufacturer
4 Stay smart	d energy company

4 As well as stirring emotions, Aristotle said that two other ways of persuading somebody are through the force of logical argument, and the fame or status of the speaker. Which way would persuade you most? In advertising in your country, which methods are used most?

Output: Presenting a hotel chain

Stage 1
Work in small groups. Your group will be allocated one of the hotel chains from the reading. You have to prepare a two-minute mini-presentation about why your hotel chain has the best prospects in the market to potential investors. You should make the presentation persuasive, and you can be imaginative in your approach.

Group A look at page 138 and read about Premier Inn.
Group B look at the information below and read about Travelodge.

Group B
Travelodge

Travelodge claims to be the fastest-growing budget hotel chain in the country, with more than 350 hotels across the UK, Ireland and Spain. Last year it opened 40 new hotels, an average of one every nine days.

'Our best prices are online. Like seats on an airline, you can book rooms up to 12 months in advance,' says a Travelodge spokesman. 'The earlier you book, the greater your chance of finding one of our Saver rooms, which start from just £19.

'You pay for rooms when you book them, rather than when you arrive, which means speedy check-in and no need for check-out. You can customise your stay by purchasing additional products from us such as breakfast or WiFi access, either when you make your booking or at the hotel.'

Stage 2
Each group should make their presentation to the whole class, and at the end all the participants should vote for the best presentation based on how persuasive they judged it to be. You cannot vote for yourselves!

3.3 Skills: Making a sales pitch

Learning outcomes

- Learn how to employ different sales techniques.
- Learn language for making persuasive presentations.
- Produce and deliver an e-presentation to promote a product or service.

Introduction

1 Look at the different ways that you can make a sales presentation of a product or service and identify some advantages of each medium.

Example: An e-presentation on the company's website means people can view it as many times as they like, at a time convenient to them, anywhere in the world. It can also be replayed or forwarded to other interested people.

- – e-presentation on the company website
- – advertisement in a newspaper or magazine
- – conversation with a prospective client at a trade fair
- – stand-up sales pitch at an industry conference
- – a printed brochure

2 What are some of the disadvantages?

Business view

Bizantra is a technology company based in London, England.

Listening: Sales presentation

 1.21

1 Listen to the sales presentation that features on the Bizantra website and answer the following questions. Circle the correct answer A, B or C.

1 What product or service is Bizantra selling?
  A software for big business
  B software for small businesses
  C software and business IT consultancy services

2 How is the presentation structured?
  A It first talks about the positive side of business and then looks at the negative side.
  B It first talks about Bizantra the company and then talks about Bizantra's main product.
  C It first talks about a business problem and then offers a solution.

2 The sentences below show the different ways in which the Bizantra presentation tries to persuade people to find out more about the company and its product. Listen to the extracts from the presentation and complete the sentences.

 1.22

1 You've got a _____ business.
2 … more administrative tasks, more _____ , more _____ channels.
3 Sound _____?
4 It's the growing pains of any successful business. But Bizantra means it _____ _____ _____ _____ this way.
5 Bizantra is a simple, _____ and _____ alternative.

3 Match the above language examples to the presentation techniques below.

a Contrast a problem with a solution.
b Use a positive adjective to show your enthusiasm.
c Group three adjectives together to give descriptions higher impact.
d Repeat the same language structure to make a powerful impact.
e Ask a question to get the audience to 'nod in agreement'.

4 Create similar descriptive sentences to prepare for a sales presentation of a product or service that you admire. Choose a product or service that you have purchased recently or a product you have with you now (e.g. a mobile phone, a calculator, a laptop, a watch, a lipstick).

Language focus 1: Presentation techniques of persuasion

1 Read the audio script for another e-presentation from Bizantra's website and try to predict what will be said by completing the gaps. Note that each highlighted part of the text illustrates a persuasion technique.

Bizantra is an integrated suite of all the essential latest-technology business tools for the smarter, 1 _____ business. It gives you everything a growing business needs, all in one place and for just a small subscription fee. Bizantra makes collaborating easy. Use as many of Bizantra's Shared Spaces as you need to connect with your team, whether they're across the office or on the other side of the world. Share documents, discussions, tasks and contacts with whomever you want, 2 _____ they are.

Whether you're on or offline, at your PC or on the web, with Bizantra you'll have access to your whole business, whenever you need it. Create opportunities and strengthen customer relationships with our powerful Contact Management and Email Marketing. Store contacts, track discussions and 3 _____ your sales efforts in one place, then set up email marketing campaigns in minutes. Stay on top of increasing staff demands with Bizantra HR. Easily manages record keeping, absence tracking and compliance 4 _____ _____ _____ informed staffing decisions, fast.

Designed for smaller businesses, our easy-to-use Finance application 5 _____ _____ an at-a-glance summary of all your finances so you can manage them easily. Giving you more time to focus on what makes your business tick. Bizantra does all that and much more. And it comes with rock-solid security, so you know that, even if your PC fails you, 6 _____ _____ . Bizantra is integrated, efficient and 7 _____ . You don't need technical expertise; you just sign up, download and away you go. And with a no-commitment, 8 _____ price, you'll wonder how you did business without it. Why not 9 _____ _____ _____ ? Sign up for a free 60-day trial now.

2 Listen to the presentation and check your answers.

 1.23

3 How is the structure of this presentation different from the first presentation? Which structure do you prefer? Why?

4 Look again at the presentation techniques in question 3 of the Listening on page 34. The first four techniques are used in the second presentation above. Find examples of the techniques in the highlighted text. (One technique has two examples.)

5 Match the remaining four highlighted parts of the text to the other persuasion techniques described below.

1 Close the presentation asking prospective clients to make contact.
2 Use two or more words together with the same consonant sound to provide memorable phrases.
3 Describe a product feature and show how it benefits the client. (2 examples)

6 Extend the description of the product or service you described in question 4 of the Listening. Write three single sentences using the new presentation techniques shown here. Read them aloud to your partner and discuss any changes you can make to improve them.

Language focus 2: Pausing and stressing words in presentations

Making a good sales presentation (or, in fact, _any_ presentation) is not simply about what you say, but also about _how_ you say it. Pausing between words and stressing particular words makes the difference between a meaningful presentation and a dull, boring one.

1 Look at the audio script below of the first part of the presentation. The underlined words show the words which are stressed. Listen to the presentation and mark where the presenter pauses between words. Mark these pauses with a |. The first one has been done for you.

Bizantra| is an integrated suite of all the essential latest-technology business tools for the smarter, smaller business. It gives you everything a growing business needs, all in one place and for just a small subscription fee.

2 What do you notice about the type of words that are stressed and where the pauses are located?

3 There are many different presentation styles that can be used. The choice of style depends on what your organisation and audience require, and also on how comfortable you feel with one style or another. Listen to the start of the Listening presentation delivered in two different styles. How would you describe the style used in each?

 1.24

A formal and authoritative
B enthusiastic and dynamic
C relaxed and friendly

Output: Make a persuasive e-presentation of a product or service

In pairs, choose a product or service that you know very well and write a word-for-word script for a short presentation (60–90 seconds), to be used on the company's website. Keep in mind the following points:

- Decide how you want to structure the presentation.
- Use a number of persuasive sales presentation techniques.

Practise presenting it to your partner, taking care to stress important words and pause in the correct places. Decide on a presentation style that suits you and the product/service you are promoting. If there is time, give the presentation to the class. When listening to other presentations, note down how many persuasive presentation techniques were used.

4 Entrepreneurship

4.1 Theory: Fostering entrepreneurship

Learning outcomes

- Learn language and importance of risk to entrepreneurship.
- Give friendly advice.
- Propose a project to foster entrepreneurship in young people.

Introduction

entrepreneur /ˌɒn.trə.prəˈnɜː/ *noun* someone who starts their own business, especially when this involves seeing a new opportunity

1 Read the definition of 'entrepreneur' from the *Cambridge Advanced Learner's Dictionary* above and select from the following characteristics the five that you think are most needed to be a successful entrepreneur.

aggressive determination
problem-solver
creative thinker
young and energetic
persuasive communicator
strategic planner
idea generator
people motivator
big personality
risk-taker
experienced manager
hard worker
unconventional attitude

Compare your list with a partner and agree on a common list.

2 'Entrepreneurship' refers to the process, learning and study of being an entrepreneur. Do you think that anybody (including yourself) can learn to be an entrepreneur? Are entrepreneurial qualities simply something people are born with, or not?

Language focus 1: The language of risk

1 Complete the gap in each question with the correct preposition to form a common word partnership with 'risk'. Answer the questions A, B or C for yourself.

1 How much of an appetite _____ risk do you have in your personal or professional life?
   A No appetite at all
   B Limited appetite
   C Big appetite
2 What is your perception _____ risk in the case of extreme sports such as rock-climbing without ropes?
   A These people are crazy!
   B I'd love to learn.
   C I'd do it, but only with ropes.
3 Has your attitude _____ risk changed over time?
   A No, it hasn't.
   B I avoid risk more.
   C I avoid risk less.

Would you classify yourself as a 'risk-taker' or not? Compare and discuss your answers with a partner.

2 Categorise the following verb/noun partnerships into three groups:

1 actions to reduce risk
2 actions to increase risk
3 actions to manage risk

> understand risk   mitigate risk   tolerate risk   spread risk
> calculate risk   minimise risk   control risk   take risks

Which one of these word partnerships would you be most likely to 'put your name to' as a personal philosophy? Explain why.

3 Categorise the following actions as posing a 'financial risk', a 'reputational risk', an 'operational risk', or a combination of these risks. Explain your answer.

1 non-payment of bills
2 introducing complex new technology
3 selling an unreliable product
4 making 80% of sales to a single client

Listening 1: New research on risk

 1.25

Business view

Dr Shai Vyakarnam is Director of the Centre for Entrepreneurial Learning, Cambridge Judge Business School, University of Cambridge.

1 Before listening to the interview with Dr Shai Vyakarnam, read the definition of 'impulsive' from the *Cambridge Advanced Learner's Dictionary* and answer the question that follows.

> **impulsive** /ɪmˈpʌlsɪv/ *adj* showing behaviour in which you do things suddenly without any planning and without considering the effects they may have: *Don't be so impulsive – think before you act.*

What do you think Dr Shai Vyakarnam will say about impulsiveness and entrepreneurs?

2 Listen to the first part of the interview and choose the correct answer (A, B or C for the following questions).

1 The Centre for Entrepreneurial Learning research involved
  A comparing test results between entrepreneurs and Psychiatry Department results.
  B using tests on entrepreneurs normally used by the Department of Psychiatry.
  C using their tests in the Department of Psychiatry.

2 The research showed that entrepreneurs and other successful people have
  A similar cold decision-making functions.
  B similar hot decision-making functions.
  C have both hot and cold decision-making functions in common.

3 The best entrepreneurs combine
  A impulsiveness and risk-taking.
  B budgeting and planning.
  C risk-taking and planning.

3 Discuss with a partner what type of decision-making you normally use: hot or cold, or a combination of the two? When do you tend to employ one type of decision-making, and when the other?

Transferable skill: Conveying meaning visually

1 Look at the two photos here and the one at the beginning of the unit on page 36. Which one best captures what entrepreneurship is all about, in your opinion?

2 If you were giving a presentation on entrepreneurship, what kind of images (other than the ones shown here) would you use on your slides?

Listening 2: Young entrepreneurs

 1.26

1 Before listening, discuss the question statement that the interviewer puts to Dr Shai Vyakarnam. How would you answer this question?

Young people take more risks so if you want to be an entrepreneur, you ought to start your business when you're young?

2 Now listen to the recording and note down the answer Dr Shai Vyakarnam gives to this question, and the reason he gives to support his answer.

Language focus 2: Giving friendly advice

 1.26

1 When giving advice informally, it is common to use verbs in the imperative form, and to use the verbs 'go' and 'get'. Read this transcript of an extract from the final part of the interview, where Dr Shai Vyakarnam discusses advice that should be given to young entrepreneurs. Complete the gaps with a verb in the imperative.

We normally tell graduates 'Go 1 _____ a proper job. 2 _____ some experience. 3 _____ some money. Learn the skills. And then 4 _____ start a company if you want to'. Whereas what we should be saying is 'Have a go to begin with when you are young, when the risks don't seem so great. 5 _____ about entrepreneurship. Maybe learn your own attitude towards risk.'

'6 _____ and find somebody who has done it before and try to learn from them. A bit like an apprentice. 7 _____ and learn from many of them. 8 _____ networking. 9 _____ your boundaries. 10 _____ things that are new and different, away from your routines. Try to get a feeling for what it is to take a risk – not just the scholarly view of risk, but actually deep down in your gut, what it feels like.'

2 Listen to this section of the interview again and check your answers.

3 Listen to two different pronunciations of these imperative phrases. Underline the words that are stressed. How does the different stress change the meaning?

 1.27

1 Go and learn from many of them. Get networking.
2 Go and learn from many of them. Get networking.

4 Of the many pieces of advice Dr Shai Vyakarnam gives to would-be entrepreneurs, which one do you think is the most valuable? Why?

Output: Propose a project to foster entrepreneurship in schools

Stage 1
In small groups, discuss an innovative way schools could teach entrepreneurship and foster an entrepreneurial spirit and understanding of risk amongst teenage students – tomorrow's future entrepreneurs. Your solution should be in the form of a project or competition that fully engages students and requires only a minimal budget. It also needs to be something that could be quickly and easily put into action with minimal organisation and effort. Possible ideas include: a link-up with a local business, a prize competition, setting up an online shop hosted on the school's website, running a snack shop at the school, etc.

Take notes of the main points of your discussion.

Stage 2
Give a short presentation (2–3 minutes) to the class, who will represent the school authorities. Explain your idea and give them friendly advice on how to implement your idea.

Whilst listening to other group presentations, make notes to help decide whose idea would work best. Use the following criteria to evaluate the presentations.

	Notes
How innovative is it?	
How simple and easy is it to implement?	
How well does it teach the concepts of entrepreneurship?	
How well does it teach understanding of risk?	
How realistic is it to do on a low budget?	
How likely is it to engage and excite teenagers?	

4.2 Practice: Jack Ma and Alibaba

Learning outcomes

- See how entrepreneurship works in action in China.
- Learn topic vocabulary and language of data quantification.
- Evaluate partners for new business opportunities.

Jack Ma addresses a business forum in Hong Kong

Jack Ma with eBay CEO John Donahoe at the annual Alibaba Netrepreneur Summit

Profile: Alibaba.com

Alibaba.com is the flagship company of the Alibaba Group. It was founded by Jack Ma (and others) in 1999 in Hangzhou in Eastern China. Essentially it is an e-commerce trading platform that provides a market place to enable small businesses (and individuals) in China and the rest of the world to do business with each other directly, without going through costly middlemen. A lot of the cross-border trade involves foreign buyers and Chinese suppliers. It has over 50 million registered users in nearly every country and region in the world. The company is valued in tens of billions of dollars, yet it employs only 22,000 people. Its shares are listed on the Hong Kong Stock Exchange.

Profile: Jack Ma

What other chairman of a multi-billion dollar technology company would say on public record: 'I know nothing about technology. The only thing I use my computer for, is to send and receive email and browse'? And in the corporate and financial world, where the shareholder is king, Jack Ma says: 'We believe the customer is number one, employee number two, shareholder three.' Jack Ma is one of the most wealthy, influential and charismatic entrepreneurs in China. He is known for his independent thinking, his simple and direct communication style, his ability to motivate and inspire and his diminutive stature. He speaks fluent English and is a former English teacher.

Jack Ma dressed as a punk rocker for the 10th anniversary celebrations of the Alibaba Group

Introduction

1 Have you ever bought or sold anything over the Internet? What are the benefits?

2 Look at the profile for Alibaba.com. What are the benefits to a small business of using this service? How do its services differ from websites you have used to buy or sell online?

3 Read the profile of Jack Ma. What characteristics does he share with well-known entrepreneurs in your country?

Martial Arts Moves

1 Jack Ma failed the college entrance examination in China twice; he barely passed on the third try. He believes that if he has been able to succeed, most people can do the same. But not everybody has set out to restructure the way business is done around the world by creating a new model for use of the Internet. By systematically putting together the elements of a new model, what he calls an 'eco-system', Jack Ma started a global movement from a small corner of China. He enabled millions of small companies to use the Internet as a primary business tool, to a degree allowing internet functions inside China to evolve beyond what they are in the West. Through use of this tool, he has effectively leveraged China's ability to trade; over the past several years, this has changed the weighting of China on the world's stage.

2 Despite Jack Ma's 'anyone can do it' claim, the fact remains that not just anyone did. Almost everything about Jack Ma is counter-intuitive – he looks at the world from a unique perspective. His greatest delight is using small to conquer big, quick to conquer slow, and intuitive insight to conquer conventional wisdom. The abstractions by which he formulates strategic plans are based on the moves of martial arts more than mathematical equations, and the mental discipline behind those moves informs his every thought. In Jack Ma, we are looking at the incarnation of a traditional martial arts master.

3 Alibaba.com is only one of the network of companies under the Alibaba umbrella. Others include an online payment service called Alipay, the largest online payment platform in China, and an online consumer marketplace called Taobao, which has all but chased eBay out of China. They include a software development company called Alisoft, which creates business software that 'lives' on the Net. All of these lie within the embrace of the Ali family and are ultimately controlled by Ali management and employees. Key investors in the network include Softbank in Japan and Yahoo! in the United States. The founders of those companies have been keys to Jack Ma's vision of creating a global company – but one that is owned and managed by Chinese nationals.

4 In reading Jack Ma's story and the story of Alibaba, it is useful to place the company in the context of global internet business. Up until the end of 1995, China officially forbade any news about the internet in Chinese media. By 1997, however, this policy was overturned, and the steep curve of internet use in China had begun. Today there are more than 230 million Internet users in the country, according to the government backed China Internet Information Center (CNNIC). China has more internet users than any other country, including the United States, which it surpassed in 2008. More than half of China's users, more than 163 million, are connected via broadband, due to the remarkable fiber network that the Chinese government has funded throughout the country.

5 While China has one of the most sophisticated internet filtering technologies in the world to censor information, the decentralisation of information technologies and their creative use for nonpolitical purposes ensure the Chinese people rapid entry into a digital age. Jack Ma's recognition of the potential for the technology allowed him to develop a model that was self-sustaining and economically viable. It focuses on ways information technology can make small companies more competitive and profitable. Since four-fifths of business in China is done by some thirty-two million small companies, the leveraging effects are substantial.

Source: *Alibaba: The Inside Story Behind Jack Ma and the Creation of the World's Biggest Online Marketplace*
by Shiying Liu and Martha Avery

Reading: The rise of Jack Ma

Skim read an extract from the book *Alibaba: The Inside Story Behind Jack Ma and the Creation of the World's Biggest Online Marketplace* by Shiying Liu and Martha Avery, and answer the questions.

1 **Match these paragraph summaries to the correct paragraphs.**

- How the Internet is used in China
- How the Internet has grown in China
- The philosophy of Jack Ma
- The achievements of Jack Ma
- Different companies connected to Alibaba.com

2 **Read the text again and complete these sentences with words taken directly from the text. Write no more than three words for each answer.**

1 China's trading ability has benefited from its small companies using Alibaba as a _____ . (paragraph 1)
2 Like a martial arts master, Jack Ma's strategy is based on _____ . (paragraph 2)
3 _____ have been important backers of the Alibaba Group. (paragraph 3)
4 The high number of broadband connections in China is ultimately driven by investment from _____ . (paragraph 4)
5 The Alibaba model helps small businesses by enabling them to be more _____ . (paragraph 5)

3 Find words and phrases in the text with the same meaning as those below.

1 level of importance (paragraph 1)
2 international level (paragraph 1)
3 against common sense (paragraph 2)
4 general consensus view (paragraph 2)
5 put together / create (paragraph 2)
6 a method for paying over the Internet (paragraph 3)
7 a sharp increase (paragraph 4)
8 supported by the state (paragraph 4)
9 reversed [a decision] (paragraph 4)
10 tools used to control online access (paragraph 5)

Critical analysis

1 Talking about Jack Ma's business practices, the text states that 'His greatest delight is using … intuitive insight to conquer conventional wisdom.' What are the pros and cons of using intuition over 'rational logical analysis' to make decisions?
2 What about you? How do you tend to make decisions?

Language focus: Quantifying data

1 There are a number of examples of language of quantity in the text.

1 millions of small companies (paragraph 1)
2 More than half of China's users (paragraph 4)
3 four-fifths of business in China (paragraph 5)

How could you express them differently without changing their meaning?

2 Which of the following expressions of quantity can describe 'internet users' and which can be used to describe 'internet traffic'? Some expressions can be used for both.

1 the vast majority of
2 a great number of
3 two out of three
4 three quarters of
5 a fair amount of
6 plenty of
7 few
8 a limited quantity of
9 millions of
10 sixty percent of

3 Each of the following sentences contains typical student errors made at Advanced level. Identify and correct each one. Some sentences have more than one error.

1 The population number of those countries vary from around 30 millions to 225 millions.
2 Global Ports Inc. only handles small quantity freight in Europe.

3 Only small fraction number of people work over 12 hours a day.
4 The great majority of UK tourists goes to France, but a significant number also goes to Spain.
5 With the new booking system, the amount of visitors is now controllable.

Output: Starting business in China

Stage 1

Work in small groups. Group A and Group B are foreign entrepreneurs who are looking to find a distributor in China. Group C and Group D are distributors and retailers in China using Alibaba.com and other channels.

Group A look at the information below.
Group B look at the information on page 139.
Group C look at the information on page 143.
Group D look at the information on page 145.

Group A

You are a company that manufactures quality metal office furniture (desks, chairs, bookshelves, etc.). You currently manufacture the goods in your own country. You would like to break into the Chinese market as you have heard there is a rising middle class of over 200 million and your products are aimed at this sector of the market. You have also heard that manufacturing costs are lower in China, so in the long term you would like to start manufacturing there.

The partner you are looking for:

- can help you get your products into the main retail chain stores in China and/or direct to the consumer through online channels.
- can help you build your brand as aspirational to the middle class.
- has plenty of warehouses and vehicles to distribute the goods across mainland China.
- has good business and government connections in China to help you set up a factory and identify reliable suppliers.

Stage 2

Using your information, make notes on what you are looking for in a business partner and think of anything else that might be useful for you.

Stage 3

Groups A and C meet to discuss what they need and can offer. Groups B and D meet to discuss what they need and can offer.

When you have finished, Group A should meet with Group D and Group B with Group C.

Stage 4

In your group decide who you would most like to do business with. Be aware of your decision-making preferences (intuitive or rational/logical) when coming to your decision.

Learning outcomes

- Compare and contrast collaborative and aggressive negotiating strategies and language.
- Consider how culture can impact negotiations.
- Negotiate effectively on price.

66 If you are planning on doing business with someone again, don't be too tough in the negotiations. If you're going to skin a cat, don't keep it as a house cat. **99**

Marvin S. Levin, management consultant and expert on negotiations

Introduction

1 Read the above quote, and discuss whether it is good advice. Why/Why not?

2 Imagine that you are trying to sell your car, and someone has offered you $1,500, which they can pay today. You then receive three more offers:

a a close friend offers you $1,400

b a stranger offers you $1,650, which they will pay in 50 days' time

c a garage offers to offset $2,000 against the price of a new car

Discuss in pairs the advantages and disadvantages of each of the four options, and then decide which one you would prefer. Consider the following issues:

- Future relationship
- Trust
- Personal benefit
- Desirability of choices

Language focus 1: Negotiating strategies

Negotiating strategies are often separated into two kinds: 'collaborative' and 'aggressive'.

1 Match these definitions with the two types of strategy, and think of an example of each.

a those that aim to look for common ground, and emphasise positive aspects of the communication/relationship

b those that utilise the power or advantage of the stronger side to pressurise the other side.

2 Sort the following negotiating strategies into the two categories.

commands	commitments
promises	open information exchanges
recommendations	threats
warnings	shared secrets
blank refusals	

Collaborative	Aggressive

3 Look at the different ways of expressing negotiating strategies. Match the phrases (1–7) with the sentences with similar meanings (a–g).

1 I command you …	a You don't perform, you're out.
2 I promise …	b We won't say anything about it if you don't.
3 I recommend this …	c Why don't you buy it?
4 I warn you …	d You have to do it.
5 We refuse …	e We'll have to say no.
6 We threaten to …	f If you don't pay, we'll withdraw your credit.
7 We will keep a secret …	g I'll definitely have the answer this week.

4 Which expressions are used more frequently – the ones in the left-hand column or those on the right?

5 While speakers may use an aggressive or collaborative approach, the desired result may be the same. For instance, imagine you want your supplier to reduce prices. You could either make a recommendation, or give them a warning (or a command). What are the advantages of each approach?

Listening 1: Discussing effective negotiating

🔊 1.28

1 Listen to a new (but experienced) salesperson talking to his sales manager about negotiating effectively.

1 Why does the salesperson like to get to the negotiation stage?
  a Because he enjoys negotiating over prices and services.
  b Because it means the other company wants to make a deal.
2 What does he say is the key difference between an inexperienced and an experienced salesperson?
  a An experienced salesperson is more likely to offer discounts only to loyal customers.
  b An experienced salesperson is more likely to offer discounts in return for concessions from customers.
3 In what situations can the company offer discounts?
  a When the other company promises to buy a longer contract.
  b When it looks like the company will miss the monthly sales target.

2 After listening, consider whether you think these colleagues prefer a collaborative or an aggressive approach. What strategies do they use?

Listening 2: A price negotiation

🔊 1.29

Listen to a manufacturer and a supplier negotiating a price increase. Match these numbers with the prices they discuss.

1	120	**a**	the new suggested price
2	126	**b**	the negotiated final price
3	125	**c**	the price suggested as a joke
4	115	**d**	the old price

Language focus 2: Collaborative negotiating language

1 Match the following types of collaborative language (1–8) with the examples from the listening extracts (a–h). The examples have also been marked in the audio script on page 152.

1	rejecting indirectly	a	it's a **two-way street**
2	frequent use of 'we'	b	**I can't justify it to** my group financial director
3	vague language	c	Well, fine. We can **probably do something**
4	metaphors	d	**What are you going to do for me?**
5	making an excuse	e	**If you can commit** this level of business to me, **this is what you're going to** pay now
6	making an offer	f	**we have** a laugh and a joke and **we do try**
7	requesting a compromise	g	**I'm hesitant to** do it
8	humour	h	**To be fair, it would look even better at a hundred and fifteen.**

2 Match the answers from exercise 1 with the functions below. Listen to the extracts again if you need to. The first has been done for you.

1 relax the mood of the negotiation   8h
2 bring sides closer while not making a concrete promise
3 comment on the relationship indirectly (to show mutual obligation)
4 propose conditions for the other side to accept
5 attempt to reach a mutually acceptable outcome
6 show a shared position and viewpoint
7 give reasons for the decision
8 not appear too forceful

Intercultural analysis

How acceptable are the following ways of influencing commercial negotiation in your culture? Are any unethical?

playing golf together, taking someone out for dinner, giving gifts, giving souvenirs from your area, taking visitors on a tour, taking spouses on trips

Output: Negotiating on cost

Stage 1: Preparing for the negotiation
In groups, look at the situations in exercise 2 of the Introduction. What types of strategies would be most effective for each of the participants in the negotiations? For example, could a close friend use threats of some kind? You can refer to the example strategies from the lesson, and any others you know of.

Stage 2: The negotiation
Role play the situation, with one person being the seller, and the others taking the roles of potential buyers (the close friend, the stranger and the garage salesperson). By the end, the seller needs to choose who to sell to.

Stage 3: Debriefing
After the negotiation, discuss which strategies you think were effective, how satisfied you are with the result, and what you could have done differently.

▶️ **Watch Sequence 2 on the DVD to find out more about Competition and entrepreneurship.**

Writing 2: Business plan and executive summary

Learning outcomes

- Structure a business plan for a new business start-up.
- Write parts of an executive summary and identify the key features.
- Write an outline business plan in note form.

Introduction

1 In what ways do you think that writing a business plan helps entrepreneurs increase their chances of success? Are there any disadvantages to planning?

2 Imagine you have a successful small business selling premium, homemade, Italian-style, yoghurt ice cream from a single city-centre location. Your plan is to become an ice cream entrepreneur and expand the business by opening a network of small kiosks located in busy city centre locations. Your first step is to set up three kiosks. You need to get a loan from a bank to finance this. What information do you think the bank will want to see before they consider loaning you the money? Make a list with a partner.

Business view

Royal Bank of Canada provides expert business advice to new business start-ups on how to write business plans.

Writing skill 1: Outline structure for a business plan

1 Royal Bank of Canada offers an example business plan for entrepreneurs seeking finance from their bank. The table on the right sets out its main sections, in the order they would appear in an actual plan. Match the sections of the plan (1–8) to the summary descriptions of their content (a–h).

2 How much of this information did you include in the list you made for the Introduction task?

3 Write a list of risks you would include in the final 'Risks and conclusions' section of a business plan for the ice cream business you discussed.

Section	What's included?
1 Introduction	**a** A description of the industry your company is in and an analysis of the competitive forces at play.
2 Executive summary	**b** This will set out forecast expenses and income and anticipated profits over the next few years and itemise any upfront costs.
3 The team	**c** This will identify the main threats that could impact on your business and summarise how you intend to counter them.
4 Business environment	**d** This gives a simple factual summary of the company in terms of when it was founded, its main products or services, and the industry sector it operates in.
5 Marketing plan	**e** The most important part of the report, which includes the highlights of the whole plan. It should be a maximum of 1–2 pages. It is best to write it <u>after</u> you have finished writing your plan.
6 Operations	**f** This will first state who your target market is and will then include sub-sections on your pricing and promotion strategy, the USPs (unique selling points) of your product and service, and how you intend to get it into the hands of your customers (distribution strategy).
7 Finance	**g** This sets out the process of how the product will be produced (or sold through the supply chain), or how the service will be delivered. As a start-up, it should also state the development stage you are at (already in business, at piloting stage, at concept stage, etc.).
8 Risks and conclusions	**h** A profile of the key people in the business – banks invest in great people as much as great business idea. They will want to know your skills, experience and qualifications.

Language focus: Key features of an executive summary

1 The executive summary draws and summarises information from the business plan that follows it. Match the paragraphs in the executive summary to the sections of the business plan. The first one has been done for you.

Paragraph number	Sections of business plan where information is drawn from
1	**a** Finance
2	**b** Team, Operations
3	**c** Team
4	**d** Marketing, Operations
5	**e** Business environment, Marketing, Finance
6	**f** Business environment, Marketing

2 Read ten key characteristics of good executive summary writing and find evidence of them in the text. Write the text reference next to each characteristic – the first one has been done for you.

1 State who the target market is. paragraph 1
2 Show there is a good market for your product or service.
3 Cite authoritative sources to back up your data.
4 Show the company's key financial performance information.
5 Show how unique and relevant your experience and skills are.
6 Use bullets to list points.
7 Show how you compare favourably with the competition.
8 Show you have support of useful network of important contacts.
9 State how much money you want to borrow over how long.
10 Show investment you have made (or will make) in the business.

Writing skill 2: Executive summary writing

In pairs, refer to the 12 highlighted sections of the text and rewrite them for the ice cream business you discussed earlier. You will need to extend the sentences and change certain words, according to your own ideas of how you see this business.

For example, the first highlighted part of the text might be changed as follows:

City Chill, located near Liverpool Street station in London, is a high-quality ice cream business specialising in the sale of homemade Italian-style yoghurt ice cream to health-conscious professionals working nearby.

Output: Writing an outline business plan

In small groups, look at the sections of the business plan for the ice cream business that you have not yet covered, and discuss the outline details. Make any relevant notes and then write the introductory paragraph for each of these remaining sections.

Executive Summary

1 Kamiko Fine Foods Inc., located in Vancouver, British Columbia, is a wholesaling company specializing in importing high-quality Japanese foods and repackaging them for sale to specialty food retailers. The business was established to offer authentic Japanese foods to the growing Asian population in the Vancouver area as well as to an ever-increasing market of urban professionals who enjoy eating more adventurous specialty ethnic foods.

2 Research indicates that the International Foods industry in Canada has annual sales of $180 million and is growing at an average rate of 30 percent per year. The Vancouver market alone is estimated to be worth $14 million. In fact, the Japanese population in Vancouver – the end user of Kamiko Fine Foods' products – is growing at 8 percent per year and an estimated 36 percent of this population purchase high-quality Japanese food products on a monthly basis. In the general population, 29 percent of people purchase specialty ethnic foods on a monthly basis. According to the Association of Canadian Food Distributors, ethnic food in general and Japanese food specifically are poised for substantial growth in British Columbia and a total of ten Japanese restaurants were opened in the greater Vancouver area in the last two years. We have reached revenues of $300,000 in our first year and project revenues of $450,000 in our second.

3 As president and sole owner of Kamiko Fine Foods Inc., I bring my ten years' experience working in my family's business in Japan to the company. I have forged long-term business relationships with three major Japanese food exporters, all of whom guarantee Kamiko Fine Foods Inc. excellent prices. In addition, I have been using the services of J. Sango, who is based in Japan and acts as a purchasing agent for the company. The company also uses the services of a sales agent, a part-time bookkeeper and a part-time delivery person.

4 There are three direct competitors for our share of the market. Although all three seem to be thriving, there are a number of fronts on which we are competing. Price is the strongest factor as all three competitors sell their products at higher prices than Kamiko Fine Foods. Our strong relationships with major Japanese exporters allow us to sell our products at a price comparable to or lower than the competition. In addition, the three competitors have focused primarily on marketing to the Japanese buyer. Kamiko fully exploits the potential market made up of non-Asian urban professionals – achieved through attractive packaging and an extensive local brand awareness campaign.

In order to support our retail customers, Kamiko Fine Foods products are advertised and promoted in a number of ways, including:

- Sponsorship of a Japanese cooking show on community access television
- Free sample product display cases in retail outlets
- A company Web site, which raises awareness of our products
- Printed coupons in community newspapers
- Distribution of flyers at gourmet stores
- Media relations

5 In addition to the staff outlined above, I have assembled a board of advisors who add strategic advice and direction. The board consists of Louis Marton, Senior Manager of Chesterton Distributing; Bryce Anderson, president of Key Connections Communications Inc.; Michelle Denison, president of Denison Publishing Ltd. and Ingrid Huxtable, a corporate lawyer and founding partner Huxtable, Grenobl, Rigby and Associates.

6 I am seeking an operating line* of $60,000 to finance our growth in year two. I have invested $23,000 in the previous years in packaging, design, product and market research and have invested an additional $15,000 towards working capital requirements at the outset.

* overdraft facility

Source: www.rbcroyalbank.com

5 Crisis management

5.1 Theory: Dealing with crisis events

Learning outcomes
- Understand the nature and impact of a crisis event.
- Compare and contrast strategy and tactics.
- Decide on tactics to deal with crisis events.

Introduction

1 Read the list of different examples of crisis events that organisations might have to face. Sort them into two categories (A and B).

A A crisis originating from outside the organisation
B A crisis originating from within the organisation

1 a conflict within a country ____
2 a huge technological breakthrough by a competitor ____
3 a major scandal resulting from management misconduct ____
4 a major computer virus attack ____
5 environmental disaster ____
6 major product recall related to product defects ____
7 bankruptcy of firm's most important client or supplier ____
8 physical attacks on the company ____
9 health and safety scare ____
10 kidnapping of company directors ____

2 Select one example from each category and discuss the following questions.

- How possible is it for an organisation to predict this kind of crisis event?
- What kind of advance warning (if any) does it get?
- What preparations (if any) can an organisation make to protect itself from this crisis event?
- What can an organisation do (if anything) to avoid or prevent this crisis event from happening?

Business view

Dr Nassim Nicholas Taleb is a founding partner in US hedge fund Universa Investments, Professor in the Sciences of Uncertainty at the University of Massachusetts and author of *The Black Swan – The Impact of the Highly Improbable*.

Reading 1: 'Black Swan' metaphor

1 Read the first part of this extract from *The Black Swan – The Impact of the Highly Improbable* by Dr Nassim Nicholas Taleb. Explain the metaphor of the first sighting of a black swan by selecting <u>two</u> answers from A, B, C and D.

A It shows how we can learn from experience.
B It is symbolic of our ignorance.
C It symbolises an unknown event.
D It symbolises exploration and discovery.

> Before the discovery of Australia, people in the Old World were convinced that *all* swans were white, an unquestionable belief as it seemed completely confirmed by empirical evidence. The sighting of the first black swan illustrates a severe limitation to our learning from observation and experience and the fragility of our knowledge.

2 Read the second part of this extract and choose the best word to complete the sentences (1–3) below, which describe a Black Swan event.

1 It is an event that is *possible/impossible* to predict.
2 It is an event which has *limited/huge* consequences and effects.
3 People *mistakenly/correctly* try to rationalise the event after the fact.

> What we call here a Black Swan, is an event with the following three attributes. First it is an outlier, as it lies outside our regular expectations, because nothing in the past can convincingly point to its possibility. Second, it carries an extreme impact. Third, in spite of its outlier status, human nature makes us concoct explanations for its occurrence after the fact, making it explainable and predictable.

3 A paraphrase of what Dr Nassim Nicholas Taleb is saying is 'things always become obvious after the fact'. What is meant by this? Can you think of any examples from your life?

1 Read this text by Nancy Green, Executive Vice President of Aon Risk Solutions, the world's largest risk management company. Are the following statements true or false?

1 To understand a Black Swan crisis event you need to feel one.

2 People exaggerate how frightening a Black Swan crisis event is.

3 After you have made a full assessment of the crisis, government and regulatory agencies will need to be responded to.

4 Cash flow, credit and liquidity problems lead to falls in the stock price.

5 You need to bring in more people during a Black Swan crisis event.

6 Managing a Black Swan crisis event is all about the survival of the company.

7 Using emotion constructively can help the company leadership manage the crisis.

8 During a Black Swan crisis, leaders should forget strategy and concentrate on tactics.

2 Match the bold words and phrases in the text to the phrases with similar meanings (1–8) below.

1 important above all else

2 really essential

3 inability to focus widely

4 finding the answer to something

5 provide time to think, free from disturbance

6 routine activities

7 a series of related events in quick succession

8 fall dramatically

3 The first section of the text outlines seven characteristics of a Black Swan event, using bullet points. If you were the main decision-maker for an organisation going through a Black Swan crisis, which point would you find the most challenging?

Keys to Success in Managing a Black Swan Event

Operating During a Black Swan Crisis Event

Companies which have been struck by Black Swan crisis events often struggle because they have a difficult time making good decisions as the event unfolds. Even the most prepared and well-run organizations can find themselves in this situation. To understand why, one needs to first understand what it feels like to operate in a Black Swan crisis event and how decision-making becomes much more complex in that environment.

The following are common characteristics of many of the Black Swan crisis events that have occurred:

- It's not just about responding to the crisis and getting the situation under immediate control; it's also about **figuring out** how to fix the problem itself.
- Often, no solution to the problem exists; rather, it must be created. To make matters worse, the organization may need to go through several solutions before finding one that works. *Do not underestimate the fear factor associated with having a problem with no known solution!*
- Public relations issues can be massive. The 24/7 news feeds as well as social media outlets such as Facebook, Google and Twitter require constant monitoring and impactful responses.
- Governmental and regulatory agencies may require a response before the size/scope of the problem has been fully assessed and any viable solutions are available.
- Productivity may be negatively impacted as employees may be concerned, uncertain and distracted.
- If publicly traded, an organization's stock price may **plummet**. The falling stock price drives additional issues which require attention and may create a further **cascading effect** on cash flow, credit, liquidity, brand reputation, consumer confidence, etc.
- Lastly, the organization must mount an effective Black Swan response while still running its **day-to-day business**.

With the chaos created by all of the above happening simultaneously, it is monumentally difficult to implement an effective crisis response, find a solution to the problem and keep the day-to-day business going. From a sheer logistics standpoint alone, it is impossible to do it with the same number of people who are already fully employed in normal operations. However, once you overlay the logistics challenge with the shock factor of being hit with an inconceivable event of staggering proportions, it is even harder to maintain a good decision-making environment.

Managing Black Swan Crisis Events

Managing a Black Swan crisis event is not simply about helping the company regroup and survive its devastating consequences. It is more about facing the event and making the best of the situation so the company will emerge better and stronger than they were prior to the event.

When a Black Swan hits, it is **paramount** for the company leadership to take emotion out of the equation. This is **an absolute must** when confronting ensuing chaos. Proven strategies to accomplish this include: Focusing on accurate, factual and objective data – numbers do not lie – and expanding access to external resources to **give breathing room** to leadership and internal resources and free up capacity to run day-to-day operations.

In the face of an overwhelming situation, leadership should break the situation down into manageable components for tactical response, but retain perspective of the whole to ensure tactics are having the desired impact and continue to align with strategy. Leadership must be confident that they will find a solution – that confidence will help overcome the fear and panic, which in turn reduces the potential for **tunnel vision** and improves the ability to see the possibilities that might otherwise have been missed. Be relentlessly persistent – do not give up.

Source: *Keys to Success in Managing a Black Swan Event* by Nancy Green

Language focus: Comparison of strategy and tactics

1 Look at the two lists of adjectives (A and B) which can be used to form common word partnerships. Which list contains words that generally partner with 'strategy', and which with 'tactics'?

A broad long-term coherent comprehensive integrated carefully planned

B useful dirty underhand common delaying illegal effective strong-arm

2 'Strategy' and 'tactics' are often described in dictionaries as 'planned ways of doing something'. What is the difference between them? Use the word partnerships from exercise 1 to help you discover the answer.

3 Match the types of tactics (1–5) to the examples (a–e) given in the table.

1	dirty/underhand tactics	a	keeping staff informed without revealing anything that will make them panic
2	delaying tactics	b	agreeing prices for competing products between competitors to keep prices high (cartel pricing)
3	effective/useful tactics	c	threatening to sack the staff or move operations to another plant
4	illegal tactics	d	paying invoices late
5	strong-arm tactics	e	taking credit for work you haven't done

4 Have you experienced or used any of these tactics?

5 For which of the following goals would you have more need of a good strategy, and for which would you need good tactics? Why?

1 To rise from fourth largest player in your industry sector to become the market leader.

2 To achieve a successful outcome in the next stage of pay negotiations with trade unions.

6 Without referring back to the text, complete the following sentence about crisis events with the appropriate forms of the words 'strategy' or 'tactics'.

In the face of [a crisis event] situation, leadership should break the situation down into manageable components for 1 _____ response, but retain perspective of the whole to ensure 2 _____ are having the desired impact and continue to align with 3 _____ .

Check your answers by looking at the final paragraph of the text in Reading 2 on page 47. Do you agree with the author's advice here? Why/Why not?

Output: Deciding tactics to deal with crisis events

Stage 1

In small groups, choose one of the following crisis event situations below and brainstorm what tactics the individuals or companies concerned could adopt to deal with them.

- Risk of job loss: A middle manager in a large city-centre high-street bank needs to avoid becoming redundant in a round of severe job cuts, where one in four staff are set to lose their jobs as a result of a huge financial crisis hitting the bank.

- Industrial action: A textile producer has made a strategic decision to move its operations to a new location. However, it now faces a major crisis as workers have gone on strike. They have physically occupied the factory and are refusing to let the company's contractors move in to pack up and transport the machines away.

- Hostile press conference: An oil company is in the middle of a crisis as a result of a huge environmental disaster caused by an oil spill. It needs to manage a press conference next week where company representatives respond to questions from a hostile press and local community.

Stage 2

Present your list of possible tactics that could be adopted for the crisis situation to another group. Discuss first how common the tactics are, and then how acceptable they are from a practical, ethical and legal viewpoint.

5.2 Practice: Successfully dealing with a crisis

Learning outcomes
- Get an insider account of a company in mid-crisis and post crisis.
- Contrast financial terms of investment, equity and capital.
- Brainstorm 'What if ...?' scenarios and devise plans to deal with them.

Profile: Ceramic Fuel Cells Ltd

Ceramic Fuel Cells Ltd (CFCL) is a successful clean-energy company founded in Melbourne, Australia in 1992. It is quoted on the London and Melbourne stock exchanges. Yet, on October 17th, at the beginning of the last global financial crisis, CFCL made an announcement with dramatic news: the company had been impacted by the crisis and had 'probably lost' a financial investment of €7 million. The money had been invested in a financial product on the advice of their external financial advisors. It represented about 30% of their total cash and investments. It was needed to fund product and technology development – a Solid Oxide Fuel Cell (SOFC) technology that converts natural gas into electricity at high levels of efficiency. At the time, the company produced virtually no income as it was still at the product development stage. The Board and senior management immediately knew the company's very survival was in jeopardy.

Introduction

1 Read the profile of Ceramic Fuel Cells Ltd that describes the announcement of the crisis event that hit the company and answer the following questions.

1 What was the crisis that hit the company and how was it caused?
2 What specific part of the company's activities would be hit as a result of this crisis?
3 How successful was the SOFC technology in the marketplace?

2 Form small groups and imagine you are the main decision-makers – the company directors. It's 6 o'clock in the evening on October 17th, just after the crisis has been announced. You're having a late meeting in the Board room.

Look at the following list of action points (a–e) and put them in order of priority. Explain the reasons behind your decisions.

a Search for new finance to cover the €7 million loss.
b Reassure existing investors.
c Conduct detailed investigation of how the €7 million financial investment was lost.
d Hold meetings with staff and explain what is happening.
e Devise a plan to speed up the development stage of the SOFC technology.

Language focus: Contrast financial terms 'investment', 'capital' and 'equity'

In an investment context, *equity* refers simply to a company's shares, *capital* refers to money used for investment purposes and *investment* is a generic word used to refer to money, property, shares or securities (government and company bonds) used to create wealth or increase income.

1 Match the words in the first and second columns of the table below to create common word partnerships. Then match the word partnerships to their definitions in the third column.

First part of word partnership	Second part of word partnership	Definition
1 investment	a capital	i The length of time investors expect to wait before they get their money back. They get their money back by selling their shares in the company.
2 equity	b horizon	ii Obtain finance for purposes of investment or to fund a company's operations.
3 raise	c stake	iii A considerable number of shares held in a company as a form of investment.

2 Complete the questions below using word partnerships from exercise 1 on page 49. Ask and answer these questions about CFCL and its industry sector with a partner.

1 Would you expect investors in clean energy / renewable energy companies to have a long or a short _____ ?

2 If you were a wealthy person, would you consider taking an _____ in a clean energy / renewable energy company? Why/Why not? What proportion of your available funds would you invest?

3 What are the different options open to companies such as CFCL to _____ new _____ ?

3 Read facts about the company and statements taken from CFCL's Annual Report in the period before the crisis hit and complete the gaps using the words 'investment(s)', 'equity' or 'capital'.

1 The Company confirmed a €12.4 million _____ in a new fuel cell manufacturing plant in Heinsberg, Germany.

2 The Company liquidated some _____ over the year.

3 The Company's long-term incentive program comprises offers of _____ under the Company's Directors and Employee Benefits Plan.

4 Valuation and performance of the [Company's] _____ portfolio is provided monthly.

5 In March CFCL raised £36 million _____ with a listing on the London Stock Exchange.

4 The statements in question 3 refer to a period of time running up to the crisis event. Discuss with a partner what each statement tells you about the company and its operations before the crisis.

Business view

Brendan Dow is Managing Director of Ceramic Fuel Cells Ltd.

Listening 1: In search of funding

 1.30

1 Listen to the first part of the interview with Brendan Dow, where he talks about how the company managed to survive the crisis. As you listen, look at the seven methods of raising capital in the list below and tick (✓) those he mentions.

1 Sell some of the company's assets.

2 Get help from the Federal Government (of Australia).

3 Raise capital from commercial partners.

4 License the company's technology to a third party.

5 Raise money from existing investors.

6 Borrow money from an investment bank.

7 Raise money from existing investors together with a new investor.

2 Which method did the company eventually use to raise new financing?

3 Listen again and make notes of the details of each source of finance mentioned.

4 Find the following terms and idiomatic phrases which have been underlined in the audio script on page s 152–3. Try to discover what they mean.

1 … [the government] sat on its hands.

2 … [capital required to] see us through.

3 [Someone who had] come out of the woodwork …

4 He had done his homework …

Listening 2: Lessons learned

 1.31

1 Before listening to the second part of the interview, try to predict what lessons the company learned from this crisis.

2 Listen to the interview and check how many of your predictions were correct. Did any of Brendan Dow's answers surprise you?

3 Listen again and complete the gaps using words from the interview. Use a maximum of <u>three</u> words for each answer.

Lesson 1 – Cash is _____ .

Lesson 2 – Don't put your money in the hands of _____ .

Lesson 3 – White knights* are _____ in a crisis.

Lesson 4 – When looking for new capital you can't rely on _____ .

Lesson 5 – Bring your employees into your _____ .

* *white knight* = an investment term that refers to a person (or company) that comes to the help of a company in difficulty; a 'friendly investor'.

Listening 3: Leading out of a crisis

 1.32

1 Listen to the final part of the interview and answer the questions.

1 How did it feel for Brendan Dow to be running a company during this crisis?

2 How did Brendan Dow's working schedule change?

3 How does he believe you should physically express confidence?

4 What does he believe you should say to be positive?

5 Who does he believe you should visit to reassure?

2 Discuss what you think top managers can do to reduce their own levels of stress during crisis events such as this.

1 In the final part of the interview, Brendan Dow stresses the importance of confident body language in difficult situations. Look at the types of body language in the table below and complete the columns to show examples of confident and insecure communication in your culture.

Body language type	Communicates confidence	Communicates insecurity
eye contact		
facial expression		
gestures		
the way you stand or sit		
the way you greet someone		

2 Body language is not universal across all cultures, and it is well known that the same action can communicate a very different message in different cultures. Look at the following situations, and discuss what impression people from one culture might make on the other.

1 In culture A, a handshake is usually very firm and brief. In culture B, handshakes tend to be very gentle, and quite long.

2 In culture A, looking someone in the eye is expected when talking to someone. In culture B, looking someone in the eye for shorter times is more appropriate.

3 In culture A, people smile a lot, even with strangers. In culture B, people would only smile with people they are close to, such as good friends and family members.

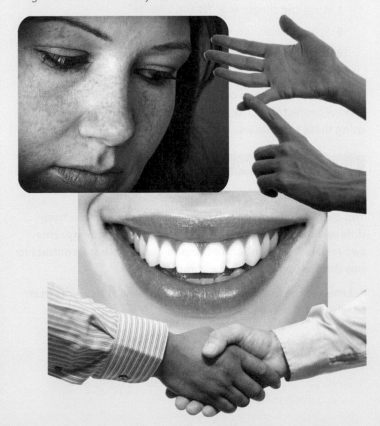

A classic crisis management technique is to imagine potentially threatening or dangerous scenarios that your organisation might face and then devise plans in advance to deal with these situations, in case such hypothetical scenarios become reality.

Stage 1

You are going to take part in a CFCL <u>post-crisis</u> scenario-planning strategy meeting, which is taking place over a weekend in a hotel up in the mountains around Melbourne. The company has now commercialised the product and is manufacturing and selling it. Get into small groups and brainstorm possible future crisis by completing the 'What if ...? scenarios table below.

Focus	'What if ...?' scenario
1 Cash and investments	What if the bank where we hold investors' money collapses?
2 Patents	
3 CFCL stock price	
4 Technology	
5 Key investors	
6 Other?	

Stage 2

Exchange the scenario table you completed in Stage 1 with another group. Taking some of their 'What if ...?' scenarios, brainstorm how the company should respond. Do some advance planning and brainstorm what kind of action the company can take now to avoid this possible crisis happening. Discuss the options, and then summarise the conclusions of your discussion in the table below.

Scenario number	Advance planning: What action can we take *now* to avoid this happening in the future?

Stage 3

Present your plans to the group who devised the 'What if ...?' scenarios. Remember to use confident body language.

Learning outcomes

- Reduce conflict in verbal communication.
- Recognise and react to aggressive language.
- Deal with difficult situations.

Why does it occur?   Where can it happen?

What can it lead to?   **CONFLICT**   When does it often happen?

Who does it happen between?   How does it increase?

Introduction

1 Look at the questions about conflict at the top of the page. Brainstorm as many answers to the questions as possible.

2 Match the tips about diffusing conflict at work (1–6) with the explanations (a–f). Which advice do you think is the most useful?

1 Don't use verbally aggressive language.	4 Be direct.
2 Be open.	5 Stay calm.
3 Focus on the problem.	6 Tell your boss.

a Accept that you may be wrong sometimes, or that you may not have all the information.

b It is always a good idea to keep your supervisor aware of any difficult situations, as he or she may be a good source of advice.

c Take a deep breath instead of responding immediately; don't get angry.

d Tell the other person in a rational way that you notice you are disagreeing, and that you would like to find a more positive result to the discussion.

e Think about how you can word your response in a non-threatening way.

f Even if the other person is attacking you personally, try to keep the discussion on the issue, not on personalities.

Language focus 1: Conflictual turn-taking

🔊 **1.33**

'Turn-taking' means the way speakers and listeners conduct a conversation, allowing each person time to speak and knowing when it is appropriate to start talking. While the content of people's talk clearly affects levels of conflict, the way people respond to the previous speaker's turn is also very important.

1 You are going to listen to some responses from a conflictual meeting. Look at what the first speaker says and predict the type of response.

a an interruption   b a direct refusal   c throwing back the criticism

	Type of response:
1 David: … the rent's stupid.	
2 David: So what else can we get out of you …	
3 John: Well, if you have an extreme problem with it then I can, er …	

2 Listen and check. How did you make your predictions?

3 Decide which of the following are appropriate techniques for reducing conflict in communication, and which are not.

1 Pause for a few seconds.

2 Use softening language before responding (e.g. 'Well …', 'To be honest …', 'Erm …').

3 Avoid eye contact.

4 Be honest about how you are feeling.

5 Give a reason or account.

6 Don't respond at all.

7 Give a vague answer (e.g. 'That might be difficult').

8 Agree then disagree (e.g. 'Yes, that's true, but …').

9 Keep your intonation very low and flat.

10 Look for areas of agreement / shared understanding.

4 Can you think of any other techniques that can reduce the level of conflict? Practise responding to the turns in exercise 1 using these techniques.

Listening 1: Opening the meeting

🔊 **1.34**

You are going to listen to a meeting between two men from different companies, David and John. David's company rents two restaurants from John's company, and also has a contract to buy drinks supplies from the company.

1 Listen to the first extract. Are the following statements true or false?

1 David and John have met before.

2 David has a clear idea about the purpose of the meeting.

3 The present agreement will continue for another five years.

4 John's company wants to discourage David's company from buying drinks from other suppliers.

Listening 2: Disagreements

🔊 1.35

1 Listen and complete the gaps in David's comments.

1 … that contract is giving us _____ from increased volume.
2 … the discounts will be _____ .
3 … absolutely beyond any _____ .

2 Compared to the beginning of the meeting, do you think the level of conflict in this part of the meeting has increased or decreased? Why/Why not?

Listening 3: Closing stages

🔊 1.36

1 Listen to the final part of the conversation and answer these questions.

1 Who is going to pay the legal fees? And the rent?
2 Do you think this meeting ends with a low or high degree of conflict? Why?

2 Listen again to this part of the meeting. Considering the tips in the Introduction, how successfully did these two men deal with conflict in the meeting as a whole?

Critical analysis

1 What are the dangers of conflict in business?
2 In what situations, if any, do you think conflict is appropriate or even necessary?

Language focus 2: Cooperative and aggressive idioms and metaphors

Idioms and metaphors can be used to make the message seem more cooperative and perhaps indirect ('Everything's moving in the right direction'), or more conflictual ('the rent's stupid').

1 Match the idioms and metaphors (1–8) from the meeting with their meanings (a–h).

1 Dive in. Grab a chair.
2 I'm a little bit in the dark.
3 It's not rocket science …
4 … the rent's stupid.
5 Not as stupid as I was trying to make it.
6 it's … beyond any business sense …
7 That's absolute madness.
8 [You must be welcomed] up and down the country.

a This is totally unacceptable.
b It's very easy to understand.
c I don't understand.
d The fee is unacceptable.
e I would've liked to raise it further.
f Everybody must hate you.
g This is not an acceptable proposal.
h Please sit down.

2 Which of the idioms and metaphors are conflictual?

3 Make the following conflictual language less aggressive.

Example: The rent's stupid. → We think the rent is an issue. / We would like to look at negotiating the rent.

1 Not as stupid as I was trying to make it. →
2 It's beyond any business sense whatsoever. →
3 That's absolute madness. →
4 You must be welcomed up and down the country. →

Output: Dealing with conflictual situations

Stage 1

You are going to discuss some common causes of conflict in the workplace. Work in pairs and look at the first scenario. Before you start, think about what you are going to say and how you are going to say it.

Scenario 1

Student A
Your colleague often takes days off, and you then have to do a lot of his/her work. You have a dental appointment next week, but your colleague has already booked to take that day off. You think you deserve to have a day off more than your colleague does.

Student B
You work much harder than your colleague, and you are in need of a day away from the office. It is your partner's birthday next week, so you have booked the day off.

Stage 2

Discuss the following questions.

- Were you conflictive or did you try to avoid being conflictive?
- Were you able to resolve the conflicts?
- If you had to do this in real life, would you handle it differently?

Stage 3

Repeat the same procedure with this scenario.

Scenario 2

Student A
Your company has recently lowered its prices but is keen to avoid any further price reductions. One of your main clients has called you about a recent quotation. The best that you can do is offer a 3% reduction.

Student B
You have a good, long-standing relationship with your supplier. You want to continue doing business together. However, a rival company has contacted you offering a reduction of 5% on your present costs. Call your supplier and see if you can get their prices reduced.

---

6 Leadership

6.1 Theory: Leadership styles and qualities

Learning outcomes
- Understand different styles of leadership.
- Describe leadership styles and qualities.
- Analyse leadership qualities in yourself and others.

Introduction

1 Think of a leader whom you admire. It could be someone from the world of politics, sport or music – or a religious leader, for example. Why do you admire this person? What qualities make the person a good leader?

2 Look at the list below. Which of these qualities would you associate with the leader you described?

intelligence	good communication skills
willingness to share experiences	respect for others
ability to inspire others	single-mindedness
good delegation skills	decisiveness
ability to stay calm	ability to listen
willingness to adapt to change	self-awareness
willingness to learn	

3 Which of these leadership skills are needed by the people in the photos on this page?

Language focus 1: Describing leadership styles

1 Match the names of leadership styles (1–6) to their characteristics (a–f).

2 The words in the box are taken from the reading text in the next section. Use the words to complete the sentences below.

> competencies inhibit dampens adrift hallmark exemplify resistant mastered

1 They are very good engineers, but it is difficult to introduce new systems, as they can be _____ to change.
2 Because of the CEO's failure to communicate his vision for the company, the staff felt completely _____ .
3 Her ambition and drive _____ the spirit that we would like to install in all of our employees.
4 I intend to coach him until he has _____ all of the necessary skills to do the job.
5 The basic training will provide you with the core _____ to be able to start doing the job.
6 It has been argued that the high taxes on business _____ growth of companies and the motivation of entrepreneurs.
7 The customer-centred approach is a _____ of the leadership's philosophy.
8 Whenever he gives a speech, instead of motivating the staff he _____ their enthusiasm.

Style	Characteristic
1 Coaching	**a** There should be equality and freedom for individuals in the team.
2 Authoritative	**b** The leader promotes the feeling of cohesion in the team.
3 Affiliative	**c** Force is used to persuade team members to do things that they are unwilling to do.
4 Coercive	**d** The leader trains and instructs the team.
5 Democratic	**e** The leader sets a high benchmark which others should follow.
6 Pacesetting	**f** The leader is able to control using knowledge and expertise.

Leadership That Gets Results

Managers often fail to appreciate how profoundly the organizational climate can influence financial results. It can account for nearly a third of financial performance. Organizational climate, in turn, is influenced by leadership style – by the way that managers motivate those who report directly to them, gather and use information, make decisions, manage change initiatives, and handle crises. There are six basic leadership styles. Each derives from different emotional intelligence competencies, works best in particular situations, and affects the organizational climate in different ways.

1 The _____ Style

This "Do what I say" approach can be very effective in a turnaround situation, a natural disaster, or when working with problem employees. But in most situations, coercive leadership inhibits the organization's flexibility and dampens employees' motivation.

2 The _____ Style

This leader takes a "Come with me" approach: she states the overall goal but gives people the freedom to choose their own means of achieving it. This style works especially well when a business is adrift. It is less effective when the leader is working with a team of experts who are more experienced than she is.

3 The _____ Style

The hallmark of this leader is a "People come first" attitude. This style is particularly useful for building team harmony or increasing morale. But its exclusive focus on praise can allow poor performance to go uncorrected. Also, these leaders rarely offer advice, which often leaves employees in a quandary.

4 The _____ Style

This style's impact on organizational climate is not as high as you might imagine. By giving workers a voice in decisions, democratic leaders build organizational flexibility and responsibility and help generate fresh ideas. But sometimes the price is endless meetings and confused employees who feel leaderless.

5 The _____ Style

A leader who sets high performance standards and exemplifies them himself has a very positive impact on employees who are self-motivated and highly competent. But other employees tend to feel overwhelmed by such a leader's demands for Excellence – and to resent his tendency to take over a situation.

6 The _____ style

This style focuses more on personal development than on immediate work-related tasks. It works well when employees are already aware of their weaknesses and want to improve, but not when they are resistant to changing their ways.

The more styles a leader has mastered, the better. In particular, being able to switch among the authoritative, affiliative, democratic, and coaching styles as conditions dictate creates the best organizational climate and optimizes business performance.

Source: 'Leadership That Gets Results' in *Harvard Business Review*

Business view

Daniel Goleman is an expert on psychology and leadership. He has written several books on these topics, including the worldwide best-seller *Emotional Intelligence*.

Reading 1: Leadership styles in practice

1 Read the article on this page quickly and complete the gaps with the six leadership styles from Language focus 1.

2 Read the article again and mark the statements below to show if they agree (A) or disagree (D) with the views of the writer, or if the writer's view is not given (NG).

1 Most managers realise how deeply the organisational climate influences the financial performance of the company.
2 The leadership style is influenced by the organisational climate.
3 The emotional intelligence competencies of the leader determine the different basic leadership styles.
4 The coercive style is useful in crisis situations.
5 The authoritative style works well with new recruits to a company.
6 A democratic leadership style can result in poor financial performance.
7 Incompetent and unmotivated employees resist changes introduced by a pacesetting leadership style of management.
8 A coaching style of leadership prioritises work-related tasks.
9 A leader who can use different leadership styles well is a more effective leader.

3 Discuss the following questions.

1 Which type of leader would you most like to have as your manager at this point in time?
2 Why do you think it is important for a leader to be able to move from one style of leadership to another?

Reading 2: Leadership qualities and Emotional Intelligence

1 Read the introductory paragraph to a text on leadership qualities and Emotional Intelligence on page 56 and complete the gaps with the words in the box.

corresponding   consists   composed

Emotional Intelligence: A Primer

Emotional Intelligence – the ability to manage ourselves and our relationships effectively – 1 _____ of four fundamental capabilities: self-awareness, self-management, social awareness, and social skill.

Each capability, in turn, is 2 _____ of specific sets of competencies. Below is a selection of the capabilities and their 3 _____ leadership traits.

Self-Awareness	Self-Management	Social Awareness	Social Skill
■ *Emotional self-awareness:* the ability to read and understand your emotions as well as recognize their impact on work performance and relationships. ■ *Accurate self-assessment:* a realistic evaluation of your strengths and limitations. ■ *Self-confidence:* a strong and positive sense of self-worth.	■ *Self-control:* the ability to keep disruptive emotions and impulses under control. ■ *Adaptability:* skill at adjusting to changing situations and overcoming obstacles. ■ *Achievement orientation:* the drive to meet an internal standard of excellence.	■ *Empathy:* skill at sensing other people's emotions, understanding their perspective, and taking an active interest in their concerns. ■ *Organizational awareness:* the ability to read the currents of organizational life, build decision networks, and navigate politics. ■ *Service orientation:* the ability to recognize and meet customers' needs.	■ *Developing others:* the propensity to bolster the abilities of others through feedback and guidance. ■ *Communication:* skill at listening and at sending clear, convincing, and well-tuned messages. ■ *Conflict management:* the ability to de-escalate disagreements and orchestrate resolutions.
Score: _____ / 15	Score: _____ / 15	Score: _____ / 15	Score: _____ / 15

Source: 'Leadership That Gets Results' in *Harvard Business Review*

2 Read the information in the table above and evaluate your own Emotional Intelligence. Give yourself a score for each of the three competencies for the four different capabilities using the following scoring system for each bullet point.

5 = excellent   4 = very good   3 = quite good   2 = OK   1 = poor

3 Compare scores with other students and discuss the following questions.

1 What do these scores say about your leadership abilities?

2 Which capabilities and competencies of Emotional Intelligence would you most like to improve on? Why?

4 Decide whether each of the following competencies (1–6) refers to Self-Management (SM) or Social Skill (SS).

1 *Change catalyst:* proficiency in initiating new ideas and leading people in a new direction.

2 *Initiative:* a readiness to seize opportunities.

3 *Teamwork and collaboration:* competence at promoting cooperation and building teams.

4 *Trustworthiness:* a consistent display of honesty and integrity.

5 *Visionary leadership:* the ability to take charge and inspire with a compelling vision.

6 *Influence:* the ability to wield a range of persuasive tactics.

5 Rank the six competencies above in terms of importance for leadership, where 1 = most important and 6 = least important. Discuss your answers with other students.

Language focus 2: Word partnerships with 'self'

Choose the best word partnership with *self* to complete the following sentences.

1 _____ can be defined as an understanding of what you do and why you do it.

  A self-determination   B self-confidence   C self-awareness

2 Making a list of your strengths and weaknesses is a useful form of _____ that can help you target your career choices.

  A self-control   B self-assessment   C self-determination

3 Mastering a new skill can really help recent graduates gain _____ in the job market.

  A self-confidence   B self-control   C self-consciousness

4 I think that the new manager could exercise some _____ instead of losing his temper with the staff all of the time.

  A self-determination   B self-assessment   C self-control

5 He puts his success in business down to _____, as he says he never takes no for an answer.

  A self-consciousness   B self-management   C self-determination

6 Managers need to avoid being too critical of staff, otherwise they can suffer from _____ and be afraid to put their opinions across.

  A self-consciousness   B self-confidence   C self-control

Output: Finding the right leader

Work in small groups. Choose a type of company that you are all keen on working for (a marketing consultancy, a small media company, a hotel chain, a large technological company, etc.) and the leadership roles that you would like to have in this company. Work through the following stages.

Stage 1

Look back at the results from the questions in Reading 2 and analyse your strengths and weaknesses as a team. What leadership traits do you have? What are your key competencies?

Stage 2

Look at the different leadership styles. Discuss which type or types of leader would be most beneficial to your group and which ones would not be suitable.

Stage 3

Agree on a set of competencies that would be essential and desired for a new manager entering your company. Create a profile for the type of person you would like to attract.

6.2 Practice: Nikki King – a business leader

Learning outcomes
- Understand what makes a good leader.
- Learn language relating to leadership.
- Analyse issues of leadership affecting an organisation in difficulty.

Profile: Nikki King

Nikki King is the managing director of Isuzu Truck UK, which serves 65 independent dealers across the UK. Her company was the first to introduce trucks produced in East Asia to the UK market. She has won several awards and honours, such as UK Businesswoman of the Year, an honorary PhD, and a Businesswoman Lifetime Achievement award. She was the first female Managing Director of a truck company in the UK, and was the first female president of both the Society of Operations Engineers and the Institute of Road Transport Engineers. As well as working in business, she is very involved with several social enterprises and charities.

Introduction

1 Read the profile on Nikki King. What has she achieved that no woman before her has ever done?

2 Discuss the following questions.

1 Why do you think it has been so difficult for women to achieve positions of leadership in the fields that Nikki King is in?
2 What leadership qualities do you imagine Nikki King has that has enabled her to rise to the top?

3 Complete the text contrasting management and leadership with the words in the box below.

management	manage	managers	leadership	lead	leaders

1 _____ is about establishing a direction for an organisation by communicating a vision, which generally involves outlining a new strategy and setting new goals. **2** _____ on the other hand is more concerned with controlling and organising staff and budgets to implement the strategy and maintain the direction decided on. In theory we can separate managers from leaders. We can say that **3** _____ have followers who are prepared to follow them because they are engaged, motivated and committed while **4** _____ have subordinates who will follow instructions as their contract of work obliges them to do so. In practice there is often an overlap between management and leadership: it's difficult to **5** _____ a team without having some leadership skills and it's difficult to **6** _____ an organisation without having some idea of how to manage one.

Listening 1: The qualities of leaders and managers

 1.37

1 You are going to listen to Nikki King talk about leadership. Before you listen, discuss the questions below.

1 What do you think are the attributes of a good leader?
2 Do you think leaders are born or made?
3 What is the difference between a good manager and a good leader?

2 Listen to the extract. How does Nikki King answer the questions?

Listening 2: Leadership in different sectors

 1.38

1 What do you think are the major differences between leading and managing in the private sector compared to social enterprises like NPOs (not-for-profit organisations) and charities? Look at the headings in the table below to help you answer the question.

2 Listen to the second part of the interview and complete the table with the information that Nikki King gives. The first one has been done as an example.

Employment status	In the private sector people work for you – in social enterprises they volunteer.
Leader communication	
Staff motivations	
Level of 'red tape' (bureaucracy)	
Commercial mindset	
Rules	

Listening 3: Advice for business leaders

 1.39

1 What advice would you give to someone wanting to be a business leader? Make a note of your ideas, then listen to Nikki King giving advice and write down her three main points.

1
2
3

2 Were any of your answers the same as Nikki King's?

3 Which of these three pieces of advice do you think is the most important for a new leader to follow? Why?

Language focus 1: The language of leadership

1 Nikki King uses the following words when talking about leadership. Use the correct form of the word to complete some common collocations.

passion: be _____ about / have a _____ for / _____s run high
vision: have a _____ / have _____s / be a _____
consistent: be _____ / act _____ / lack _____
inspire: seek divine _____ / be _____ / _____ your followers by example
dictator: avoid a _____ approach / be a _____ ruler / be a real _____
persuade: be _____ / have _____ arguments / lack powers of _____
motivate: have the ability to _____ others / be highly _____ / be _____ by greed

2 Which of the collocations are unusual or inappropriate for business leaders?

3 Which of the above qualities do you think are the most important for a leader? Are there any other qualities that are needed – for example, charisma?

Language focus 2: Understanding proverbs

Proverbs are used in business to evaluate or comment on something or someone, and as such are used more by people with power and influence. They are not common in meetings, but may be used more when people are talking <u>about</u> business.

1 In the interview, Nikki King uses the proverb 'Practise what you preach'. What does this proverb mean?

2 Discuss what the following proverbs mean, and how they might relate to business. For instance, 'Practise what you preach' relates to the way good managers should behave.

1 Better late than never.
2 A bad workman always blames his tools.
3 A bird in the hand is worth two in the bush.
4 Give a man a fish, feed him for a day, teach a man to fish, feed him for a lifetime.
5 Too many cooks spoil the broth.

3 Discuss the following questions.

1 Do the same or similar proverbs exist in your first language?
2 What kind of proverbs are commonly used in your culture?
3 How could these proverbs relate to a business context?

Critical analysis

Read what Nikki King says about women at work, and discuss these questions.

Nikki King: I'm actually part of Women in Transport, which is an organisation to encourage women into the transport logistics business. And as a result of that I meet a lot of women of all ages, and one thing that really has hit home to me is that women are hampered in their careers generally not because companies are sexist, not because there's an innate sexism in the work place, mainly because women tend to have to bow to external pressures far more than men do. So they're the ones that have to cope if mum and dad are ill. They are the ones that have to cope if they have young children. And actually it's very rarely work-related things that stop women progressing; it's actually their private lives that stop them. And that's really quite interesting, because men don't have to make those sort of sacrifices.

1 What issues does she say women face that men don't?
2 Do you think the issues that Nikki King describes also exist for women in your country?
3 Do you think the points Nikki King raises explain why there tend to be so few women business leaders?

Output: Advising an organisation on leadership

You are part of a team that has been asked to advise an NPO about how it can turn around its performance. The NPO is losing money, and if it continues to do so it will have to be closed down.

Stage 1

Read through the description of the organisation and its practices, and pinpoint the issues that need addressing within the organisation.

NPO Mission
To raise people's awareness in the rich industrialised world of problems in the world's poorest areas and to raise funds to finance projects there.

Premises
The NPO is based on a floor of a large office block in central Frankfurt, the 'financial capital' of Germany.

Staff
There are a total of 200 people working in the organisation. The numbers break down as follows:
- 70% of staff are unpaid volunteers and work either part-time or full-time. These unpaid volunteers are generally aged over 65 or are recent graduates in their early 20s.
- 30% of staff are paid employees.
- Staff are roughly equally divided between men and women.
- Morale in the workplace is low and is characterised by a certain level of hostility between paid and non-paid staff and between younger and older volunteers.

Management Team
- The CEO of the NPO is Peter Hofmeister, aged 62. He has held the position for the last 10 years. His whole career has been spent working in the NPO sector. He is responsible to the Chairman and Board of Directors, who must approve any decisions that he makes.
- The management team consists of 26 people. Most of them are men in middle age or above. Most have a background in the NPO or public sector.

Funding and operations
- The NPO has been successful in obtaining financial support from government agencies; however, government budget cuts mean that money from this source is drying up.
- They raise only 10% of their funds from private non-governmental sources.
- There is very limited use of new technology and new ways of working.

Stage 2

The Chairman and the Board of Directors have asked you to address a number of key questions surrounding the leadership of the organisation. Read through the questions below and discuss in small teams how best to answer them. Take notes on your discussions to form the basis of a presentation to the Board of Directors.

- How effective do you think the leadership of this organisation is?
- What changes would you make to the leadership and management structure?
- How would you improve motivation and morale in the organisation?
- What can be done to reduce the levels of conflict amongst staff members?
- What can the leadership team do to make the organisation more commercial without alienating staff or detracting from the organisation's mission and goals?

Stage 3

Deliver your presentation.

Learning outcomes

- Understand different approaches to motivating staff.
- Analyse types of motivational language.
- Take part in a meeting about staff motivation.

Introduction

1 Look at the pictures on the right. How is each manager's style different?

2 Brainstorm as many ways as you can of motivating others to work or study harder. Which types of motivation would make you try harder?

3 What methods would you expect the two managers in the pictures use to motivate their staff?

Business view: David Prasher

David Prasher is the Managing Director of Haymarket Consumer Media, a major publisher of consumer magazines and websites.

3 What reasons does David Prasher give for a change from transactional to transformational styles of motivation?

4 Look again at the pictures above. Which manager appears more transactional? Why?

Listening 1: Describing transactional and transformational motivation

 1.40

According to David Prasher, there are two types of motivation: transactional and transformational. Whereas a transactional approach involves the manager instructing and giving orders to the staff, a transformational approach is more interactive and collaborative.

1 Listen to a short interview with David Prasher. Which of the following examples does he classify as transactional? Which are transformational?

do what the boss says	telling
experience tells us what to expect	doing
need to work in new ways	togetherness
consulting	pointing

2 Listen again and use the information from the interview to summarise the two approaches to motivation in your own words.

Listening 2: Motivating different types of people

1.41

You are going to listen to David Prasher talk about different types of employees and how managers can motivate them.

1 David Prasher describes the following four types of people. What features do you think each type of person shows in terms of ability and motivation?

- stars
- strivers
- problem children
- coasters

2 Listen to the extract and complete the diagram below. Each square relates to one of the four types of people.

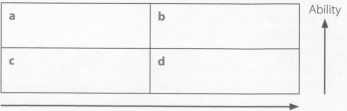

3 How are stars and problem children motivated differently? Do you agree with the advice given on how to motivate them?

4 Which type are you?

Listening 3: Team-building meeting in a hotel

 1.42

According to David Prasher, 'The language that you use in outlining the vision has to excite people, and make them think "Yeah, I want to be part of this team." That is the first step in motivation.'

Now listen to a hotel manager, Brad, trying to motivate a team after they received a low score on their team appraisal. The team is made up of middle-aged women from outside the UK, and most of them are intermediate-level English speakers. Do you think what he says would motivate this team? Why/Why not?

The audio script is given below.

> ### Audio script
> **1.42**
>
> **Brad:** You know, once you get a hundred percent as a team, like you did last year and the year before, a hundred percent becomes the expectation.
> **Jeanne:** Yeah.
> **Brad:** You know, if Gina gives me a hundred percent, I am singing from the rooftops.
> **Jeanne:** Yeah.
> **Brad:** I'm gonna be 'Wow'. But you do begin to expect success all the time. You start to say, like the manager at Manchester United, 'Well, yeah. I expect us to win the Championship every year. You know, the talent is here so we can win. And we've proven it time and time and time again.' So that's why your score this time was, you know, disappointing. OK, so we're going to go through some of the procedures in this meeting. And I'm very excited about this. I guess this is now my fourth meeting within a department to discuss these changes. I think the feedback's been tremendous.

Language focus: Using transactional and transformational language

1 The following comments were made by managers directly to staff. Decide which are transactional and which transformational.

1 You actually feel you could be using the time more productively, I feel. Would that be right?

2 We'll do the thinking and planning and we'll just tell you how you fit into the plan. Right?

3 Well, this is what we believe you need to do now.

4 We've got to be a bit more proactive.

5 When I say feedback I don't mean it as a criticism, as these are comments that people are making to me and I just think it needs passing on.

6 I'm not asking you to fill this in now because it will depend when you need to do it.

7 You need to get better sales figures next month.

8 Anything else you want to cover this morning?

9 Do you think that's worthwhile doing or do you think it's a waste of our time and effort and resources?

10 You have to check every single day.

2 Look at the following four scenarios and decide whether a transactional or a transformational approach would be more appropriate, and what the manager could say.

a A problem child keeps missing deadlines.

b A star seems to be becoming a little bored with the present task.

c A coaster has been coming to work late recently.

d A striver has just won a big contract for the company.

Intercultural analysis

Transformationally minded or transactionally minded managers may be more common in one work culture than another. For instance, David Prasher says in creative media and publishing, technology is driving change at such a pace that transactional styles are not appropriate.

1 Can you think of any work environments where a transactional style would be appropriate?

2 Can you think of any disadvantages of working for a transformational manager?

3 Discuss how a transactional manager working with staff who expect a transformational style might appear, and vice versa.

Output: Motivating a staff member

Work in pairs. You work for a company that publishes lifestyle magazines. Student A is a manager who is concerned with the motivation of a member of staff; Student B is the member of staff.

Stage 1
Student A look at page 139.
Student B look at page 143.

Prepare what you are going to say and then hold the meeting.

Stage 2
Read the update for your role below and then have the meeting.

Manager
A month after the first meeting, the situation has not really improved. Decide what to do and call another meeting.

Employee
You've been trying to do some of the things your boss said in the last meeting. Your boss has called another meeting. You think that you should be promoted.

> **Watch Sequence 3 on the DVD to find out more about Management and leadership.**

Writing 3: Writing effective emails

Learning outcomes

- Learn features and language for writing effective emails.
- Contrast different styles and types of email writing.
- Write short messages in a fast email exchange.

Introduction

1 Discuss the following questions with a partner.

1 How is meeting someone face-to-face a more effective means of communication than sending an email?

2 In what way is it easy to misinterpret people via email communication?

2 What do you find most difficult when communicating by email?

Language focus: Features of effective emails

1 Do you agree with these general guidelines of email etiquette? Write 'agree', 'disagree' or 'depends' for each one.

> **Email Etiquette at Work – The Guidelines**
>
> Don'ts
> 1 Don't write anything to anyone you wouldn't say to their face.
> 2 Don't write words in CAPITALS to emphasise points.
> 3 Don't overuse abbreviations (btw) and exclamation marks!!!
> 4 Don't use email to discuss confidential matters.
> 5 Don't write an email with more than one message in it.
> 6 Don't just convey information in a dry way; instead use language that recognises that email exchanges are between <u>people</u>.
>
> Dos
> 1 Take care (and a little extra time) to spell and punctuate correctly.
> 2 Be brief wherever possible.
> 3 Use a short subject line that people can recognise and refer to.
> 4 Keep to a minimum the word 'urgent' in subject headings.
> 5 For long emails use a proper structure, including paragraphing.
> 6 Use friendly/courteous greetings and sign-offs at the start and end.

2 Compare and discuss your answers with a partner.

3 The following table shows formal and polite phrases that are used in email writing. Match them to the functions.

1 Opening comments	a Please find [my comments / the file] attached.
2 Final comments	b Please let me know if you want me to …
3 Offering to help / do something	c Please let me know if you are happy with this.
4 Making a request	d I wanted to follow up on [yesterday's meeting regarding …]
5 Indicating an attachment	e I wonder if we could [postpone the meeting]?
6 Referring to a communication	f I'm writing in response to …
7 Taking further action	g With reference to [your last email / call yesterday …]
8 Checking acceptance	h I look forward to …

4 What other formal and polite phrases can you think of for these different functions?

Writing skill 1: Writing short messages in fast email exchanges

1 The five short emails on page 63 are between colleagues in the same organisation who know each other well. Read the emails and put them in the correct order.

2 How would you describe the style of writing in these emails?

a Informal and friendly   c Quite formal and polite

b Informal and professional   d Formal and polite

3 Think about the guidelines you read in the Language focus. How closely are they being followed in this email exchange?

4 Read email A in detail and find phrases which are examples of the following common features of this 'informal professional' style of correspondence.

a more informal greetings and endings

b use of more informal words and phrases

c use of a dash in place of a comma, a full stop or a word

d omission of subject pronoun

e omission of article 'the'

f use of shortened forms

5 How could you write these phrases in a more formal style?

6 Re-write emails A, B and C in a more formal style using some of the language in the Language focus table.

A

> Hi Marlene – good job – the last bit works very well too – concise and gets across message that the clients are getting a lot here..
> I've put a few comments down with a couple of alternative wordings for a couple of bits (see attached). I'll leave it to Sylvie to decide which ones she likes.
> All best
> Max

B

> Looks good to me. Lets go with this. Another piece in the puzzle nicely done.
> best
> Max

C

> Hi guys,
> Here are my comments. Very nice introduction.
> All the best,
> Sylvie

D

> Hi Max and Sylvie
> Thanks for your comments. I'll make a couple of tweaks here and there and then get it finalised.
> Marlene

E

> Subject: Brochure – Edited Version
> Dear Max and Sylvie,
> Here is the slightly edited version of the brochure.
> Let me know if it is OK.
> Best wishes,
> Marlene

Writing skill 2: Writing a longer email

1 The relatively long email below has a formal structure. Read the email. What is the purpose of each of the paragraphs?

Paragraph 1: State purpose of writing

Paragraph 2: _____

Paragraph 3: _____

> **File** **Edit** **View** **Insert** **Format** **Tools** **Message** **Help**
>
> Subject: Astra
>
> Dear Zac and Sam,
>
> I wanted to follow up on the design and production meetings and flag my concern with the planned launch dates for our Astra sofa range. Launching in November means we would lose a whole year of sales.
>
> In the sales cycle, we present to buyers from major store chains in the Spring and they then select their choices around May/June. They typically place their orders with us in July/Aug, ready for display in the stores starting end of Sept/beginning of Oct. A Nov launch date will not get any significant sales until the following Autumn. Stores in Russia, in particular, are very keen to get our six-seater models so if we can serve this market next year, it will considerably influence our sales potential.
>
> Is there any way this schedule can be brought forward?
>
> Many thanks
>
> Dina

2 How many features of the 'informal professional' style (described in Writing skill 1) are used here?

3 Find the formal words and phrases in the email that match the more informal ones below.

1 normally

2 next

3 really want

4 have a big impact on

4 The language used in this email is quite indirect – this is a typical way of making points whilst still showing a high level of politeness and respect. Look at the underlined phrases and re-write them in a style that is more appropriate for a manager with a direct communication style.

Output: Write a fast email exchange to make an agreed decision

You are going to have a fast three-way email exchange. You need to arrive at a group decision on how to deal with the problem of the schedule, outlined in the email in Writing skill 2.

Stage 1

Divide into groups of three and read about the thinking and circumstances of each of the three correspondents below. Each person in the group should choose one of the three roles.

Sam – Head of Design: You think that you 'can't rush good design'. A quality product takes time to create. Your team are working on many projects, not just Astra.

Dina – International Marketing Manager: You are eager to get the product out on time as it's no use having the 'perfect sofa' too late! You are under pressure to develop new markets.

Zac – Production Manager: You are sympathetic to both Sam and Dina's positions. If you knew a bit more detail about the design schedule from Sam, and expected unit sales from Dina, you might be able to adjust production schedules to save time.

Stage 2

Write an email exchange between the three of you. Keep the emails very brief and to the point (1–3 lines maximum per email) and make sure you address both participants in all mails, either directly or via cc. Sam should start the correspondence by responding directly to Dina, cc-ing Zac.

Stage 3

Review the emails you wrote and discuss whether the language and style used were correct and appropriate for the task.

7.1 Theory: Culture in international business

Learning outcomes

- Understand the role of culture in international businesses.
- Learn key intercultural words and concepts.
- Advise companies on reconciling cultural differences.

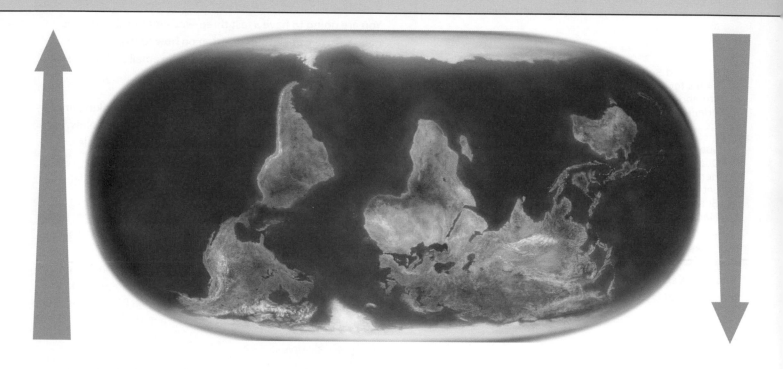

Introduction

1 'Culture' is a difficult word to define, as it can mean various things. Look at the examples of culture in the box and discuss which ones are relevant to doing business internationally.

> Classical music
> Dress at work
> Poetry
> Customs of professional groups (e.g. sales staff compared to technical staff)
> Punctuality
> Art
> Theatre
> Directness of communication
> Decision-making style
> National customs
> Attitudes to power
> Customs of organisations (e.g. Microsoft compared to The University of Cambridge)

2 Doing business in a foreign culture has been described as entering a world 'turned upside down'. What do you think you personally would find most challenging about living and working in a culture very different from your own?

3 'Culture' in terms of business is often defined as 'the way we do things round here'. What communication difficulties have you had with people from other countries as a result of them 'doing things differently'? Why is it important to go beyond simply describing (or complaining about) cultural difference in business?

Business view

Dr Fons Trompenaars is a consultant in cross-cultural communication. He is the President of Trompenaars Hampden-Turner, and has written a number of books on business and culture.

Language focus: Key intercultural words and concepts

1 You are going to hear an interview with Dr Fons Trompenaars. Before you listen, match the terms he uses with their definitions.

Terms	Definitions
1 stereotypes	**a** how respectful a person is about cultural differences
2 culture	**b** the standards, beliefs and customs of a group
3 globalisation	**c** how successfully an individual can communicate with members of other groups
4 intercultural communication	**d** how competent a person is at realising the actions necessary to implement the reconciliation of cultural differences
5 practices	**e** fixed prejudgements somebody has about members of another group
6 values	**f** how competent a person is at bringing together cultural differences
7 recognition	**g** something that is usually or regularly done – often as a habit, tradition or custom
8 reconciliation	**h** the increase of trade around the world, mainly by large multinational companies trading goods in many countries
9 intercultural competence	**i** the deeply, sometimes unconsciously held beliefs of a group
10 respect	**j** communication between members of different groups, such as nations or professions
11 realisation	**k** how competent a person is at noticing cultural differences around him or her

2 The four terms 'reconciliation', 'respect', 'recognition' and 'realisation' are a series of sequential steps for successful intercultural communication, developed by Dr Fons Trompenaars. The first step is recognition – put the other steps in a logical order.

3 Match each of the intercultural problems described below to one of the four steps. Comment on how these problems are caused and what impact they could have on individuals and organisations. The first one has been done for you.

1 They seem to think it's OK to arrive late for meetings, but to us this seems rude.

   Example: *Recognition – the person saying this might not recognise or appreciate that different cultures have different attitudes to time and punctuality.*

2 I can see that they do things differently from us, but we can't reach a shared understanding.

3 I don't know how to manage this multicultural team, because I don't have the skills.

4 They think that their solution is the best but they should listen to our ideas too.

Listening 1: International organisations and their cultures

 1.43

Dr Fons Trompenaars talks about three types of organisation.

a globalisation-focused organisation
b multi-local organisation
c trans-national organisation

1 What do you think the differences are between these types?

2 Listen and match the points (1–8) below with one of the organisation types (a–c) above.

1 universal approach
2 multicultural top management
3 is value driven
4 particular approach
5 one size fits all
6 have multi centres
7 local offices have complete autonomy
8 learns locally but globalises best practices

3 Which type of organisation does Dr Fons Trompenaars think is the most successful in international business, and why? Do you agree?

4 Discuss what qualities and skills you think someone who wants to work in a trans-national company would need.

Listening 2: Merging companies with different cultures

 1.44

1 Think about international mergers and acquisitions (M&As), when one company merges with a competitor or acquires a smaller company from a different country. Do you think culture might be an obstacle? Listen to Dr Fons Trompenaars discuss this issue, and see if your opinions differ.

2 Listen again. Are the following statements true or false?

1 Between 15% and 18% of M&As fail due to human issues.
2 Many consultancy companies only consider the organisational, IT or downsizing aspects when advising about integrating.
3 Culture is sometimes used to excuse the mistakes of the CEO.
4 Only after all the cultural dilemmas have been reconciled can successful dialogue occur.

3 Dr Fons Trompenaars states that we should 'not overestimate the role of culture in business'. Discuss what you think he means by this. Do you agree?

Transferable skill: Avoiding stereotyping others

Dr Fons Trompenaars argues that recognising cultural differences and stopping there can be dangerous because 'Recognition is just neutral or very often leading to negative comments on cultures because they are different from yours.'

1 Many experts argue that such comments then lead to stereotypes, which mean we prejudge individuals on the basis of our view of their culture, rather than as individuals. Which of the following are stereotypes? Why?

1 People from country X are arrogant.
2 People from company Z are lazy.
3 People from company A work 7.5 hours a day on average.
4 Women from country X are 1.65 metres tall on average.
5 I can't trust people from country B.

2 Read some suggestions for improving different aspects of your intercultural competence. Discuss which you think are useful or appropriate for you. Do you have any other ideas?

- Read about different cultures.
- Read the literature of other cultures.
- Watch foreign films.
- Actively search out people from different cultures to communicate with.
- Join multicultural groups, such as online discussion groups.
- Live abroad.
- Work for a foreign company.

3 How can having negative stereotypes of cultures be bad for business when dealing with people from these cultures?

4 How important do you think it is to understand the culture of a country when you are doing business there?

Output: Advise companies on reconciling cultural differences

H.L. Corp., a large Korean electronics manufacturer, has decided to acquire a small but dynamic German electronics company (Kripp) as part of its strategy to transform H.L. Corp.'s traditional culture. By learning about the best practices of Kripp, the CEO intends to make H.L. Corp. a truly innovative and global corporation.

Your consultancy company has been hired to make a presentation to each company about the other's culture, and to predict possible areas of initial conflict. In small groups, read the description of management styles of H.L. Corp. and Kripp, and list the potential areas of cultural conflict. Then think of some suggestions for <u>reconciling</u> at least two of the areas, and for encouraging <u>respect</u> between the companies.

H.L. Corp.

1 They are very hierarchical, with many layers of management, although this has been changing slowly over the past decade.
2 They are extremely punctual, and always arrive on time for meetings, etc.
3 While at work, levels of formality (e.g. in the way people address each other) are high, although this changes when colleagues go out together.
4 Women tend to hold few management posts in the business, but again this is changing slowly.
5 They prefer a very direct style of communication, but make criticisms very indirectly.
6 Working long hours is valued as much as productivity, as it reflects loyalty to the company.
7 Generally speaking, the English language level is reasonably high.

Kripp

1 Over half of the management posts are held by women.
2 The company employs a very flexible attitude to time.
3 The company has a crèche so that children can be looked after while parents are working.
4 The time spent in the office is relatively short, and many people choose to work at home for part of the week.
5 In this company, friendliness is displayed through humour, and staff address each other using first names.
6 There is little socialising outside the office between colleagues.
7 English language levels are very high.

7.2 Practice: Internationalising a company

Learning outcomes

- Discuss the role of English in international business.
- Link ideas and information together.
- Make a set of guidelines for improving English in the workplace.

Profile: Rakuten

Rakuten is the largest online shopping site in Japan, and is among the top ten biggest in the world, along with Amazon and eBay. The company was founded in 1997 by CEO Hiroshi Mikitani, a Harvard MBA graduate. According to the company website, 'Rakuten's flagship shopping portal, Rakuten Ichiba, connects some 40,000 merchants to customers looking for a one-stop shop for products from electronics to pajamas.' While overseas business accounted for only 1% of the company's turnover in 2010, the CEO has stated the company goal is to raise this to 70%. In order to achieve this, he is implementing a radical English language policy.

Introduction

1 Read the profile of Rakuten and discuss in pairs whether you agree or disagree with the following three statements. Even if you both have the same opinion, try to think of reasons supporting the opposite viewpoint.

1 Companies that want to work internationally should use English at all times.
2 In an international company, people who cannot speak English should not be employed.
3 In an international company, it is the company's responsibility to train employees to speak business English.

2 Do you think your workplace or college should be an 'English-only' environment?

Reading 1: Initiating policy

1 Read through the first part of the article on page 68 and answer these questions.

1 How strict will the official policy towards English be?
2 How many non-Japanese speakers need to be present for a meeting to be held in English?
3 According to the experts, what factor(s) will affect the success of this policy?
4 What proportion of staff are receiving company-sponsored English lessons?

2 Do you think sufficient support is being offered to the staff by the company? Why/Why not?

Part 1

Rakuten's all-English edict a bold move, but risky too

By MINORU MATSUTANI
Staff writer

Internet shopping mall operator Rakuten Inc. surprised the public **by** announcing early this year it will make English its official language.

All internal meetings will be in English **whether** foreigners are present or not. Board meetings and weekly all-company meetings have been in English since March, and President Hiroshi Mikitani has said board members who can't speak English in two years will be fired. Cafeteria menus are now in English.

The Rakuten group has 6,000 employees globally, **of whom** about 400 are non-Japanese, spokesman Naoki Mizushima said. The firm doesn't keep track of how many non-Japanese it has in Japan, **while** the 16 board members at its headquarters in Tokyo are all Japanese, he said.

Japanese companies looking to expand their overseas sales don't deny the merit of having employees proficient in English, **but none has gone as far as to** require their Japanese employees to speak English to other Japanese employees. Experts are unsure if Rakuten's ploy will succeed, **saying it** depends entirely on employee commitment.

'Of course, Japanese is the best language for Japanese to communicate with each other, and of course other companies should also try to improve their employees' English skills,' said Minoru Ohki, the business development supervisor at Temple University Japan's Corporate Education. 'The significance of Rakuten's announcement was that Mikitani forced the employees to make the commitment.'

Rakuten is one of a very small number of Japanese companies able to push English as its official language because Mikitani, who has an MBA from Harvard, is fluent in English and is very charismatic, analysts say, **though** making such a decision **and** getting positive results are two separate things.

'Rakuten has a culture of uniting under Mikitani's top-down decisions,' UBS Securities Japan Ltd. analyst Sumito Takeda said. 'For Mikitani, Rakuten is doing something normal at a normal speed, but the speed is very fast for other firms.'

Rakuten employees are under a lot of pressure to learn English. Spokesman Mizushima said 200 employees out of 3,000 working at the headquarters take lessons from Berlitz Japan Inc., a language school chain that has an exclusive contract to send English teachers to Rakuten.

'A lot more people applied for the lessons, but we had a capacity of only 200 due to space limitations,' Mizushima said, **adding that** other employees are taking English lessons elsewhere. 'Everybody spends their own money for lessons and is committed to learning English.'

Rakuten is not providing financial support for lessons, but Berlitz offers a discount, Mizushima said.

For its part, Berlitz believes success at Rakuten would give it an enormous business boost, **while** it also feels the pressure to produce. 'Our responsibility is huge. Our mission to improve Rakuten employees' English skills has just begun,' Berlitz Japan Sales Manager Gan Yaguchi said.

Source: *The Japan Times*

Part 2

In a similar move, Fast Retailing Co., operator of the Uniqlo inexpensive clothing chain, said last month it will make English an official language starting in March 2012, **but** meetings among Japanese employees and e-mail exchanges with Japanese won't have to be in English, spokeswoman Naoe Tsunashima said.

Now, some meetings are in Japanese and foreign participants later ask Japanese who speak English about what was discussed. But mixed meetings will be conducted in English, she said.

Other major firms have long focused on improving the English proficiency of their employees **as** they look to expand overseas amid the declining labor pool at home.

However, few have made it a rule to adopt English as their official language.

For example, Nissan Motor Co., which is headed by Carlos Ghosn, who is not fluent in Japanese, 'has no rules on languages,' a spokesman said. 'If non-Japanese are in a meeting, Japanese need to speak English.'

Nomura Holdings Inc., which acquired U.S. securities firm Lehman Brothers' Asian and European businesses, also has no rules, but many Japanese now have to communicate in English with foreign colleagues, a spokesman said.

Rakuten has also acquired foreign companies, including Buy.com Inc. in the United States, and it has a major stake in a joint venture with Baidu Inc. in China. But the degree to which English is necessary at Rakuten is far lower than companies like Nissan and Nomura, **and thus** critics say it is questionable whether Rakuten employees' commitment will last.

'Even people who absolutely have to learn English give up learning. Many Rakuten employees don't need to speak English. I don't think Rakuten will succeed,' said Giri Suzuki, who teaches Japanese linguistics at Taisho University in Tokyo and edited *Ronso: Eigo ga Koyogo ni naru Hi* (*Dispute: The Day English Becomes an Official Language*).

Mikitani insists English is a must for all the employees, saying in a recent magazine interview, 'English is like "soroban" (abacus, meaning math) in "yomi kaki soroban" (reading, writing and arithmetic). Employees who can't speak English are out of the question.'

Source: *The Japan Times*

Reading 2: Other companies and reactions

1 Read the second part of the article, and make notes on how each company's policy compares with Rakuten's.

Uniqlo	Nissan	Nomura

2 What is the opinion of Giri Suzuki, and how does it contrast with Hiroshi Mikitani's view?

3 Do you believe that Rakuten employees will be committed to learning English? Why/Why not?

4 Having read the article, what is your opinion on Rakuten's policy? Do you think it is a good one, and do you think it will succeed?

Critical analysis

Discuss whether you agree with these statements about international business English.

1 Successfully building a relationship is more important than accurate language.
2 Grammar mistakes are only important if they obscure the meaning.

Language focus: Linking ideas and information together

A complex sentence has at least two parts, with the second part adding either supporting or contrasting information.

1 Find the words and expressions which are highlighted in the reading texts. Write them in the table according to what they are used for (A or B).

A adding extra information or explanations	B adding contrasting information

2 Which of the expressions do you think would not be appropriate in spoken English?

3 Look at these sentences about internationalisation. Make each pair of sentences into one sentence using the words in brackets. The first has been done for you.

1 Our domestic market is shrinking. We need to open overseas markets. (as)

Example: As our domestic market is shrinking, we need to open overseas markets.

2 New markets will want these products. It does not matter if we are present. (whether)
3 We have 2,000 employees. 700 speak good English. (of whom)
4 Many companies move their manufacturing plants abroad. This company has moved its head office. (but none has gone as far as to)
5 Staff will receive support. They will be expected to reach a satisfactory English standard. (and thus)

Output: Developing an English policy for an international company

The charismatic CEO of the internet retail company you work for has decided that, in order to survive in the shrinking domestic market, the company must fully internationalise and the staff need to be able to use English in business. (The company is based in a country where English is not spoken as a first language.)

Stage 1

Work in two groups, managers and staff. Imagine that you have been put in charge of improving the English ability of the company's employees. You need to consider the following issues:

- Who has to learn English?
- What is the timeframe?
- What types of communication should be in English?
- When should English be used in the workplace?
- Who should pay for training?
- What incentives are there?

Managers turn to page 140 and read the information.

Staff turn to page 143 and read the information.

Take a few minutes to discuss your aims.

Hold a meeting between managers and staff to negotiate an agreement on the company's English policy.

Stage 2

After the meeting, managers should write a list of summary bullet points to other managers who were unable to attend the meeting and staff should write to other staff members. Remember to use the Language focus to help you.

Example: We spoke to the staff, most of whom were concerned about the issue of learning English.

We managed to negotiate a 20% subsidy for all courses, though these will have to take place out of work time.

Learning outcomes

- Raise awareness of potential problems in intercultural communication.
- Use collaborative turn-taking strategies.
- Develop guidelines for improving intercultural communication in a company.

'Turn-taking' means the way speakers and listeners allow each person time to speak, and know when it is appropriate to start talking.

1 Here are some commonly used turn-taking strategies. Match the strategies with the language.

1 Checking shared viewpoint	**a** So do we all agree that …
2 Handing over to another speaker	**b** Well, actually, what I mean is …
3 Summarising the discussion so far	**c** So, what you're saying is …
4 Reformulating another person's meaning	**d** Maya, could you update us on …
5 Repairing misunderstanding about your intended meaning	**e** Sure. Absolutely.
6 Actively supporting the speaker	**f** So, just to sum up, …

Introduction

1 One aspect of culture is the physical distance required between speakers, for both speakers to feel comfortable. In small groups, stand up and talk to each other while varying the distance between you. Does your level of comfort change according to the distance between you?

2 Discuss how comfortable you are with the following.

1 Being touched on your arm or shoulder in public by friends.
2 Being touched on your arm or shoulder in a more formal setting, like a job interview.
3 Standing 40 cms from a colleague you are talking to.
4 Standing 90 cms from a colleague you are talking to.
5 People making jokes in meetings and seminars.
6 People coming 15 minutes late to a meeting or seminar.
7 People arriving 5 minutes early for an appointment.
8 Businesspeople wearing shorts to work.

3 Sort (1–8) above into categories – for example, 'touching'. Which of these categories are strongly affected by culture? Do you think you are typical of your culture?

2 You are going to hear six short extracts from successful international meetings. Listen to each extract, and match it with one of the turn-taking strategies in exercise 1.

🎧 1.45

3 Choose one or more of the strategies to help with the following communication problems.

a You are explaining a new process, and your listeners are looking confused.
b You are the chairperson of the meeting, and you want to make sure that everybody has the same opinion.
c You are the chairperson, and you want to briefly repeat what has been discussed so far, to make sure everyone understands.
d Your colleague is making a suggestion, but seems very nervous.
e You are not sure you fully understand what your colleague means.
f You are the manager, and you know one of your staff has a good solution to the problem being discussed.

4 Why do you think these strategies are so important in __international__ meetings?

Critical analysis

The amount of silence that happens between turns can vary according to the individual and culture. Some people prefer very little silence between speakers, and they may be happy to interrupt each other. In contrast, others may prefer longer silences between turns, and they may feel that interrupting is generally unacceptable.

1 How about you? Do you interrupt very much? Why/Why not?
2 What communication problems can occur when somebody who dislikes silence between turns and interrupts a lot communicates with someone who does not? Can you think of any solutions to such problems?

Listening: Expert advice

 1.46

You are going to listen to people giving advice on good intercultural communication.

1 Note down the key point each person makes.

2 Compare your notes with a partner, and discuss which you think is the best advice.

Speaker 1: Professor Hiro Tanaka, Professor of International Studies at Meisei University and Senior Consultant at Transnational Management
Key point:

Speaker 2: Nikki King, MD of Isuzu Trucks UK
Key point:

Speaker 3: Charlie Peppiatt, Vice President of Global Operations, Laird PLC
Key point:

Intercultural analysis

Look at the following cross-cultural problems, and select the advice you heard in the Listening that would address each problem.

1 You are having a meeting with your new partner from Saudi Arabia, but you are not sure of his level of English.
2 You are going to be transferred to Ethiopia for three years to manage a new office there. You know nothing about the country and have never been there before.
3 You are visiting Thailand, and are surprised by how much people smile in public and when they meet strangers (this is unusual in your culture). How should you respond and how could you find out more about this cusom/behaviour

In pairs, role play situations 1 and 3.

Output: Intercultural consultancy work

Stage 1

You have been invited to observe the communication in an international company, and make recommendations about how it can be improved. Although the company's offices are based in Argentina, most of the senior management are from the USA.

Look at the list of problems below and discuss possible solutions. Remember to use turn-taking strategies.

1 The senior management seem to have minimal knowledge of Argentina, and never socialise outside of their circle. Virtually none of them speaks Spanish.
2 The English used by the management tends to be very idiomatic, with lots of US humour and references to US culture. The Argentinian staff do not seem to understand a lot of what is discussed in meetings, and directives are often not implemented. This has led to much bad feeling between the staff and the management.
3 The company has a policy in meetings where one of the middle-ranking employees chairs the meeting, in order to motivate them. But you have noticed that in practice, this means that the topic is not fully discussed, and some of the members do not seem to follow the direction of the meeting.
4 There is a lot of sarcasm in meetings, and several staff never contribute to the discussions. There is, however, a small group of younger Argentinian staff who take a very aggressive approach, and often interrupt their US managers and question many aspects of company policy.
5 Presentations tend to be very long and very boring. Delivery techniques are very poor, and there is little awareness of the audience.
6 At lunch and in the evening, there is no contact or communication between the Argentinian and American employees.

Stage 2
Report your findings to the rest of the class.

8 International outsourcing

8.1 Theory: Avoiding outsourcing pitfalls

Learning outcomes
- Understand issues that companies face when deciding to outsource.
- Learn key terms and phrases linked to the topic of outsourcing.
- Discuss cases of extreme outsourcing.

Introduction

Read the dictionary entry from the *Cambridge Advanced Learner's Dictionary* and answer the questions below.

> **outsource** /ˈaʊtsɔːs/ *verb* If a company outsources, it pays to have part of its work done by another company. *Unions are fighting a plan by universities to outsource all non-academic services.*

1 Why do unions often fight plans by companies to outsource activities such as cleaning, catering and IT services?

2 Why would companies pay outsourcing providers to do activities that they previously did themselves?

3 When would companies use local outsourcing providers and when would they use offshore ones?

Language focus: The language of outsourcing

1 Match these key words and phrases to their definitions.

1	core business	**a**	discuss again the terms of a contract with the same supplier or partner, with the goal of changing the terms
2	back office	**b**	reducing staff numbers and becoming smaller (often as a result of outsourcing)
3	outsourcing provider	**c**	bring back in-house activities or functions that were previously outsourced
4	downsizing	**d**	a complex strategy that allows a company to keep its stock levels to a minimum, by placing a lot of small stock orders of just the right quantity at just the right time. This means the company no longer needs large stock rooms.
5	switch providers	**e**	essential activities and functions of an organisation, from where it derives its competitive advantage.
6	reintegrate activities	**f**	a company that sells outsourcing services
7	renegotiate a contract	**g**	end a contract with one outsourcing provider and sign a contract with another
8	logistics	**h**	administration activities and functions where there is no direct contact with the client
9	shortfall in inventory	**i**	complex process of managing the company's supply chain to ensure it has the right components / raw materials in the right amount at the right time in the right place
10	just-in-time (JIT)	**j**	not having enough stock

2 In small groups, brainstorm some reasons to explain the following.

1 Why a company might decide to switch outsourcing providers.
2 Why downsizing is often the result of outsourcing.
3 Why core services are not usually outsourced.
4 Why a company might want to reintegrate activities it had previously outsourced.
5 Why a company might want to renegotiate its existing outsourcing contract.

Business view

Jérôme Barthélemy is Professor in the Department of Management at the ESSEC Business School in Paris. His research area is strategic outsourcing.

1 Read the executive overview of an extract from a journal article written by Jérôme Barthélemy titled 'The seven deadly sins of outsourcing' and answer the questions that follow.

1 What are the main benefits of outsourcing?
2 What is the source of the author's findings and conclusions?
3 Why is not much heard about the down side to outsourcing?

2 Quickly read the examples of each of the seven deadly sins of outsourcing and then write the name of each sin, found in the executive overview, in the title gaps.

Executive Overview

While outsourcing is a powerful tool to cut costs, improve performance, and refocus on the core business, outsourcing initiatives often fall short of management's expectations.

Through a survey of nearly a hundred outsourcing efforts in Europe and the United States, I found that one or more of seven "deadly sins" underlie most failed outsourcing efforts:

(1) outsourcing activities that should not be outsourced; (2) selecting the wrong outsourcing provider: (3) writing a poor contract; (4) overlooking personnel issues; (5) losing control over the outsourced activity; (6) overlooking the hidden costs of outsourcing; and (7) failing to plan an exit strategy.

Outsourcing failures are rarely reported because firms are reluctant to publicize them.

The seven deadly sins of outsourcing

First Deadly Sin: 1 _____
A European bank outsourced its entire telecommunications network to cut costs and refocus on its core business. This endeavor turned out to be a complete failure, with increasing costs and decreasing service quality. The main reason for the failure was that the management had rushed to enter the relationship with the outsourcing provider. Too little time was spent on developing a good contract and several mistakes were made. The contract, though very long, was not precise. For instance, the bank had to pay extra fees even for basic services. There were no objective performance measurement clauses either.

Second Deadly Sin: 2 _____
The newly appointed top managers of a car rental company decided to outsource information technology (IT) to reduce costs. At that time, IT costs stood at five per cent of revenue, which was higher than the industry average (three to four per cent). Three years into the outsourcing contract, IT costs stood at ten per cent of revenue and the car rental firm could not get out of the contract. According to the chief information officer: "The entire IT department has been outsourced, but we should have kept applications development and maintenance in-house. These activities are too close to our core business."

Third Deadly Sin: 3 _____
A European department store had to close for two days because its 70 facilities management personnel went on strike. The shutdown took place during an important sales promotion and resulted in the loss of several million Euros. This strike was partly due to constant rumors that facilities management would be outsourced and the company downsized. These rumors were essentially fueled by the fact that retiring facilities management employees were never replaced. Basically, their colleagues were afraid of being transferred to the outsourcing provider (with lower pay and benefits) or being laid off.

Fourth Deadly Sin: 4 _____
One retail company outsourced several IT activities that senior management considered to be non-core (data centers, applications maintenance, and user support). However, outsourcing failed due to high costs and low performance. Though the vice-president of information services wanted to get out of the contract, he was reluctant to cancel it. Indeed, he knew that an outsourcing provider switch would take over six months while reintegrating the activities would require as much as ten months. All he could do was to renegotiate the contract.

Fifth Deadly Sin: 5 _____
The table below shows the hidden costs of a manufacturing firm which outsourced its entire logistics function. There are two main costs; the first one is the upfront cost involved in the search for the ideal outsourcing provider together with the legal costs to negotiate the initial contract. There is also the annual management cost to ensure the outsourcing provider fulfills its contractual obligations. As a proportion of the total contract amount, these costs are significant (6.2% and 15% respectively).

Contract amount	$4 million
Total search and legal costs	$250,000
Ratio of total search and contracting costs to total contract amount	6.2%
Annual management costs	$600,000
Ratio of annual management costs to total contract amount	15%

Sixth Deadly Sin: 6 _____
Acting on instructions from its U.S. headquarters, a European equipment manufacturer outsourced its entire logistics activity. The U.S. top management was not sure that the internal logistics department of their European subsidiary had a sufficient level of expertise to implement a just-in-time logistics operation. As the headquarters asked for the move to be made very quickly, the managers of the subsidiary had to find a third-party logistics provider, within only six months. Shortly after the contract was signed, things started going sour as the third-party provider did not live up to expectations. Goods were either delivered too late or not delivered at all. There were large shortfalls in inventory.

Seventh Deadly Sin: 7 _____
Outsourcing at a specialty retail firm had resulted in the total dismantling of the internal IT department. Shortly after the outsourcing decision had been made, the Chief Information Officer (CIO) was left alone to manage the outsourcing provider. Outsourcing ended up as a downright failure. The five-year contract was cancelled three years after it was signed. According to the CIO, outsourcing had resulted in "a total and dangerous loss of control over IT, inability to cope with the changing environment and command over the future."

Source: _The seven deadly sins of outsourcing_ by Jérôme Barthélemy

3 Read the text again and answer the questions about each of the seven sins.

1 What was wrong with the contract that the European bank had signed with its outsourcing provider?

2 How much higher than the industry average were the car rental company's IT costs, three years after outsourcing its IT function?

3 Why did the facilities managers at the European department store think that the company was going to be downsized?

4 Why did the retail company not cancel its contract with its costly low-performing IT outsourcing provider?

5 What are the three types of hidden costs that need to be taken into account when evaluating the option to outsource?

6 Why did the European equipment manufacturer outsource its logistics function?

7 What were the three reasons given for the speciality retail firm cancelling its contract with its IT service provider?

4 In a later part of this article, the author identifies the two sins that had the greatest impact on the success of the outsourcing efforts. Which two sins do you think he refers to? Discuss the reasons for your answer.

Transferable skill: Considering the other side of the argument

1 How useful is it is to consider the other side of an argument, in your view? Put the following benefits in order of importance.

1 You are more effective in debates and discussions.

2 It helps you prepare for negotiations by anticipating the other side's moves.

3 It helps you build relationships at work by better appreciating colleagues' positions.

4 You become a more creative thinker and gain new insights into issues.

2 Look at the list of 'non-academic services' provided by universities. Which do you think universities should not consider outsourcing? What is the other side of the argument – how could universities actually outsource these services, and what benefits could that bring?

> accounts payroll IT support cleaning security
> software development canteen student registration
> student residences library services career advice

3 Why have universities not outsourced academic services, such as teaching and course design? Considering the other side of the argument, who could actually provide these services and what benefits could they bring?

Output: Discuss cases of extreme outsourcing

You are going to discuss the cases of two US fashion designer brands selling premium-priced branded clothing in the USA and across most major country markets. These companies have taken an extreme position regarding outsourcing.

Stage 1

Divide into small groups and discuss the following two companies who have both recently made a strategically important business decision. Which one of these companies is more likely to succeed in the long term?

- Marcus Clothing has recently made a radical strategic decision to outsource all its component services to outside contractors based in the USA and abroad. A case of extreme outsourcing, where it keeps in-house only three main functions: coordinating and monitoring outsourcing providers, strategic planning and sales. Everything else, from marketing, design, manufacturing and IT to cleaning the offices, will be outsourced.

- Whilst its competitors are outsourcing more and more of their activities, Jason K Fashions has made a radical strategic decision to outsource none of its component services. It will keep everything in-house.

Stage 2

Look at the table below showing the major component services that a company could outsource. Which of these services do you think the two companies should consider outsourcing, and which not? Decide also whether it would be best to outsource to providers locally in the USA, or to providers abroad. Discuss your answers and note down the main reasons behind your decisions in the table.

Component service	Consider outsourcing Y/N	If 'Yes', use local or offshore provider?	Reason for decision
Cleaning offices			
Garment manufacturing			
Clothes design			
Marketing, branding and PR			
Payroll processing			
Accounts and invoicing			
Website design and maintenance			
Logistics/IT			
Customer care call centre			

Stage 3

After completing the task, report your findings to another group.

8.2 Practice: Offshore outsourcing provider's perspective

Learning outcomes

- Understand how the outsourcing industry in the Philippines works.
- Learn to use different stances to tone up or down a message.
- Resolve misunderstandings between client and offshore outsourcing provider.

Profile: Business Processing Association Philippines (BPAP)

BPAP is the country's industry association for business process outsourcing in the service sector. This includes 'voice services', which are call centres to handle customer enquiries, and back-office services, as well as 'non-voice services' such as accounts, payroll processing, data inputting and IT services. These services are provided to international clients. According to its website, BPAP's vision is 'to make the Philippines the number one destination for voice and non-voice services worldwide'.

Introduction

1 Read the profile above to understand what is meant by the term 'business process outsourcing'. Do companies and/or government departments in your country do much of this type of outsourcing to service providers abroad? Why/Why not?

2 Many banks, airlines, telephone service providers and even train operators in the UK and the USA have outsourced some or all of their customer care services. They use offshore call centres, in places such as Bangalore in India and Manila in the Philippines, to handle their customer enquiries. What do you think are the advantages and disadvantages of doing this for the end-user customer?

Business view

Gigi Virata is Senior Executive Director of Business Processing Association Philippines (BPAP), which promotes the country as an international outsourcing destination.

Listening 1: Benefits of offshore outsourcing

🎧 2.02

1 Listen to the first part of the interview with Gigi Virata and tick (✓) the reasons mentioned below for why companies outsource offshore.

1 They want to become more efficient and competitive.
2 They need to hire skilled labour on a large scale.
3 They are looking for a range of skills that are difficult to find at home.
4 They are looking for new ideas from a more culturally diverse work force.
5 They want to save money.

2 Listen again and make notes on the example given of international companies' need for skilled labour. Is the example presented for illustration purposes or presented as fact?

Critical analysis

Look at the photo showing protesters demonstrating against outsourcing in Washington DC and discuss the following questions.

1 How sympathetic are you to these workers' protests?
2 Do you think these workers' jobs would be protected if US companies stopped outsourcing offshore?
3 Who would lose out and who would gain if companies in the rich industrialised world stopped outsourcing offshore?

Listening 2: Why companies choose the Philippines

 2.03

1 Listen to the second part of the interview and answer the questions.

1 What kind of outsourcing work is done in the Philippines for companies from non-English speaking countries?
2 How does the Philippines compare to India for IT outsourcing?
3 How does the Philippines compare to India for call centre outsourcing?
4 What examples are given of the Philippines 'embracing western culture'?
5 What is driving the growth of call centres in the Philippines?

2 Look at the following figures from the Listening. Can you remember what they represent?

a 100 million   b 400,000   c 70%

3 Listen again and check your answers.

Intercultural analysis

In the interview, Gigi Virata states that American companies are choosing the Philippines over India because there is greater cultural affinity between the two countries.

1 How might cultural affinity be important for call centre customer interactions?
2 Why is cultural affinity less important for other sectors of business process outsourcing such as IT support, software development and accounts?

Listening 3: Challenges facing the industry

 2.04

1 Listen to the final part of the interview and complete the notes below which summarise what was said about the challenges facing the industry in the Philippines. Use a maximum of four words to complete each gap.

2 Practise presenting this information out loud, in as much detail as possible, using your completed notes below.

Language focus: Taking different stances to intensify or tone down the message

1 The sentences below are taken from the interview with Gigi Virata and show the stance (or position) she takes to present her point of view. Choose two descriptors from the box that best describe this stance.

1 Our accent seems easier to understand, for Americans …
2 … companies tell us that we are a little bit better than India.
3 That can be a challenge [in, for example, a smaller city] …

assertive / very direct   hesitant   diplomatic / tactful
evasive   critical   confrontational   highly subjective / one-sided
defensive   objective / balanced

2 In the sentences (1–3) above, underline the words that show evidence of the stance. Rewrite the sentences to make them more assertive and direct.

3 Tone down the following statements to make them less assertive and direct, and consequently more tactful and indirect.

1 This isn't any good. You've got to completely rewrite that report.
2 You're totally wrong. There's no way we were responsible for that.

4 Look at the words and phrases in the box below and categorise them into two groups (A and B).

A = 'tone-down' words used to soften a message
B = words that intensify a message

very   completely   sort of   totally   so   absolutely   kind of
basically   a (little) bit   such   like (adverb)

Main Problems
* Not enough potential recruits 1 _____ .
* Of those that apply, not enough have right level of 2 _____ .

Industry challenges

Typical recruitment scenario
* Of 100 people that apply, 10 are 3 _____ .
* A further 20–30 are hireable after 2–3 weeks' 4 _____ .

BPAP action to solve problems
Two things BPAP can do:
* Make the hiring, recruitment and 5 _____ more efficient.
* Have more awareness campaigns to change 6 _____ of the industry.

5 Use the words in question 4 to complete the gaps in the following sentences. In some cases there is more than one correct answer.

1 That's why it's _____ fun to work here.
2 Well, _____ , what happens is, you have to have some form of contract that …
3 The new product has _____ had a negative impact on our reputation.
4 It's going to be fantastic, _____ amazing!
5 Because otherwise it'll have, you know, _____ three or four requests.

6 The words 'actually', 'really', 'just' and 'quite' are used both as softeners and intensifiers. Which of the following sentences show these words used as softeners, and which as intensifiers?

1 I'm just writing to ask if you could send me your report sometime before Thursday.
2 It's not a big seller really.
3 It's really easy to do.
4 You could actually smell all the smoke coming up … it was horrible.
5 It was quite an experience!

7 Listen to the pronunciation of these sentences and repeat what you hear. What do you notice about how 'actually', 'really', 'just' and 'quite' are stressed when these words are used as intensifiers, compared to when they are used as softeners?

🔊 2.05

8 Which sentence below (A or B) refers to 'tone-down' softening words and which to intensifying words?

A They are most often used between colleagues making small talk to build relationships at work. In this context, they are also used to heighten drama and tell good anecdotes.

B They are most often used between managers and subordinates to politely convey information or instructions.

Output: Resolve misunderstandings between client and outsourcing provider

You are going to participate in a meeting between Star Air (an international airline based in North America) and Rock Solid Support (an offshore outsourcing provider based in Asia) who deal with their passenger bookings and information services. There are problems on both sides which need resolving.

Stage 1
Divide into small groups.

Group A look at the information for StarAir on this page.
Group B look at the information for Rock Solid Support on page 143.

Read through the list of problems and prepare for the meeting.

Group A

You work for Star Air. A number of problems have occurred with your passenger booking and information service. This is run by Rock Solid Support in Asia, who you have contracted to do the job for you. In your group, read through the problems and brainstorm practical steps you want taken to resolve them.

Problem 1: Initial contract clause not being followed
The contract states that the call centre should respond to all calls promptly, which for you means 'within 2 rings'. This is not happening, especially at peak times. Too many first calls are also being referred to supervisors, as front-line staff are unable to deal with them.

Problem 2: Poor level of written English communications to passengers
Approximately 30% of emails sent to passengers to confirm new travel arrangements are full of English grammar and spelling mistakes, leading to passenger confusion and an unprofessional image being presented.

Problem 3: Passengers complaining of unfriendliness
Passenger satisfaction surveys show call centre representatives' tone of voice and overall manner is unhelpful and unfriendly. 'They don't seem to relate to me in any way' is an often-quoted problem.

Problem 4: Lack of action to fix problems
Results of poor customer satisfaction surveys and direct (negative) feedback from passengers is being sent to the outsourcing provider but it is not being acted on.

Stage 2
You are going to have a meeting with the people from the other group to try to resolve your differences. Before the meeting, assign at least one person in your group to each of the following roles:

■ Someone to take an assertive and direct approach
■ Someone to take a tactful and diplomatic approach
■ Someone to build relationships and keep the atmosphere positive

After you have decided on your roles, get together with the opposing team and have the meeting.

Stage 3
After you have finished your meeting, discuss which approach was more effective: assertive and direct, tactful and diplomatic, or relationship building – or a combination of these approaches.

8.3 Skills: Dealing with Q&A

Learning outcomes
- Understand how to manage Q&A sessions during presentations and meetings.
- Learn how to ask and answer a variety of question types.
- Manage a Q&A session discussing staff redundancies.

Introduction

1 When giving a presentation, some presenters prefer taking questions from the audience <u>during</u> the presentation whilst others prefer to wait to <u>the end</u> of the presentation and then take questions in a short concentrated question and answer (Q&A) session. What are the advantages and disadvantages of each approach?

2 In pairs, ask each other the main question in the chart below and then follow the 'Yes' or 'No' route and ask and answer the subsequent questions.

> Do you have personal experience of giving a presentation with a Q&A session?

Yes
- What are the type of questions you are asked?
- How confidently do you answer questions?

No
- What type of questions are experienced politicians and business leaders asked by journalists?
- What do they do to answer these questions effectively?

3 Why do you think it is a good idea to plan and prepare for a Q&A session?

Listening 1: Managing a Q&A session

🔊 2.06

1 Listen to the start of a Q&A session and decide what kind of meeting (A, B, C or D) it is.

A Press conference
B Annual shareholder meeting
C Internal staff conference
D Meeting with banks and potential investors

2 Listen again and answer the following questions.

1 What are the two 'ground rules' mentioned?
2 How should people at the meeting ask their questions?

3 Listen again and complete these six introductory phrases used to set up the Q&A.

1 It's now time to begin _____
2 I want to review _____
3 We look forward to _____
4 We do, however, reserve the right to _____
5 And we really do not plan _____
6 If you wish to ask a question _____

4 Practise saying the Q&A set-up aloud, using your notes.

Language focus 1: Inviting questions from the audience

🔊 2.07

1 Complete the gaps in the sentences below which show how presenters invite questions from the audience.

1 Are there any questions about how we're going to p_____?
2 I'd be h_____ to take questions at the end of the talk.
3 If you have any questions, please raise your h_____ .
4 So, any questions anybody? Please f_____ away.
5 Right, are there any questions before we s_____?
6 I'll move straight over to Graham and o_____ it u_____ for any questions from the floor.

2 Listen and check your answers.

3 Which sentence above is more formal than the others, and which is more informal?

4 Which sentences would you probably not hear in a Q&A session?

2.08

1 The table below shows the types of question that can be encountered during a meeting or presentation. Listen to the five questions posed at the annual shareholder meeting and match them to the question types in the table.

Question type	Question number
Non-question	
Straightforward question	
Difficult question	
Hostile question	
Multiple question	

2 Look at the strategies for answering questions in the table below. Listen again and tick any of the strategies used by the presenter to deal with each of the questions.

Question asked	Strategies used in answer
1 Straightforward question	**a** Be short, simple and concise. **b** Use humour to engage with the audience.
2 Multiple question	**a** Acknowledge a multi-question has been asked. **b** Admit that you don't know the whole answer. **c** Ask if someone else in the audience knows the answer. **d** Answer all parts of the question.
3 Non-question	**a** Clarify what the question is. **b** Attack the questioner. **c** Defend your position/organisation.
4 Difficult question	**a** Be honest and admit it when things have gone wrong. **b** Carefully avoid the question. **c** Be optimistic when facing difficulties.
5 Hostile question	**a** Confront criticism head on. **b** Challenge 'facts'. **c** Answer a different question from the one asked. **d** Defuse conflict by empathising with the questioner.

3 Which of the strategies listed do you think are most effective? Discuss your answers and explain your reasons.

Language focus 2: Replying to questions

1 Look at the strategies (1–9) a presenter could use to deal with questions and match them to the phrases (a–i) that the presenter could use.

1 Be straight and to the point.	
2 Acknowledge that a multi-question has been asked.	
3 Ask if someone else in the audience knows the answer.	
4 Admit that you don't know the answer.	
5 Be honest and admit it when things have gone wrong.	
6 Be optimistic when facing difficult questions.	
7 Confront criticism head on.	
8 Challenge 'facts'.	
9 Defuse conflict by empathising with the questioner.	

a There are many questions there …
b I don't know how true the information you have is.
c Yes, it is important. Does that answer your question?
d We didn't do it because I don't believe that the risk was worth it.
e I promise I'll try to get back to you within 48 hours with an answer.
f I am aware that we may have been guilty of that …
g That's OK, I know where you are coming from.
h Is Bill here? Do you want to comment?
i It's going to be a difficult six months, but we will come out of it stronger …

2 Work in pairs. Think of some difficult questions to ask your partner about their work or studies. Answer your partner's questions using the language above to help you.

Output: Q&A session discussing staff redundancies

You work for Arco Design, a small chain of 12 kitchen design shops located in your city. There are about 120 members of staff, mainly sales people and kitchen designers. You are in a presentation where the senior management have just explained that the company has experienced a fall in sales over the last six months and that orders for the next six months are well below normal levels. They have informed staff that shop closures, redundancies and relocation of some staff will be inevitable. You are now going to take part in the Q&A session at the end of the meeting.

Divide into small groups.

Group A look at page 139 and read about the senior management position.

Group B look at page 144 and read about the staff position.

▶◀ **Watch Sequence 4 on the DVD to find out more about Globalisation.**

Writing 4: Writing follow-up emails

Learning outcomes

- Contrast transactional and interpersonal language and goals in business.
- Request, remind and explain in writing.
- Write follow-up emails.

Introduction

1 In business, a distinction is often drawn between 'transactional' communication (which focuses on the task) and 'interpersonal' communication (which prioritises or focuses on the relationship). Decide whether the following are primarily transactional or interpersonal.

1 So, I think we've got to look at production capacities …
2 Good morning, Colette.
3 It was just a pain getting down here.
4 … you have to send it in writing.
5 I think we should make a start …

2 The terms 'transactional' and 'interpersonal' can also be applied to business culture and practices. Decide whether the following views are more transactional or interpersonal.

1 Long-term relationships are valued over quick profits.
2 Relationships in business should begin and end quickly.
3 Business relationships are built up slowly, and are based on trust.
4 Business communication and services should be quick, efficient and to the point.

Writing skill: Contrasting transactional and interpersonal emails

The email on the right was written by Pete Jones, the director of sales for an American agricultural equipment supplier. He is writing to foreign business people who have expressed an interest in his products after a visit to the United States.

1 Look at the email and choose the correct words in italics to complete it.

2 The email did not receive any response from the potential foreign clients. Read it again and discuss whether it has a more transactional or interpersonal focus. Give examples to support your opinion.

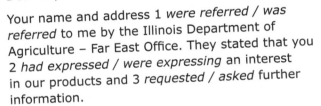

Dear Sir,

Your name and address 1 *were referred / was referred* to me by the Illinois Department of Agriculture – Far East Office. They stated that you 2 *had expressed / were expressing* an interest in our products and 3 *requested / asked* further information.

I am therefore 4 *enclosing / enclosed* a brochure which 5 *itemizes / lists* up our products and services. Please let me know your exact requirements. I will be happy to 6 *provide you / give you* with further details.

Thank you for 7 *participating for / participating in* the Illinois Slide and Catalog Show.

I look forward to your reply.

Sincerely
Pete Jones
Director of Sales

3 Pete Jones' email was not as successful as he had hoped it would be, because it was not interpersonal enough. Look at the following points, and discuss which ones you think he should have followed in his email.

1 use the recipient's name to open the email
2 mention the clients' visit to the USA
3 make 'small talk' – for example, about the weather
4 thank the recipient for visiting the USA
5 say something about the history of his company
6 state the reputation the company has
7 say something about his company's desire to have good relations with the recipient's country and company
8 request the recipient contact his company

4 Look at the example below of a more interpersonal email and see which of the above points the writer follows.

Dear Mr. Yen Zen-jiu,

I have recently spoken to my colleague Sid Cowans, who told me about your visit to the United States. I hope that you enjoyed your stay and that your trip home was a comfortable one. I am writing as Mr Cowans has informed me that you have expressed an interest in our products, and would like further information about our company and the products we provide.

Please let me firstly tell you a little about us. We are a fairly large company based in Bloomington, Illinois with over 10 years' experience in selling both livestock and livestock equipment. We have trade relations with more than 45 countries and we have built up a solid reputation and good relationships in the industry as a whole.

We are very interested in building a relationship with clients in China and would be very keen to hear if any of our products would be of interest to you. I am also enclosing a price list of our products and will be happy to answer any questions or queries that you have.

May I thank you again for interest in our company. We very much look forward to hearing from you in the future.

Yours sincerely,
Tan Wen-lan

Intercultural analysis

1 In your culture, which style of communication would be more successful in attracting clients?
2 Do you think that cultures can be accurately distinguished according to whether they are more transactional or interpersonal – for instance, 'deal oriented' for the USA and 'relationship oriented' for China? Do you think there are any problems with such generalisations?

Language focus: Reminding, explaining and requesting in follow-up emails

1 Emails which follow up on an initial enquiry often include the following stages. Put the stages in an appropriate order.

a requesting a response
b reminding the reader of the initial discussion or request
c explaining the value of the product or service

2 Look at the following examples and sort them into the categories (a–c) in exercise 1.

1 In light of these factors, we request your comments on the effect of the proposed regulation.
2 The uniqueness of our product line and the existing untapped vast market paves the way for our success in the market.
3 The company's broad product line has applications in numerous industries.
4 … we remind you that the procedure continues to be available.
5 And it really is a great product. I think the product itself has got a lot of uses that we haven't even thought of yet.
6 … if you remember from our previous discussions, we have said we [are offering …]
7 Please let me know your exact requirements.
8 We request your comments on whether we should progress with the order.
9 If you could send us those comments that would be great.

3 Look at the examples in exercise 2 and underline the language that is used for requesting and reminding. Can you think of other examples? Which examples seem more formal, and which less?

Output: Writing to a potential client

One month ago, your garden tools manufacturing company was asked to send some sample equipment and literature to two big foreign wholesalers. You sent the materials, but have not heard back. You recently checked the accompanying emails, and found that they were not written in the same style as the original requests: your company sent a transactional response to an interpersonal request from one wholesaler, and an interpersonal response to a transactional request from the other wholesaler.

Write an appropriate follow-up email to each company in the same style as the original mail, and make sure to do the following:

1 Remind them of the initial discussion.
2 Explain the value of your products.
3 Request a response from them.

9 Affordable innovation

Learning outcomes
- Understand low-cost innovation emerging from developing countries.
- Learn innovation concepts and definitions.
- Debate low-cost innovation solutions.

automobile sector

telecommunications

computer software

pharmaceuticals

internet services

consumer electronics

Introduction

1 Read the definition of 'R&D' from the *Cambridge Advanced Learner's Dictionary* below and answer the question.

> **research and development** *noun* (*ABBREVIATION* **R and D**) the part of the business that tries to find ways to improve existing products, and develop new ones.

The sectors shown in the image above consistently have the highest R&D spend of all industry sectors. Give some examples of improvements to existing products and development of new products that come out of companies in these sectors.

2 Look at the findings of a recent EU Commission report listing the top seven drivers that make EU companies increase their R&D investment. What do you think are the top three factors, in order of importance?

a Need/desire to improve productivity
b Competition from other EU companies
c Competition from US/Japanese companies
d Competition from Chinese/Indian companies
e Technology push (exploit new technologies and opportunities)
f Market pull (demand from customers)
g Need to conform to new product regulations

Do you think this order will change over the next 10–20 years?

Language focus: Concepts of innovation

1 What is the difference between invention and innovation? Use the two words to complete the gaps in the definitions from the *Cambridge Advanced Learner's Dictionary* below.

1

_____ the use of a new idea or method: *the latest* _____ *in computer technology.*

2

_____ something which has never been made before, or the process of creating something which has never been made before: *The world changed rapidly after the _____ of the telephone.*

2 Which of the following words are more likely to partner with 'innovation' and which with 'invention'?

> patented   foster   marketing   ingenious   license (an) product   encourage

3 Match the following concepts of innovation to their definitions in the table below.

1	radical innovation	a	doing more for less
2	affordable innovation	b	traditional innovation done in R&D centres, initiated by senior management
3	top-down innovation	c	innovation through partnerships
4	bottom-up innovation	d	innovation coming from consumers or employees
5	collaborative innovation	e	a step-by-step approach to innovation using the existing knowledge and resources the company has
6	incremental innovation	f	breakthrough innovation using new knowledge and resources

4 Complete the following sentences using word partnerships from exercise 3. You will need to make some words plural.

1 Amazon.com's internet-based approach to selling books was a _____ at the time as nobody had done it before.

2 The task is to find _____ in the medical field that the world's poorest will have access to.

3 Google's work with Carnegie Mellon University is working towards more _____ between big business and university research centres.

4 The company has not made any major breakthroughs, but owes its success to smaller _____ .

5 CEOs are increasingly being asked to implement _____ as part of their role as business leaders. On the other hand, _____ is viewed by many organisations as a useful way of using the knowledge of the whole of the organisation's workforce.

5 What types of innovation are most/least likely to lead to success in your organisation, or in one you know well? Why?

Reading: Reverse innovation

1 Read the first <u>three</u> paragraphs of the article 'Made in India for the World' on page 84. After reading, choose the correct words in italics to complete the summary below.

Summary

Reverse innovation is about developing global product innovations and low-cost solutions to worldwide problems in **1** *developed / developing* countries. In the past, international companies produced products for rich country markets and then **2** *standardised / adapted* them for high-income consumers in developing countries. Today, the location of the R&D centres of international companies in developing countries is about meeting the specific needs of the **3** *local population / large multinational corporations*. In the initial phase, however, the main reason to locate R&D in developing countries was the **4** *availability of skilled workers / need to cut costs*.

2 Read the rest of the text and match the examples of reverse innovation below to the following companies. One company has two examples.

Mahindra & Mahindra   Deere & Company   Renault-Nissan   PepsiCo

1 Made efficiency savings in India and then transferred that knowledge back to the USA.

2 Realised at a relatively early stage that it could sell low-cost innovations in the USA that it developed in India.

3 Didn't initially think to sell low-cost innovations in the USA that it developed in India.

4 Achieved similar quality of innovations in India as it did in rich developed countries, but at a fraction of the cost.

5 Set up a centre in India to access ideas imbedded in the local culture. This centre is now responsible in part for the development of a future global product.

3 Read the text again and find words and expressions in the article that have similar meanings to the following definitions.

1 an idea expressed in a few words (paragraph 1)
2 small modifications (paragraph 2)
3 the force behind a new plan or a change (paragraph 3)
4 basic (paragraph 4)
5 mainly (paragraph 4)
6 way of thinking (paragraph 6)
7 simple and economical (paragraph 7)
8 of equal value (paragraph 7)
9 created / produced for the first time (paragraph 7)
10 expertise (paragraph 8)
11 launched (paragraph 8)
12 exploit something from another place (paragraph 8)

Made in India for the World

1 There are variants to the theme of reverse innovation bandied around in boardrooms and business schools – some call the trend 'polycentric innovation', for instance – but in a nutshell, it is about innovating products and solutions primarily in emerging markets with an aim to serve both developing and developed nations.

2 Reverse innovation as a concept would have been complete fiction as recently as the beginning of this decade. Historically, the multinational innovated in cloistered research and development (R&D) centres typically located in the US, Europe or Japan and sent products – with minor tweaks – to markets as varied as India and Ethiopia. Such products, mostly, found takers among the middle class and rich or, in rare instances like personal care products, even the poor.

3 'R&D stayed at home as late as the end of the 20th century,' says Jaideep Prabhu, Nehru Professor of Indian Business and Enterprise at the Judge School of Business, Cambridge University. 'In the first phase (of innovation shifting away from the developed world), the driver was talent in countries such as India. Now, the driver is the local market.'

4 For multinational corporations chasing growth, India presents a sweet intersection of low-priced talent and a mass market – making it a new innovation destination in the world. If multinational companies fail to act, local companies in emerging economies will innovate and disrupt their rich, home markets. This almost happened to Deere & Company, the world's number one maker of tractors (sold under the John Deere brand) by revenues. While its R&D facility in Pune had developed a no-frills tractor model for India, it never thought of selling it in the US, a market that predominantly buys tractors powered by engines upward of 80 hp and those that come with air-conditioned cabins, global positioning systems and other developed-market add-ons.

5 But when Indian tractor maker Mahindra & Mahindra began targeting customers such as hobby-farmers or those who do not need advanced features in the US in 2001 (it had entered the market in 1994), John Deere woke up to an all-new market. It quickly modified the India model (added more power) and launched it in the US as the 5003 series. Today, about half the tractors Deere makes in India are exported.

6 'The emergence of frugal mindset among consumers in developed markets and increasing demand for "value for money" products is accelerating the drive for reverse innovation,' points out Navi Radjou, Prabhu's colleague and Executive Director, Centre for India & Global Business at Judge Business School.

7 Carlos Ghosn, Chairman and CEO of the Renault-Nissan Alliance, recently related the story of his company's India experience on an engineering solution. A team each in France, Japan and India worked on identical specifications (for a problem Ghosn declined to detail) and produced solutions that were all on a par in quality. The difference, Ghosn told reporters in Chennai elaborating on India's 'frugal engineering' DNA, was that the Indian solution cost one-fifth what the French and Japanese engineers came up with. The trend extends into processes, brands, consumer insights and even business models, adds Radjou, who believes the results will be comparable to the impact the Internet had on businesses.

8 Elsewhere, PepsiCo is transferring know-how it got in India on reducing water consumption to other locations. It brought down water required to produce a litre of beverage from 7.3 litres to just 2.4 litres through process efficiencies. India's diversity offers many lessons, too. Renault-Nissan chose to set up a design studio in Mumbai not just to design cars for India but also tap into trends that are unique to the country. 'Indians want to stand out in a crowd. That explains why there are so many different colours in the interior of a car,' says Jean-Philippe Salar, Studio Chief Designer, Renault-Nissan Design India. Over the last few years, the studio has gained such an expertise that it has been given the exclusive responsibility to do the colour and trim of Renault-Nissan's global concept car that is to be unveiled this year.

Source: *Business Today*, India

Output: Debate low-cost innovation solutions

You are going to debate the effectiveness and viability of a developing-world innovation solution to the problem of high-cost medical treatment in developed countries.

Stage 1
Read the motion below.

> High costs of medical treatment in the rich developed world are best addressed with radical innovation solutions provided by developing countries.

Turn to page 139 and read the arguments in the table. Mark whether each is <u>for</u> (F) or <u>against</u> (A) the motion by completing the right-hand column.

Stage 2
Divide into small groups and choose either to support the motion (<u>for</u>) or oppose the motion (<u>against</u>). Prepare for the debate in the following ways.

1 Expand and support the relevant opinions expressed in the table with reasons, examples or personal knowledge.
2 Challenge, question and try to dismantle the arguments listed in the table that do not support your case.
3 Create new reasons to support your position.

Stage 3
After completing your preparation, have the debate. One person should read aloud the motion. The <u>for</u> team should then present their arguments and respond to any questions from the other side at the end of the presentation. The <u>against</u> team should then respond and present their case, and answer questions at the end.

On concluding your debate, have a vote to decide whether to pass the motion or not – vote according to your personal views and the arguments you heard during the debate.

9.2 Practice: GE Healthcare – low-cost reverse innovation in practice

Learning outcomes

- Understand how reverse innovation strategy works in a multinational company.
- Learn word partnerships connected to 'international business strategy'.
- Devise a reverse innovation marketing strategy.

Profile: GE Healthcare

GE Healthcare is a business unit of US giant General Electric (GE). It is headquartered in the UK with sales of over US$17 billion, employing more than 46,000 people worldwide and operating in over 100 different countries. Its major product sectors include medical imaging, medical diagnostics and patient monitoring systems. GE has five integrated multidisciplinary Research and Product Development Centers in New York, USA; Bangalore, India; Munich, Germany; Shanghai, China and Rio de Janeiro, Brazil, where it conducts research, development and engineering activities for all of its diverse businesses worldwide.

Introduction

1 How do you think healthcare needs in developing countries are different from those in rich industrialised ones? Think about types of illness and disease, different ageing populations, affordability issues, etc.

2 Read the profile of GE Healthcare. Why do you think the majority of their research and product development centres are located in emerging markets?

3 Look at the findings of a recent EU Commission report, which lists the top six drivers influencing EU companies' decisions on where to locate their R&D centres. What do you think are the top three factors, in order of importance?

a Economic and political stability
b Proximity to other company activities (e.g. closeness to manufacturing plant or HQ)
c Access to markets
d High availability of researchers
e Access to specialised R&D knowledge
f Reliable legal framework (e.g. protection of Intellectual Property Rights)

4 For which of these six factors do you think developing countries would score highest and lowest?

Business view

Professor Vijay Govindarajan is Chief Innovations Officer for General Electric (GE), and Professor in residence at Tuck School of Business, USA.

Listening 1: GE Healthcare in China

🎧 2.09

1 Look at the photos of different ultrasound machines used to 'see inside' people's bodies. The small portable machine was designed and built in China by GE Healthcare but then later sold in the USA. How do you think the user needs of this machine are different in the two countries?

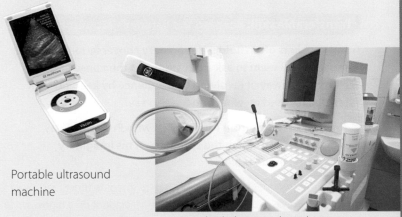

Portable ultrasound machine

Standard ultrasound machine

2 Listen to the first part of the webcast by Professor Vijay Govindarajan and answer the questions.

1 How much does this portable ultrasound machine cost in China compared to top-of-the-range models in the USA?
2 What are the two advantages of the GE portable ultrasound machine for the Chinese market?
3 How big is the global market for this product?
4 How is this product being used in the USA?

Listening 2: GE Healthcare global strategy

🎧 2.10

1 Listen to the second part of the recording and answer the following questions.

1 Why has reverse innovation become so important today?
2 What were the four regions of the world that GE used to have a strategy for?
3 What are the three regions of the world that GE now has a strategy for?
4 What thinking is described as 'outmoded'?

Critical analysis

Professor Vijay Govindarajan states in the recording that 'we need to bring the five billion poor into the consumer base'. He is talking about turning non-consumers into consumers through ultra-low-cost innovation. How realistic (or desirable) is it to achieve this objective? Discuss both sides of the question.

Tata Nano, the world's cheapest car, costs $2,000.

Aakash, the world's cheapest tablet computer, costs $35.

Transferable skill: Keeping the listener's attention

Good speakers often hold an 'imaginary conversation' with their listeners. They seem to ask a question and then answer it. This is an effective way of involving the audience by keeping their attention focused on what you have to say.

1 Read the extracts from the webcast with Professor Vijay Govindarajan and match the two parts of his imaginary conversation in the table below.

1 You may wonder how come reverse innovation has become such an important strategic priority for companies today.	a Imagine there is an accident on a highway; an ambulance is going there.
2 Let me just describe one application of this in the US.	b It is really because of the great recession …

2 Underline the language used to engage in this imaginary conversation with the audience.

3 Other language can be used for a similar purpose of involving the listener when making a case or presentation.

Have you ever heard of …   I bet you're thinking …
If you're a …

Use some of the language from questions 2 and 3 to explain what factors influence companies' decisions on where to locate their R&D centres. Practise saying it aloud.

Reading: Disrupting international business strategy

1 Read an extract from this text from the *Harvard Business Review*, written jointly by Professor Vijay Govindarajan, Professor Chris Timble and GE CEO Jeffrey Immelt, and complete the gaps using the phrases in the box.

glocalization approach   emerging economies
rapid development   global scale   substantially lower costs
local customization   slowing growth   pioneering new uses

How GE Is Disrupting Itself

General Electric announced that over the next six years it would spend $3 billion to create at least 100 health-care innovations that would 1 _____ , increase access, and improve quality. Two products it highlighted at the time – a $1,000 handheld electrocardiogram device and a portable, PC-based ultrasound machine that sells for as little as $15,000 – are revolutionary, and not just because of their small size and low price. They're also extraordinary because they originally were developed for markets in 2 _____ (the ECG device for rural India and the ultrasound machine for rural China) and are now being sold in the United States, where they're 3 _____ for such machines.

We call the process used to develop the two machines and take them global 'reverse innovation', because it's the opposite of the 4 _____ that many industrial-goods manufacturers based in rich countries have employed for decades. With glocalization, companies develop great products at home and then distribute them worldwide, with some adaptations to local conditions. It allows multinationals to make the optimal trade-off between the 5 _____ so crucial to minimizing costs and the 6 _____ required to maximize market share. Glocalization worked fine in an era when rich countries accounted for the vast majority of the market and other countries didn't offer much opportunity. But those days are over – thanks to the 7 _____ of populous countries like China and India and the 8 _____ of wealthy nations.

Portable electrocardiogram device (ECG) used to monitor patients' heartbeat

2 Are the following statements true or false?

1 The electrocardiogram device was initially intended for India and the USA.

2 A glocalisation approach no longer works for international companies today.

3 A glocalisation strategy is about producing products in local markets.

4 Rich countries are still by far the biggest markets for international companies today.

Language focus: Marketing of innovation – word partnerships

1 Use the words 'global' and 'local' to fill the gaps to create common word partnerships in the sentences below.

1 American companies would do well to follow in Islamic countries the same glocalisation strategies – _____ reach, _____ implementation – that have served them well in other parts of the world.

2 The more naturally a culture glocalises, i.e. the more it absorbs foreign ideas and _____ best practices and moulds them with its own traditions, the greater advantage it will have.

2 Discuss the following two questions.

1 How open would you say your country's culture is to foreign ideas and global best practices?

2 As a customer, what experience do you have of American companies' glocalisation strategies in your country?

3 The commercialisation and marketing of the product is the last stage of the innovation process. Complete the sentences below with words from the box to form common word partnerships found in marketing for 'price range', 'distribution channel', 'promotion' and 'product features'.

core   price   multiple   enhanced   wide   appropriate
internet   initial

1 People are attracted to the website due to the _____ price range of goods, meaning there is something for everyone.

2 When the product was launched, the _____ price range was considered too high and had to be slashed.

3 The growth of e-marketing and selling online has led to _____ distribution channels for companies to choose from.

4 When you enter a new market you must identify the _____ distribution channel for your goods.

5 We could offer discounts for people who buy multi-packs, as part of our _____ promotion.

6 Viral advertising, where one person emails an engaging advertisement to all of their friends, has become a part of _____ promotion.

7 Many goods produced in developing countries are cheaper as they only deliver the _____ product features with no extra add-ons.

8 Technological innovation has led to _____ product features, which have led to further customer satisfaction.

Output: Developing a reverse innovation marketing strategy

You are going to discuss a possible reverse innovation marketing strategy to sell a motorised vehicle in the USA (or another rich industrialised country you know well). Look at the photo and read the brief product description.

Tuk-tuks are named by the sound these three-wheeler auto-rickshaws make. Tuk-tuks are a distinctively Thai mode of transportation, but variations are found throughout developing countries in Asia. They're relatively cheap to buy compared to cars, they are often customised in bright, fun colours. However, safety can be an issue and their two-stroke engines make them noisy. They also produce a lot of pollution.

Stage 1

In small groups, discuss who might want to buy a tuk-tuk in the USA (or another developed-country market that you know well), and for what reason. (Target groups of customers could come from sectors such as leisure, transportation, retail, food and drink, publicity, etc.)

Stage 2

Discuss and take notes on what kind of marketing strategy you would implement to sell the product to <u>one</u> of the target groups of customers you identified in Stage 1. Complete the following table as a summary of your discussions.

Target market group – _____	
How much will these customers be willing to pay? (price range)	
Where will be a convenient place for these customers to buy the product? (distribution)	
What communication channels and messages would you employ to persuade this target group to buy? (promotion)	
What product features would you add / take away to customise the tuk-tuk for this target group? (product)	

Stage 3

Present a summary of the key points of your marketing strategy to another group and make sure to use language that keeps the listeners' attention whilst giving the presentation.

9.3 Skills: Dealing with criticism

Learning outcomes
- Understand negative and constructive criticism.
- Criticise directly and indirectly.
- Apply strategies to react to criticism.

Introduction

1 If you were criticised for any of the following things at work, which would upset you the most? Why?

- your clothing
- your timekeeping
- your time management skills
- the quality of your work
- your presentation style
- your command of English

2 Are there any that you wouldn't be upset by? Why not?

3 Can you remember the last time somebody criticised you, or you criticised somebody else? What happened? How direct was the criticism?

Language focus: Recognising and reacting to criticism

 2.11

1 Criticism can be direct or indirect, negative or constructive. Match these definitions with the four types of criticism.

1 It is useful and intended to improve or help something.

2 It is suggested rather than explicit.

3 It offers no suggestions about how to improve, and only focuses on the problem.

4 It is very explicit and sometimes rude.

2 Listen to and read the following two extracts from meetings. Which one is direct and negative? Which one is indirect and constructive?

Audio script

 2.11

Extract A

Manager: Why is it always you? Why is it you that has the new Renaults breaking down? Why is it you that has a problem with the centres? Why is it you that breaks the machines?

Employee: Why is it me?

Manager: Yeah?

Employee: I don't know.

Manager: 'Cause you're an idiot, that's why.

Extract B

Manager: Well, do you know why you've fallen behind with this?

Employee: Because I just get so bored and tired when I have to do too much stuff.

Manager: Well, why don't you do a little bit of the project every day?

Employee: Mm.

Manager: Just set yourself so many pages. That's what I've been doing. And some days I haven't been able to do any, but then I try to make up for it a little bit by setting a few more the next day. It's just a suggestion.

Employee: That might help.

3 Discuss what language helped you to decide on the answer to exercise 2.

4 When we receive criticism, there are several strategies for dealing with it. Read the tips below (a–h), and match each one with the appropriate language (1–8).

a	Show that you are really listening to what the critic is saying.	**1**	I've made a mistake and I've signed the wrong one off.
b	Acknowledge that the person's opinion may be correct.	**2**	The reason I'm bringing those in now is advertising costs a lot of money.
c	Don't react immediately – say you need time to think about the criticism.	**3**	I hear what you are saying and will take your comments on board.
d	Explain sincerely the reasons for your actions.	**4**	I just need a while to digest it all.
e	Admit your mistakes.	**5**	I don't know why you're talking about this.
f	Question why the critic is telling you this.	**6**	I'm not prepared to accept that.
g	Question the relevance of the criticism.	**7**	That's very interesting.
h	Say something positive to avoid criticising your critic.	**8**	We are certainly not happy with our losses in the digital aspects of our businesses either.

5 Look at the following examples of criticism. How would you respond to each of them?

1 I have no idea why you didn't consult me before agreeing to the contract.
2 Your mistake has cost us an absolute fortune.
3 That is the stupidest idea that I've ever heard.
4 I can't believe it. I never had these problems with my old supplier.
5 It's all your fault. What are you going to do about it?

6 Listen to the responses. Which tips from question 4 did the speakers use in their responses?

 2.12

Listening: Discussing the results of an exhibition

 2.13

You are going to listen to part of a marketing meeting at a company that produces a magazine for heavy industry. Sally, the Managing Director, is concerned that Mark, the Marketing Manager, has wasted money on an exhibition.

1 Listen and answer the following questions.

1 What is the initial figure that Sally says was spent on the exhibition?
2 Why does Mark think that attending exhibitions is important?
3 Why hasn't his team always followed up with possible customers after exhibitions?

4 Why does Sally think that the exhibition cost more than the initial figure?
5 Why does Sally think that some people will have seen the exhibition as a success?
6 Why does Sally think that it is important to be patient about seeing the results?

2 Listen again and discuss the following.

1 How direct is Sally at the start of the meeting?
2 How effective do you think her style of criticism is?
3 How well do you think Mark deals with the criticism?
4 How positive is the end of the discussion?

Critical analysis

Do you agree that managers should always try to offer constructive as opposed to negative criticism? Why/Why not?

Output: Making and taking criticism

Stage 1

Work in pairs. Student A is a manager and Student B is an employee. You both work for a manufacturer of children's educational games.

Student A turn to page 144 and follow the instructions. Student B look at the instructions below.

Student B

You are the employee. Your boss is angry with you for spending a large amount of last year's advertising budget on TV advertising. This hasn't led to an increase in sales yet, but you think that it will in the future. Think about what other justifications there could be for your actions, and what strategies you will use to deal with the boss's criticism.

Stage 2

Role play the situation.

Stage 3

Exchange roles so that Student B is the manager and Student A is the employee. This time the manager should try to be constructive and more indirect.

Stage 4

Work in small groups. Discuss the outcomes of your role plays. Which one was the most successful in your opinion? Why was this?

10 Design and invention

10.1 Theory: Design in business

Learning outcomes
- Understand the function of innovation and design in a business context.
- Analyse error corrections and make noun compounds with 'design'.
- Create an innovative design solution for an everyday problem.

Introduction

1 Discuss the following questions.

1 Look at the photos showing the evolution of data storage systems. How have other products and services (such as telephones, televisions and methods of payment) evolved over your lifetime?

2 What products do you own (or services do you use) which you think have been particularly well designed? Explain why. What about badly designed services and products?

Business view

Dr Clare Brass is a designer and Lecturer in Innovation Design Engineering at the Royal College of Art, London.

Listening 1: Design and people

 2.14

1 Listen to the first part of the interview and answer the questions below.

1 What two professional groups of people are being compared?

2 What company and product are given as an example of good design?

2 Listen again and take notes to expand your answers to the questions above by making notes on the following two points.

1 How the two professional groups are different

2 How the good design company and product are different from their competitors

🔊 2.15

Listen to the second part of the interview and answer the questions below.

1 Complete the table of the 'Dos and Don'ts of design' with words from the interview.

Design point	Don'ts	Dos
Example	1 Don't focus on designing a new t _____ .	2 Focus on a new way of t _____ .
Method	3 Don't focus on design as a n _____ .	4 Focus on design as a v _____ .
Perspective	5 Don't look at the o _____ .	6 Look at everything s _____ the o _____ .

2 Are the following statements true or false?

1 To understand users' needs, you need to just watch them carefully.

2 Users do many things that people generally don't realise.

3 Fully understanding users' needs helps designers design things differently.

Language focus: Noun–noun partnerships with 'design'

1 The following sentences about design show mistakes made by Advanced level learners of English. Find the mistake in each sentence and correct it.

1 She is responsible for all types of designing work for our company.

2 Her main responsibility is design new products.

3 She is responsible for the company products design department.

4 The shopping malls sell lots of very cheap designed clothes.

5 The whole house has used one systematic design and colour scheme.

6 She will be the core member of the designing team.

7 The restaurant's designs reflects aspects of a country's culture.

2 The word 'design' is often used as a compound noun (i.e. connected to another noun – for example, 'design quality'). Check your answers to exercise 1 and find examples of compound nouns with 'design'.

3 Write compound nouns with 'design' to express the following phrases more concisely.

1 the proposal for the design

2 the design of the software

3 the company that deals with design

4 the way designers think

5 the trick with design

6 all the professionals who work in design

7 the brief given to designers

8 the department where they work on design

Critical analysis

❝ If I had asked people what they wanted, they would have said a faster horse. **❞**

Henry Ford, founder of the Ford Motor Company

❝ It's really hard to design products by focus groups. A lot of these people don't know what they want until you show it them. **❞**

Steve Jobs, co-founder of Apple Inc.

1 Dr Clare Brass says that she thinks the best way for designers to innovate is to go and talk to users. How does this view differ from those in the quotes above?

2 Why might the results of asking people what they want be different for an innovator and an inventor?

3 How can designers try to ensure that their research with users is effective?

The Model T Ford

Apple's iPhone

You are going to take part in a design competition to enter an innovative design that solves an everyday problem. Read the task instructions below and keep in mind the design guidelines presented in this unit.

Stage 1: Problems and inspirations
In small groups, select one of the problems/inspirations below and then explore how this problem affects people. Have you (or anyone you know) had similar experiences? Ask each other questions on the <u>how</u>, <u>what</u>, <u>when</u>, <u>where</u> and <u>why</u> of the problem to really understand the issues and behaviour surrounding the problem.

Stage 2: Designing a solution
In the same groups, discuss designing something that solves this problem and clearly addresses people's needs. If possible you will want to delight the users with your design solution and provide some indication that it's environmentally friendly too. Sketch out a preliminary design of how the solution might look and add labels and notes to show how it might work.

'It's so frustrating – I can never find my keys when I need them'

'A runaway shopping trolley hit my Dad's brand new car in the supermarket car park last week. He was furious.'

'I always lock my bike in the bicycle parking places yet I've still had my bike stolen twice this year.'

'We can't be bothered to sort our organic waste for collection. It's pretty smelly and to be honest, we just throw it in with the normal rubbish.'

'We've got a mouse in our house but we don't know how to get rid of it – we really don't want to use a trap or poison to kill it.'

10.2 Practice: Dyson – a design-led company

Learning outcomes
- Understand how a design-focused company thinks and works.
- Describe how products and processes work.
- Explain and talk about the benefits of a new invention.

> 66 The more original your idea, the more resistance you will meet. 99

James Dyson

Profile: Dyson

Dyson is a British manufacturing company employing 3,600 people worldwide, with an annual turnover in 2011 of over a billion pounds. Its global HQ and main R&D centre is located in the UK, with a further R&D centre in Singapore and a manufacturing centre in Malaysia. Dyson is widely recognised for the high quality and innovative design of its products and technology. The product the company is best known for is its bagless vacuum cleaner, but it also produces air fans and hand dryers. It takes its name from its founder Sir James Dyson, who is a designer, inventor and entrepreneur. James Dyson has also set up a foundation to 'promote design and engineering education' and 'inspire young people about design engineering'.

Introduction

1 Read the quote and profile of Dyson and look at the photos of the company's inventions. What are your first impressions of the company?

2 Choose an electrical household product that you regularly use (e.g. a hairdryer, an electric razor, a microwave oven). Which three of the factors below would most influence your buying decision if you had to buy one today?

reliability strength performance design look and feel
ease of use brand customer satisfaction rating cost
customer service guarantee latest technology

Reading: The Dyson story

1 Read the three section titles in the box below, then quickly read the sections from the company's website that follow and match them to the titles.

A cautionary tale   Against the odds   Research and development

1 _____

It took 15 years of frustration, perseverance, and thousands of prototypes for James to finally launch the Dyson DC01 vacuum cleaner under his own name. Within 22 months it became the best-selling cleaner in the UK.

'I wanted to give up almost every day. But one of the things I did when I was young was long-distance running. I learned determination from it.'

'A lot of people give up when the world seems to be against them, but that's the point when you should push a little harder. I use the analogy of running a race. It seems as though you can't carry on, but if you just get through the pain barrier, you'll see the end and be okay. Often, just around the corner is where the solution will happen.'

2 _____

New ideas are the lifeblood of Dyson. Every year, we invest half our profits back into harnessing them – in 2010 we spent £45m. There are over 700 engineers and scientists based at our research and development laboratory in Wiltshire. Thinking, testing, breaking, questioning.

They're a varied bunch, too. Many are design engineers developing new ideas and technology. Then there are specialists who test and improve different aspects of each machine, from the way they sound to what they pick up. Some will have years of experience. Others are fresh out of universities like the Royal College of Art, Brunel or Loughborough.

They share some eclectic engineering pastimes – from building vintage cars to reconstructing medieval catapults. One design engineer also has a jet engine he'll fire up in the back garden once in a while.

3 _____

When James invented the Ballbarrow he assigned the patent to a company to manufacture and market it. At first James had a controlling interest, but as turnover grew the company needed more investment to fund its cash flow and James was not in a position to provide funding.

His business partners introduced more cash in return for shares and soon James found he was a minority shareholder. Against his wishes, the majority shareholders decided to sell his invention. There was nothing James could do about it, except learn from his mistake.

2 Find words and phrases in the text that match the meanings below.

1 first models of a new invention (section 1)
2 ability to continue trying to do something that is difficult (section 1)
3 an idiom meaning 'very soon' (section 1)
4 the thing that is most important to continued success of something (section 2)
5 occasionally (section 2)
6 unusual / highly individual hobbies (section 2)
7 formally hand over the registered rights to an invention (section 3)
8 owners of over 50% of the company (section 3)

3 Read the texts again and answer the following questions.

1 What guiding philosophy of work is communicated in Text 1?
2 What do Dyson engineers have in common?
3 What mistake did James Dyson make with his Ballbarrow?

4 How would you describe the style in which these web pages are written? What does it communicate about the kind of company Dyson is?

5 Brainstorm a list of adjectives that you could appropriately use to describe the company.

Language focus: Describing products using multiple adjectives and analogies

1 When describing products, people often use a combination of adjectives, such as 'It's a large red pneumatic ball.' Sort the following adjectives into the correct order.

a / wooden / red / eighteenth-century / square / beautiful / large / Chinese / painted box

2 Using your answer to exercise 1 as a model, sort the following in the order that the adjectives would usually appear before a noun.

material / colour / age / shape / opinion / size / origin / observation noun

3 It is unusual for speakers to use all these categories when talking. However, remembering this order can help you to position adjectives before a noun. Look at the following phrases with the noun 'product' or 'products' and put them in the correct order.

1 products / a / range / of / huge
2 products / sweet-smelling / cosmetic / beautiful
3 old / imported / product / inefficient / an
4 great / paper / products / American
5 European / exciting / innovative / products
6 innovative / fantastic / product / a

4 Another way to describe products positively is through analogy – for instance, by comparing one thing with another using 'like'. Look at this example: 'The Dyson Airblade™ hand dryer works like a windscreen wiper'. Why is this such an effective product description'?

5 What do the analogies below mean?

1 Their staff turnover makes the company look like a revolving door.
2 In her new role she's like a fish out of water.
3 Talking to her boss is like talking to a brick wall.
4 Making great adverts is like good Italian cooking: if the raw ingredients are right, creating the dish is very simple.

6 Choose a product you like, and create a clear and interesting analogy for it – for instance, its appearance ('it looks like …'), or its function ('it works like …').

Business view

Sir James Dyson is an inventor, entrepreneur and the founder of Dyson.

Listening: James Dyson talks about design and invention

2.16

1 Listen to a short interview with James Dyson. What would be an appropriate title for this interview?

2 Listen again and answer the following questions.

1 What is the 'myth about inventors'?
2 How do inventors benefit from failure?
3 What does the number 5,000 refer to?

Intercultural analysis

'So the moral of the tale is keep on failing. It works.' These are the words James Dyson uses to conclude the interview. How does this view compare to the attitudes to failure in the organisation you work or study in, or the country you live in?

Transferable skills: Thinking differently

This is sometimes referred to as 'thinking outside the box' or 'thinking laterally' – using techniques to think differently about a difficult issue or a complex problem, in order to arrive at an innovative solution or answer. This type of thinking is particularly useful when traditional and usual ways of thinking have been exhausted with no solution being found. The principle is to 'jump' you out of your 'mental tramlines'.

1 Read a short list of some techniques. Mark each one 1–5 depending on how likely you are to try it out.

1 = Not likely at all to try this
5 = Very likely to try this

1 Go for a walk (Stop what you are doing. Get up from your desk and have a walk outside to breathe some fresh air and clear your head. Have a think on a park bench.)
2 Throw the dice (Write an option for action for each of the six numbers on the dice to solve a problem. Throw the dice. Whichever number is thrown, do the action that corresponds to that number.)
3 Ask a child for advice (Children are not limited by the same mental blocks that adults have; asking a child for advice allows for the possibility of a completely fresh view on the issue.)
4 Forced association (Open any book or magazine and and stab your finger blindly on to the page. Note down the word you 'selected' and make ten associations to your problem or issue, to show new ways of looking at it.)

2 Compare your answers with a partner.

Output: Explaining unusual inventions to potential investors

You are product designers who developed a product for fun. You now believe it has potential and have built a prototype to convince investors to bring it to market.

Stage 1

Work in small groups. Look at the photo of your prototype invention and discuss the following questions.

1 What problem are you solving with this product?
2 Who is the target market for this product?
3 How does the product work and how is it assembled?
4 What variations could you make to the product with extra funding?

Group A turn to page 140.
Group B turn to page 144.

Stage 2

Practise giving the presentation within your group.

Stage 3

Find another group with a different invention and take turns to make the presentation. Show them the photo of the product and talk through the four points. At the end of both presentations, discuss which one of the two inventions is more likely to be a commercial success.

10.3 Skills: Communicating negative information in a positive light

Learning outcomes

- Discuss how managers may describe a difficult situation to staff.
- Understand euphemisms and excuses.
- Communicate bad news while maintaining the relationship.

Introduction

1 Which of the following would be most difficult for a manager? Why?

1 Telling your team about the loss of a key supplier
2 Telling your team why two of them will have to be laid off in the next six months
3 Discussing a drop in sales with the team
4 Explaining to your team why everyone (except you) has to have a 20% pay cut for the next six months
5 Announcing that the company is reducing the number of paid holidays from 20 to 15 days a year, but will give an extra 5 days to the best salesperson

2 Discuss how a manager could communicate the above information positively, and the challenges in doing this. Think about content of the message, where best to tell the bad news, language, tone of voice and body language.

3 How would you prefer to receive bad news like in the examples in exercise 1?

Language focus 1: Understand how euphemisms provide a more positive alternative

A euphemism is 'a word or phrase that is used to avoid saying an unpleasant or offensive word'. For example, 'let someone go' means 'fire somebody'.

1 Look at the following sentences and decide which definition A, B or C is closest to the real meaning of the underlined words in each sentence.

1 I'm afraid that the company is going to have to <u>restructure</u>.
   A relocate   **B** make employees redundant
   C buy new furniture
2 Our CEO is <u>leaving to pursue other opportunities</u>.
   A has resigned   **B** is going on a business trip
   C is going home early
3 We're afraid that you are <u>overqualified</u> for this job.
   A too old   **B** too rude   **C** too slow
4 We think that you <u>have been economical with the truth</u> on your application form.
   A have shown a lot of skills   **B** didn't complete it   **C** lied

5 We think that your <u>youth and enthusiasm</u> would be better suited to another role.
   A overexcitement   **B** good looks   **C** inexperience
6 We have experienced a lot of <u>customer churn</u> over the last year.
   A complaints   **B** customers leaving   **C** new customers

2 Look at these euphemisms and discuss what they could really mean. You will hear them used in the Listenings on page 97.

1 the department is thin on the ground
2 we've got some real challenges
3 they will be tough doors to knock on

3 Find the euphemisms in the extract below which mean the following.

1 a group of difficult customers
2 there are many difficulties we have to confront
3 try harder

The chemical sector is a really complex set of customers who we manage, and we've got some real challenges there, that a lot of you have already been involved with, and you've really got to focus in on how we look after that sector next year, and grow it.

Listening 1: Talking about the customers

🔘 2.17

You are going to hear part of a presentation. The sales director of a large telecommunications company is talking to managers about how next year's sales targets are going to be met. Listen and answer the following questions.

1 Which of the following reasons does the sales director give for customers churning?

1 They didn't pay.
2 They were forced to leave.
3 They chose to leave.

2 Which of the following reasons does he give for trying to get back churned customers?

1 The company has improved its service so customers may consider returning.
2 They will be easy to attract because they already know the company.
3 They will be hard to attract but easier than finding new customers.

3 What is his message about teamwork?

Listening 2: Talking about marketing support

🔘 2.18

1 Listen to the next part of the presentation and answer the following questions.

1 What does he hope the sales staff are going to do?
2 Why have the marketing workforce had problems and what euphemism does he use to explain their current situation?
3 Which of the following are true about 'Front Line'?
   a It is a new department.
   b It will monitor all sales activity and opportunities.
   c Some people are using it now.
4 What financial position is the company in at the moment?

2 Discuss the following questions.

1 If you were a staff member, how would you react to the talk just given by the sales director?
2 If you were the director, how would you communicate the financial and staffing circumstances the company finds itself in?

Language focus 2: Making excuses

1 Another way of dealing with negative information and situations is to make excuses. Match the types of excuse (1–6) with the examples (a–f).

1 Claim ignorance.
2 Say it is unusual.
3 Pass the responsibility on to someone else.
4 Say it is not your responsibility.
5 Blame others.
6 Give a reason.

a Well, I'm not in the accounts department so it's not me who's to blame.
b We do it this way because it will save us time in the long run.
c Have a word with Charles if you're stuck.
d Well, I can't understand why. That is totally their fault.
e But at the end of the day that's not really happened before.
f To be honest with you, Robert, I don't know a great deal about them.

2 Imagine you are a manager who has to fire somebody because of cost-cutting in your company. Would you use any of these excuses or would you use a different strategy?

Critical analysis

In business, using euphemisms and making excuses carry risks. Would you prefer a manager who regularly uses euphemisms, or one with a more frank approach? Why?

Output: Communicating negative information

Stage 1
Discuss the following scenarios, and how you can communicate the information while trying to keep the goodwill of the listeners. Decide whether using euphemisms or excuses might be appropriate in any of these scenarios.

Scenario 1: The visionary MD of your IT company has quit because of high levels of stress. Make an announcement to shareholders.

Scenario 2: You have decided not to promote Mr/Ms X, because of a lack of experience and some confidence issues. Tell him/her.

Scenario 3: Your company has decided not to award the contract to Company X because the costs of their services are too high. Tell them.

Scenario 4: Your board of directors has decided to move production overseas (to a different continent), but has offered managers the choice of moving with the company. Announce this to the managers.

Stage 2
Choose one of the scenarios, and role play it.

▶◀ **Watch Sequence 5 on the DVD to find out more about Design, technology and innovation.**

Writing 5: Writing for meetings – notes, minutes and agenda

Learning outcomes

- Take notes during a meeting with reference to the agenda.
- Learn guidelines on how to take notes and draw up minutes.
- Produce an agenda for a workplace meeting and transform notes into minutes.

Introduction

1 Complete the following sentences using words from the box.

after   agenda   are   before   is   minutes

1 The purpose of the _____, which _____
   distributed _____ the meeting, is to provide an official
   record of the main points of the meeting, any decisions taken, and
   who will take action on any given point.

2 The purpose of the _____, which _____
   distributed _____ the meeting, is to provide a structure
   by stating the points the meeting covers.

**2 Which of the things that happen in meetings below is it best
not to take notes on for the purposes of writing minutes?**

Jokes	Introductions
Decisions made	Confidential information
Disagreements	Background information
Private discussions	Action to be taken
Agreements	Name of person speaking
Relationship-building discourse	Name of person to take action

Writing skill 1: Taking meeting notes and interpreting an agenda

🎧 2.19

**1 Look at the agenda on the right from a meeting of
technicians for a large corporate training provider in the UK.
Answer the questions below.**

1 When and where is the meeting taking place?
2 Who has the agenda been circulated to?
3 Look at points 1, 2, 3 and 9, which often appear on meeting
   agendas. What do you think they mean?

**2 Listen to the meeting and take appropriate notes for the first
five items on the agenda that they discuss.**

**3 Look at the conventions for a standard note-taking style below.
Which of these did you use when you took notes on this meeting?
Which of these do you generally use when you take notes?**

- Use acronyms (IMF, UN, NASA)
- Use short forms ('she's', 'we're')
- Use abbreviations ('info' instead of information, 'tech' instead of
  technology, etc.)
- Use symbols (= to show 'means', < to show 'less than',
- Omit articles ('the', 'a', 'an')
- Use standard shorthand (e.g. = 'for example', w/ = 'with')
- Omit small words with no real content information ('of', 'for', 'and')
- Use bullet points or mind-maps to structure information

**4 Listen again and then check that your notes cover the main
points listed in the 'draft minutes' in the Language focus on
page 99. (Note that the draft minutes are written up from notes
you take in the meeting and have their own writing style.)**

Agenda v2

To: Dave Sinclair   Emile Lahar
     Peter Chen   Elizabeth Willis
     Paula Summers

SB Technical Assistance Team Monthly Meeting – May

Date: 28 May at 10.00 am
Room: S224 Stamford Building

Items

1. Apologies
2. Approval of April minutes
3. Matters arising
4. Liaison arrangements with IT dept
5. Feedback from results of equipment user survey
6. Fault reporting
        6.1 Review procedure for logging faults with equipment
        6.2 Set up system for investigating main causes of faults
7. Leads and cables
        7.1 Quality issues
        7.2 Storage and tracking
8. Security labelling of equipment
9. AOB

Language focus: Structure and style of meeting minutes

1 Look at the draft minutes of the first part of the meeting you have just heard and then refer to the guidelines below on how to write minutes. Which guidelines have been applied?

Draft Minutes

SB Technical Assistance Team Monthly Meeting – May

Date and venue: 28 May Room S224 Stamford Building

Present:

Dave Sinclair (Chair)   Emile Lahar
Peter Chen   Elizabeth Willis

Apologies: Paula Summers

Item No:	Item/Comments/Action	By Whom
1.	**Apologies**	
1.1	Paula Summers in Paris setting up trade fair stand	
2.	**Approval of April meeting minutes**	
2.1	Agreed	
3.	**Matters arising**	
3.1	Agreed it would be useful for SB Technical Assistance Team to have minutes of 'User-First' interdepartmental meetings. **Action:** DS to circulate 'User-First' meeting minutes.	Dave
4.	**Liaison arrangements with IT dept**	
4.1	Decided to delete this item from agenda as this is covered by cross-departmental 'User-First' meetings.	
5.	**Feedback from results of equipment user survey**	
5.1	As above (See item 4.1)	

Guidelines – writing minutes

1 The numbering of the minutes follows the item number in the agenda.

2 Each action point is separated out from its corresponding minute and highlighted.

3 The person who is responsible for the action point is identified.

4 People are generally referred to by their initials and/or name.

5 The action points are stated using this structure: person's name + to + infinitive verb.

6 The main points and decisions are summarised in short sentences.

7 When there is agreement on particular points, this is generally highlighted.

8 There is frequent omission of words such as 'the' or subject pronouns.

9 Minutes are written up in formal language.

2 Why are points summarised using formal language when the tone and content of many meetings can be quite informal?

---

3 Listen to four short extracts from different meetings. Rewrite them as 'Action points' for the minutes. Change any information that is vague, to make it precise – this reflects standard checks you would do post-meeting, to ensure the minutes are accurate. The first one has been done for you.

 2.20

1 Dina Ahmed **Action:**
DA to investigate incident of client being injured tripping over projector leads last Wednesday (May 15th) in Caroline Woodhead's office.

2 Alfonso Garcia
Action:

3 Steve Knox
Action:

4 Magda Zboina
Action:

Output: Produce an agenda, notes and minutes of issues affecting your workplace

You are going to write an agenda and have a short meeting concerning issues affecting your workplace (or place of study). You will also take notes and draw up minutes on another group's meeting.

Stage 1

In small groups write out a short agenda of items you would like to discuss. They should be about your place of work or study and be relevant to all the people in the group. Use the model on page 98 as a template. Possible items could include: problems with the canteen, rest breaks, new ways of working – flexible work (or study) schedules, quality of facilities, agreeing rules on use of mobile phones on the premises.

Stage 2

Get together with another group and show them the agenda you have prepared. Allow the other group to select one item from the agenda for you to discuss. Within a five-minute time limit, discuss that item in a meeting. The other group should listen and take notes. Swap roles and repeat the process.

Stage 3

In your original groups, use your notes to write up the draft minutes and then pass them back to the other group for approval or revisions.

11 The economic environment

11.1 Theory: Government influence on the economic environment

Learning outcomes

- Understand how governments and central banks influence the business environment.
- Learn financial and economic terms, concepts and word partnerships.
- Assess impact of government and central bank action on a family household.

> ❝ Government's view of the economy could be summed up in a few short phrases: If it moves, tax it. If it keeps moving, regulate it. And if it stops moving, subsidise it. ❞

Ronald Reagan, former President of the USA

Introduction

1 Read the quote above and discuss the questions that follow.

1 Do you share this view of government influence on the economy? Why/Why not?

2 What would governments say in their defence to justify taxing, spending and intervening in the economy?

2 Read the quote below, from a character in a Shakespeare play, and discuss the questions that follow.

> ❝ Neither a borrower nor a lender be. ❞

1 Why do you think Shakespeare's character gives this advice?

2 How good is this advice today for individuals, businesses and national governments?

Language focus 1: Financial and economic word partnerships

1 'Interest rates' represent the cost of borrowing money. If interest rates rise, it becomes more costly to borrow money.

How might interest rate rises on a mortgage for a home change the way in which a family live?

2 Governments and central banks (such as the Federal Reserve in the USA or the European Central Bank in the Euro area) can stimulate the economy by 'putting money into' the economy or they can slow down economic activity by 'taking money out' of the economy. They can do this using three main mechanisms: tax, spending and interest rates. Label the following as S = stimulate or SD = slow down.

1 Increase government spending
2 Cut government spending
3 Increase taxes
4 Cut taxes
5 Raise interest rates
6 Cut interest rates

3 Which one of these six options do you think the government or central bank in your country should implement right now? Why?

4 Match the words on the left with the groups of words which often follow them on the right.

Key word	Common partnering words
1 financial	**a** collection evasion declaration/ return revenue planning
2 economic	**b** spending/ expenditure policy intervention funding
3 government	**c** activity downturn/slowdown recovery
4 tax	**d** currency economy prices interest rates outlook
5 stable	**e** crisis sector markets advisor

5 In small groups, ask each other questions to check you understand the differences in meaning between the terms in each group.

Example: What is the difference between tax planning and tax evasion?

6 Complete the following sentences using word partnerships from the table above.

1 Mexico's government badly needs more _____ . It collects only 11% of GDP in tax.
2 It's the most profound _____ since the stock market crash of 1929.
3 Job growth in the current _____ has been slower than in most previous upturns.
4 The chairman of the Federal Reserve said that he expected the dollar to remain a 'strong and _____ '.
5 The new Finance Minister says he wants to reduce _____ in business by abolishing price controls in several sectors.

Business view

Dr Tatiana Damjanovic is an Associate Professor at the University of Exeter, UK. Her primary research areas are Macroeconomics and Banking. She has also worked for the International Monetary Fund (IMF) and the Russian Ministry of Finance.

Listening 1: Government and central bank objectives

 2.21

1 Listen to the first part of the interview with Dr Tatiana Damjanovic and answer the questions.

1 What is the reason stated for why governments manage economies?
2 What is poor people's view of taxation and government spending, compared to that of rich people?
3 What is the main objective of the central banks?
4 What is the foundation for achieving this objective?

2 Do you agree with Dr Tatiana Damjanovic about the reason for governments wanting to manage economies? Why/Why not?

Listening 2: The impact of government spending

 2.22

1 Listen to the next part of the interview and answer the questions.

1 List the three reasons why government revenues are lower during an economic crisis.
2 What is the reason stated for why some people think governments should cut their expenditure in times of economic crisis?
3 What are the three reasons stated to justify government expenditure in an economic crisis?

2 Discuss what you think governments should do in times of economic crisis. Cut spending or increase it? Why?

Listening 3: Taxation

 2.23

1 Listen to the final part of the interview and tick ✓ the three subjects from the list below that are discussed by Dr Tatiana Damjanovic.

tax rates   tax evasion   tax planning   tax collection

2 Listen again and answer the questions.

1 What do the following numbers refer to?
   a 60%   **b** 0%   **c** 13%   **d** 20%   **e** 10%
2 What reasons are given to explain the tax rates in the Arab Emirates, Scandinavia and Russia?
3 Read the quote below and discuss what it says about taxpayers and paying tax. Is this a problem in your country? Compare your answers with other students.

❝ It's strange how a person with no sense of humor can come up with such funny answers on his/her tax return. **❞**

Anon

Critical analysis

In what way is the cartoon below criticising government management of the economy? Try to explain it using some of the economic and financial terms presented in this unit.

Language focus 2: Verb patterns in finance

1 Look at the sentences below and answer the questions which follow.

- The government are thinking of <u>moving</u> the elections in the hope of economic recovery.
- The government aim to <u>cut</u> spending.
- Next year inflation will <u>fall</u>.
- The new policy has been put in place to get the economy <u>moving</u>.

1 Which of the underlined verbs <u>must</u> be followed by an object (known as a transitive verb)?
2 Which of the underlined verbs <u>cannot</u> be followed by an object (known as an intransitive verb)?
3 Which of the underlined verbs is both transitive and intransitive?

2 Which of the following sentences can be changed into the passive form? Write new sentences where it is possible.

1 We will <u>reduce</u> spending in the public sector.
2 We will make sure that inflation <u>falls</u>.
3 We will <u>cut</u> taxes.
4 The currency will not <u>collapse</u>.

3 Choose the correct word in italics to complete this rule.

It is not possible to use the passive form with *intransitive/transitive* verbs.

4 Look at the following mistakes made by learners of English. Are the underlined verbs in each sentence transitive, intransitive or both?

1 She was able to <u>rise</u> turnover by 5%.
2 TV sales will <u>raise</u> by 10%.
3 The government has <u>disappeared</u> the deficit.
4 The economy has <u>impacted</u> because of falling exports.
5 The company's assets will <u>freeze</u> if he doesn't pay the bill.
6 The company had to <u>fall</u> its prices due to the recession.

5 Correct the mistakes in the sentences.

Output: Assess impact of government and central bank action on a family household

You are going to assess the financial position of a family household and determine what impact a major government spending and tax review, together with a central bank interest rate decision, will have on their lives. You will consequently advise them on what steps they can take to respond to their changed set of circumstances.

Stage 1
In small groups, read a summary of the main points of the government and central bank action below.

Tax
- VAT rise from 17.5% to 20% plus new band of 25% for 'luxury goods'
- Income tax rises from 40% to 50% for top-rate taxpayers earning over $60,000 per annum. Basic rate of tax is unchanged at 23% for people earning less than $60,000.

State benefits
Maternity benefits frozen

Government department spending
Health spending cut by 12%, education by 15%, police by 20%

Interest rates
Central bank raises interest rates from 2% to 2.5%

Commercial banks today raised their mortgage interest rates by 0.5% following the central bank rise, and increased their credit card rates for customers to an average of 17%.

Stage 2
Turn to page 140 to read the financial profile of the household and follow the instructions.

Stage 3
Get together with another group and compare your assessment and recommendations for the Chen family. Discuss any differences and try to resolve any disagreements in order to ensure the best financial advice is given to this family.

11.2 Practice: Managing economic and financial risk – Unilever

Learning outcomes
- Understand how a large multinational company assesses its business environment.
- Learn key terms related to financial and economic risk management.
- Identify and manage risk factors facing a small business.

Profile: Unilever

Unilever is one of the world's largest corporations. It is an Anglo/Dutch consumer goods multinational with a turnover of 40 billion euro and 163,000 employees worldwide. Its main brands are market leaders in three main sectors: food, homecare (washing powders, cleaning products, etc.) and personal care (soaps and shampoos, etc.). Many of its products require raw material commodity ingredients (such as sugar, coffee and wheat) that can be in short supply and can change sharply in price. It has operations in 170 countries, with more than half its sales coming from developing and emerging markets in Asia, Africa, Latin America and Central and Eastern Europe. This is presently its fastest-growing geographical market by far.

Introduction

Discuss the following questions in small groups.

1 What kind of risks do you face in your home, work or place of study? (Example risk areas include: health and safety, crime, job loss.)
2 How high are the risks you have identified and what can be done to reduce the risks or avoid them completely?
3 Read the company profile above and brainstorm the kind of risks Unilever might face and how it can manage these risks.

Language focus 1: Economic and financial terms and phrases

1 Match the bold words and phrases in the table on the right with the definitions (a–i) in the box below.

a moving constantly up and down
b difference between cash coming in and cash going out
c unfavourable
d capability to survive
e reserve strategies in case circumstances change unexpectedly
f give as a working example
g amount of money left open to risk
h an amount less than expected
i a measure which moves up and down with the rest of the market

2 The table below lists economic and financial terms and phrases that appear in the reading text in the next section. Match the risks (1–6) to the strategies (a–f).

Description of risk	Corporate risk management strategy
1 Significant **shortfall** in **net cash flow**	a Monitor and review the health of trading partners.
2 Volatile commodity prices	b **Model** the impact of different economic scenarios.
3 **Adverse** economic conditions	c Use forward foreign exchange contracts which guarantee a specific exchange rate between two currencies at a specific time in the future.
4 Changes to relative value of currencies	d Regularly update cashflow forecasts.
5 **Fluctuating** market interest rates	e Have **contingency plans** to secure alternative material supplies.
6 **Viability** of customers and suppliers in doubt	f Aim to achieve an appropriate balance between **floating rate** and fixed rate **exposures** (investments and loans).

3 Discuss the following questions.

1 What examples of adverse economic conditions can you think of? How have any of these impacted on your organisation, or one you know well?
2 What are some of the reasons why end-user customers might increase or decrease their consumption of branded goods from companies such as Unilever?

The following text is an extract titled 'Outlook and risks' from a recent company annual report from Unilever, written at a time of a global economic downturn. The report sets out the possible risks facing the company in the year ahead and what they propose to do to manage these risks.

Description of risk	What we are doing to manage the risk
Economic	
1 _____ *a* _____ Unilever's business is dependent on continuing consumer demand for our brands. Reduced consumer wealth driven by adverse economic conditions may result in our consumers becoming unwilling or unable to purchase our products, which could adversely affect our cash flow, turnover, profits and profit margins. In addition we have a large number of global brands, some of which have a significant value as **intangible assets**: adverse economic conditions may require us to **impair** the brands' **balance sheet value**.	The breadth of Unilever's brand portfolio and our geographic reach help to mitigate local economic risks. We carefully monitor economic indicators and regularly model the impact of different economic scenarios. We monitor consumer behaviour through regular market research and adopt a flexible business model which allows us to adapt our portfolio and respond quickly to develop new offerings that suit consumers' and customers' changing needs during economic downturns.
2 _____ During economic downturns there could be constrained access to credit. This could impact on the viability of our customers and suppliers and could temporarily inhibit the flow of day-to-day cash transactions with suppliers and customers via the banks.	We regularly monitor and review the health of our customers and suppliers and **implement credit limits**. These reviews are undertaken more frequently during economic downturns.
Operations	
3 _____ Our ability to make products is dependent on securing timely and cost-effective supplies of production materials, some of which are globally traded commodities. There are constant changes in commodity prices according to global economic conditions, which can have a significant impact on our product costs.	We have strategies and policies in place to monitor short- and long-term raw material demand forecasts. We have contingency plans to enable us to secure alternative key material supplies at short notice, to transfer/share production between manufacturing sites and to use substitute materials in our product formulations and recipes.
Financial	
4 _____ As a global organisation Unilever's asset values, **earnings** and cash flows are influenced by a wide variety of currencies, interest rates, tax jurisdictions and differing taxes. If we are unable to manage our exposures to any one, or a combination, of these factors, this could adversely impact our cash flow, profits and/or profit margins. A significant shortfall in net cash flow could undermine the company's credit rating, impair investor confidence and hinder our ability to raise funds.	A key target for the Group is to manage our financial affairs so as to maintain our **A1/A+ credit rating**, which gives us continued access to the global **debt markets**, even when the overall financial markets are under stress. We regularly update cashflow forecasts and assess the range of volatility due to interest rates and currencies.
5 _____ We are exposed to market interest rate fluctuations on our floating rate debt. This could increase the interest cost of our floating rate debt and increase the cost of future borrowings.	In order to minimise interest costs and reduce volatility our interest rate management policy aims to achieve an appropriate balance between fixed and floating rate interest exposures on forecast net debt levels for the next five years.
6 _____ Because of the breadth of our international operations we are subject to risks from changes to relative value of currencies which can fluctuate widely and could have a significant impact on our assets, cash flow, turnover, profits and/or profit margins.	In order to manage currency exposures we maintain a policy whereby operating companies manage trading and financial foreign exchange exposures within prescribed limits and by the use of forward foreign exchange contracts.

Glossary of financial terms

intangible assets – assets that are not in physical form such as the value of a brand or patents.
impair – verb meaning 'to negatively affect something'.
balance sheet value – formal value of an asset as stated in the balance sheet. This value might be different to its actual value.
implement credit limit – set a limit to the amount of credit customers can have. They are not given credit beyond that limit.
earnings – gross profits (i.e. profits before tax has been deducted).
A1/A+ credit rating – an evaluation by Standard & Poor's international credit rating agency (A1/A+ rating = 'very strong capacity to meet financial commitments'). Ratings range from D to AAA.
debt markets – markets that companies can go to in order to raise money by selling bonds.

1 Look at the subheadings (a–f) below. Skim read the text in a few minutes and put the subheadings in the correct positions (1–6). The first one has been done for you.

a Decline in business during an economic downturn
b Managing currency fluctuations
c Managing interest rate differences and movements
d Avoiding customer and supplier default
e Securing raw materials
f Funding the ongoing operation of the business

2 Read the text again and answer the following questions.

1 What factors might lead to Unilever revising down the value of its brands?
2 How does Unilever's range of brands and geographic markets protect it from local risk?
3 What is the possible cause of customers and suppliers going bankrupt?
4 What would Unilever do if the raw materials from its usual sources were no longer available?
5 Why is it important for Unilever to keep its A1/A+ credit rating?

3 What other risks do companies face that have not been described in the text on page 104?

4 What different risk exposures do small businesses have compared to big companies?

Language focus 2: Financial terms

1 Complete the gaps in the following sentences using words and phrases listed in the glossary of financial terms on page 104.

1 If house prices fell by more than 20 percent, that would _____ the banks' ability to offer credit.
2 BMI has become the first airline to put a _____ on its take-off and landing slots.
3 GE executives say the company's _____ and vast cash resources put it in a strong position to make acquisitions.
4 It's difficult to measure some of the company's _____, such as goodwill from customers and the trademarks we own.

2 Discuss what you think would happen to …

1 … Unilever's earnings if it sets credit limits for its supermarket customers too high or too low.
2 … Unilever's ability to raise finance in debt markets if its credit rating was cut to lower than A1/A+ grade.

Output: Advise a company on managing risk

Working as management consultants, you are going to assess the risks facing a small company and advise on how best to manage them better.

Stage 1

Form small groups and then read the company profile of MokaTorre. Address the following two issues.

- Identify the main risks facing the company and then rank them in order of priority and urgency.
- Decide how these risks can best be managed. What recommendations would you make to the Company Directors?

MokaTorre – company profile

Activity:
Roasting and grinding coffee beans to supply to coffee shops and restaurants.

Owners and staff:
Private company founded ten years ago by three brothers; Paulo does the accounts, Luigi and Mario look after clients. Luigi and Mario don't speak to each other. They employ six people.

Customers:
Supply coffee to 500 outlets in the San Francisco area. Three of their customers have chains of 50–60 shops. The others are individual restaurants/cafés. Customers have payment terms of 60 to 90 days.

Supplier:
Wholesale importer who obtains beans from Costa Rica and Guatemala.

Financial position:
They have an overdraft facility of $50,000. They pay 5% over central bank interest rates when overdrawn. This helps MokaTorre with cash flow, as clients often pay late, but they must pay their staff on time. They have a fixed interest loan of $150,000 which they used to buy a competitor. The loan is secured against the owners' houses.

Business environment:
The local economy is booming, but interest rates and inflation are rising.

Stage 2

Present your recommendations to another group and agree a common set of action points to present to the directors at MokaTorre.

Learning outcomes

- Understand and analyse statistical information presented in a chart.
- Structure a description of a slide with a chart and highlight key data.
- Prepare and present a slide with statistical information in chart form.

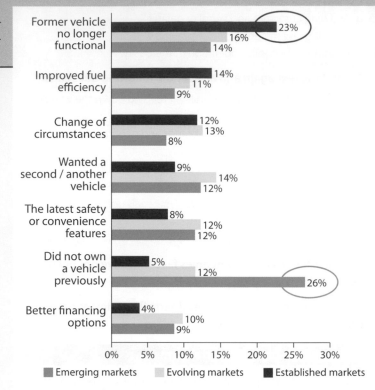

Introduction

1 How do you feel in the following situations?

1 You are giving a presentation to a room full of people.
   a Totally terrified.
   b It depends on what I'm presenting and who the people are.
   c I generally enjoy it and get a real adrenaline rush.
2 Someone asks you to help them understand some graphs and statistics.
   a They've come to the wrong person.
   b No problem, statistics and graphs are fascinating.
   c You'll try to help but you know it'll be difficult.

2 Compare your answers with a partner. Ask each other questions to understand why the other person feels this way. In what way do you think you can improve your understanding and presentation of graphs and statistics?

Business view

Josh Crandall is President of Netpop Research in partnership with Google, and author and presenter of the webinar presentation titled 'Driving International Success: Reaching Auto Consumers Globally'.

Listening: Analyse a chart in a slide presentation

 2.24

1 Look at the chart on this page, which formed part of Josh Crandall's webinar presentation. The presentation showed findings of survey results of purchasers of new cars. Answer the questions below to analyse the meaning of the chart.

1 What do the colours represent?
2 What do the numbers represent?
3 What is the purpose of the two circles?
4 What tense would a presenter use to describe these statistics during a presentation?
5 How would you summarise what the chart is about? Choose one answer (a–d).

a New car purchasers' customer satisfaction ratings
b Different information searches by new purchasers on Google
c The different reasons why people buy new cars
d A comparison of new car purchasers' experiences

2 Listen to the presentation and check your answers.

3 Is there any information in the chart that surprises you? Discuss the statistics that most and least surprised you about reasons for new car purchase in different geographical markets.

4 The information presented here is in a bar chart format. Discuss why it would <u>not</u> be advisable to use a pie chart, a line graph or a table format to present this information.

Language focus: Structuring and describing a chart

 2.25

1 Discuss and complete the following questions about the chart on page 107, which was used in the same presentation.

1 What is the chart about? Write an appropriate introduction for it. Start with: 'Now let's look at …'
2 An alternative way to introduce a chart is to change the title into a rhetorical question (a question that you answer yourself). Write an appropriate alternative introduction of this slide. Start with: 'So, wh___ …'
3 Looking at the information presented in this chart, what do you

think is the key point the presenter needs to make? Write this out in two different ways, to reflect what the presenter would say here. Start with: 'As you can see …' and 'When we compare …'

4 Find another piece of data that stands out as unusual and can be mentioned as a secondary point. Write a single sentence for the presenter to introduce this secondary point at the end of the slide presentation.
Start with: 'Finally, it's interesting to note …'

2 Listen to the description of the chart and compare what you wrote with what the presenter actually says.

3 The presentation of a slide containing charts or statistical information can be broken into four stages. Put the stages below in the right order.

a Explain and explore the key point(s) with reference to the data and add highlighting.

b State what the chart is about.

c Mention any secondary point(s) and add highlighting.

d State key points you want to make with reference to the data and add highlighting.

4 Check your answer by listening again to the description of the chart while looking at the audio script on page 162. Mark the audio script with // to show the breaks between each of the four stages.

5 Complete the following sentence descriptions of the chart titled 'First Source for Research'.

1 Auto dealerships are the s_____ m_____ popular source of information.

2 H_____ a_____ used newspapers, TV or private sellers as a source of information.

3 Over t_____ a_____ m_____ people in emerging markets used the Internet compared to friends and family as a source of information.

First Source for Research

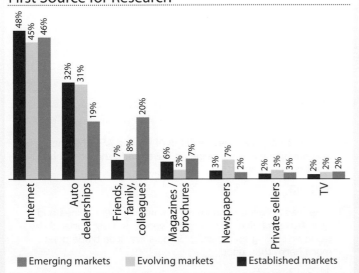

Emerging markets **Evolving markets** **Established markets**

1 Answer the following questions about highlighting key data on the chart.

1 How do you think the presenter highlights the key point on the chart during the presentation? Mark it on the chart.

2 The presenter also highlights the secondary point during the final part of the presentation of this chart by circling the relevant data with a coloured circle. Mark it on the chart with an appropriate colour.

2 Turn to page 140 and compare the highlighting you marked on the chart to the highlighting actually done by the presenter. Answer the questions below.

1 How effective is this highlighting in helping the audience understand the chart?

2 In this case, the highlighting was added <u>during</u> the presentation of the chart. Do you think there are also benefits to having the highlighting on the chart from the beginning? Why/Why not?

You are going to produce a chart showing how you divide your time spent on the Internet. You are then going to present this information.

Stage 1
Work individually and draw a pie chart with a breakdown of how you divide your time on the Internet, expressing numbers as percentages. Choose a maximum of six factors. You can choose from the list below or create your own.

- Using social network sites
- Using chat and internet telephony
- Writing emails
- Gaming
- Doing research for study or work
- General surfing
- Shopping

Stage 2
Form small groups. Transfer the information for all of you on to a single bar chart (in a similar format to the charts shown in this unit) and highlight the key points. Decide whether to add the highlighting at the beginning or during the presentation. Prepare your presentation, which should be timed to a maximum of two minutes and should follow the four-stage structure studied. Practise giving the presentation in your group.

Stage 3
Get together with another group and give the presentation to them.

Learning outcomes

- Understand arguments for and against free trade.
- Improve speed-reading techniques.
- Make your points more powerfully in arguments and debates.

Introduction

1 Complete the definitions of 'free trade' and 'protectionism' using phrases from the box below.

> a barriers to trade
> b different industry sectors
> c government economic policy
> d trade liberalisation

Free trade refers to the free movement of goods and services across frontiers without government interference. Free trade is achieved through **1** ＿＿＿＿＿＿ , which progressively removes the **2** ＿＿＿＿＿＿ that stop countries from trading freely with each other, such as import tariffs (import taxes) or special protection given by governments to national companies or industries.

Protectionism is a **3** ＿＿＿＿＿＿ designed to keep out imports from other countries. This is done through imposing high import tariffs or import quotas that limit the imports to a fixed level for **4** ＿＿＿＿＿＿ . This policy aims to protect national industries and companies.

2 Complete the quiz and discover how pro- or anti- free trade you really are.

Add up your score for the four questions and read your profile on page 141. Compare your answers and profile with another student and give reasons to support your position.

Business view

Joseph Stiglitz is a Nobel prize-winning economist, writer and professor at Columbia University, USA.

How much of a protectionist are you?

Do you agree or disagree with the following opinions about international trade?
Answer the questions individually by circling the number that reflects your opinion.
(1 = strongly agree, 5 = strongly disagree)

1 We should raise import taxes to keep out a lot of foreign-made goods and services to protect our own industries and companies.

1 2 3 4 5

2 Large multinational companies are the main beneficiaries of trade liberalisation. We are better off with national companies.

1 2 3 4 5

3 Trading blocs (such as the EU, NAFTA and ASEAN) and international trade agreements have made the rich richer and the poor poorer.

1 2 3 4 5

4 Free trade means consumers are paying lower prices and have better choice, but people's wages in most parts of the world are falling as a result. On balance, free trade does more harm than good.

1 2 3 4 5

Transferable skill: Improving speed-reading techniques

Speed reading involves reading in stages. Answer the questions below, making sure you check your answers after each stage.

1 The first stage is to skim read the text to understand the general meaning. Skim reading involves passing your eyes quickly over the text. This is very different from reading word by word.

Skim read the extracts (A–F) below from Joseph Stiglitz's book *Making Globalization Work*. Decide which extracts are pro-free trade and which are anti-free trade.

2 The second stage of general reading comprehension is to create a 'map of the text' which tells you where all the key 'points of interest' are within the text. You can create this by summarising the meaning of each section. Complete the summaries of the extracts using no more than <u>four</u> words.

A Bringing down trade barriers tends to …
B Trade liberalisation can …
C NAFTA shows why trade liberalisation …
D Free trade allows countries to specialise in what they …
E Economic theory and historical experience show the …
F Globalisation can impact negatively on government finances in …

Reading: Making globalisation work

1 Read the following questions and decide in which extract (A–F) the answers are likely to be.

1 Why are developing countries not as able as advanced industrial countries to take advantage of the opportunities of trade liberalisation?
2 How does free trade lower government income in less developed countries?
3 How can trade liberalisation be done fairly?
4 How is comparative advantage defined?
5 What were the main arguments in favour of the creation of NAFTA?
6 Who have been the biggest losers due to trade liberalisation in advanced countries?

2 Read each extract and answer the questions.

3 After reading the extracts, have you changed your mind at all regarding where you stand with free trade? Are you more or less favourable to free trade or is your position unchanged? Discuss your opinions in small groups.

A If free trade barriers are brought down, not everyone is equally in a position to take advantage of the new opportunities. It is easy for those in advanced industrial countries to seize the opportunities that the opening up of markets in the developing countries affords – and they do so quickly. But there are many impediments facing those in the developing world. There is often a lack of infrastructure to bring their goods to market, and it may take years for the goods they produce to meet the standards demanded by the advanced industrial countries. These are among the reasons that, when Europe unilaterally opened up its markets to the poorest countries in the world, almost no new trade followed.

B Trade liberalisation can, when done fairly, when accompanied by the right measures and the right policies, help development. The most successful developing countries in the world have achieved their success through trade – through exports. The question is: can the benefits that they enjoy be sustained, and be brought to all the people of the world? I believe they can be; but if that is to be the case, trade liberalisation will have to be managed in a very different way from that of the past.

C Understanding why NAFTA failed to live up to its promise can help us to understand the disappointments of trade liberalisation. One of the main arguments for NAFTA was that it would help close the gap in income between Mexico and the United States, and thus reduce the pressure of illegal migration. Yet the disparity in income between the two countries grew in NAFTA's first decade – by more than 10 per cent.

D The British economist Adam Smith, the founder of modern economics, was a strong champion of both free markets and free trade, and his arguments are compelling: free trade allows countries to take advantage of their comparative advantage, with all nations benefiting as each one specialises in the areas in which it excels.

E Politicians and economists who promise that trade liberalisation will make everyone better off are being disingenuous. Economic theory (and historical experience) suggests that people will actually be worse off: even if trade liberalisation may make the country as a whole better off, it results in some groups being worse off. And it suggests that, at least in the advanced industrial countries, it is those at the bottom – unskilled workers – who will be hurt the most.

F Globalisation has limited the ability of governments to respond. Not only does liberalisation require removing tariffs – which are an important source of public revenue for less developed countries – but to compete, a country may have to lower other taxes as well. As taxes are lowered, so are public revenues, forcing cuts in education and infrastructure and expenditure on safety nets such as unemployment insurance at a time when they are more important than ever in order both to respond to the competition and to help cope with the consequences of liberalisation.

Source: *Making Globalization Work* by Joseph Stiglitz

Language focus: Emphasising key points through inversion

Speakers and writers of English can emphasise key points by using certain words and phrases and changing (inverting) word order or the order of information. Pausing, and stressing certain words also allow speakers to add emphasis.

1 Rewrite the following sentence, starting with the inversion phrase 'not only'. Then read Extract F to see if the author organised the information in the same way. (Note: the sentence in the text includes extra information.)

> Liberalisation requires removing tariffs – but to compete, a country may have to lower other taxes as well.

2 Listen to the sentence from the text read aloud, and notice how the speaker uses pauses and stress to add more emphasis. Repeat the sentence with the same pausing and stress and get feedback from a partner on how persuasive you sound.

 2.26

3 Look at the examples below and underline the inversion language which helps to add emphasis to the key point in each sentence.

1 As you've said, not only are we trying to make tourism more sustainable, but essentially it should still be fun.
2 I suspect the amount of money made would have been significantly more had we not got such poor results in the first quarter of the year.
3 Well, I've got the minutes of the last meeting that say 'Under no circumstances can the price go up.'
4 Were we to face another crisis on this scale, we would be in a much better situation to deal with it.
5 Such was the extent of speculation about the nature of their relationship that she was moved to other duties.
6 At no time did I suggest that she should lie to the board.
7 Only by increasing taxes on corporate wealth will we be able to finance the project.

4 Reformulate the following sentences by adding the words in brackets and changing the word order and structure of the sentence in order to add emphasis through inversion. The first has been done as an example.

Example: Only by working together can countries achieve true globalisation.

1 When countries work together they can achieve true globalisation. (only by)
2 The reduction of inequality has been a more pressing issue. (at no time)
3 The free movement of people between countries should be allowed. (under no circumstances)
4 The power of multinational corporations means fair trade is not possible. (such)
5 The most powerful countries always win and they also ensure that their corporations have unfair trading advantages. (not only)

5 Reformulate the following pairs of sentences into single conditional sentences using the words in brackets to add emphasis through inversion.

Example: Were there no trade barriers, developing countries could become richer.

1 There are trade barriers. Developing countries stay poor. (were)
2 International trade agreements are unfair. The global economy is unstable. (were)
3 The UK didn't adopt the euro 14 months ago. It is suffering from a grossly overvalued currency today. (had)

6 Check your answers to exercises 4 and 5 by listening to a recording of the example sentences read aloud.

 2.27

7 Listen again and repeat the sentences. Make sure to pause and stress the words as the speaker does, in order to add further emphasis with your voice.

Output: Debate arguments for and against free trade

You are going to debate arguments for and against free trade.

Stage 1
'Fair trade is not possible – in practice, the most powerful countries will always win.'

As a class prepare a list of all the arguments for and against the motion above.

Stage 2
Work in two groups. Group A support the motion and Group B are against the motion. Spend five minutes preparing your argument, using language of emphasising to help you make your points forcefully.

Stage 3
Get together with an opposing group and choose someone to act as an independent chair to direct the debate. The chair should ensure the procedure below is clearly followed.

1 Two spokespeople from Group A should start by presenting their group's arguments while Group B listens and notes down key points made. The chair should allow <u>one</u> minute for each spokesperson.
2 Two spokespeople from Group B should respond, presenting the opposing arguments, while Group A listens and notes down key points made. The chair should allow <u>one</u> minute for each spokesperson.
3 Have an open discussion, countering the opposing team's arguments and adding any new ones. The chair should try to encourage participation from everyone present and ensure that the debate is conducted in an orderly fashion.
4 After hearing both sides of the argument, the chairperson should decide whether to 'pass' the motion or not, based on how effectively each team argued their case.

12.2 Practice: NAFTA and Mexico

Learning outcomes
- Understand how NAFTA has impacted on Mexico.
- Learn language of economic convergence and divergence.
- Take part in a meeting to discuss the merits of free trade.

Profile: NAFTA

NAFTA stands for the North American Free Trade Agreement. It was signed in 1992 by the three member states – Mexico, the USA and Canada – and came into force in 1994. The agreement created the world's largest free trade area. The aim of NAFTA is to promote trade and investment between the three countries through the elimination of barriers, most notably import tariffs (import taxes). Cross-border trade and investment has indeed flourished, but opinions are very divided in all three countries regarding how much employment and unemployment it has created and what effect it has had on the economy and on wage levels in each country. For these reasons the formation of NAFTA has been very controversial.

	Population (millions)	Average income per head ($USD)
Canada	34.4	$41,950
Mexico	114.8	$8,930
USA	313.1	$47,240

Sources: UN and World Bank

Introduction

1 Read the profile on NAFTA and find out why the formation of NAFTA has been controversial.

2 There are potential opportunities and threats when neighbouring countries with very different economies and population sizes are members of the same trading blocs. What are your views on the questions below?

- Migration – a new source of labour, or a cause of social and economic problems as people cross borders in search of work?
- New markets – export opportunities or import threats?
- New investment – a chance to attract foreign companies to set up production bases, or the beginning of the end of locally owned national industries?
- Competition – will it make local national companies internationally competitive or will they be killed off?

Business view

Carlos Piñera is Chief Representative, NAFTA Office of Mexico in Canada.

Language focus: Terms of economic convergence and divergence

1 The following terms are all used to talk about international trade. Complete the sentences below with the correct terms.

economic integration
removing trade barriers
regulatory cooperation
growing polarisation
compliance with [international standards]
protectionist trade policies
inward investment
increased bilateral trade
duty-free trade
income disparity
export-orientated economy

1 The improved political relationship between Russia and China has led to _____ between the two countries.

2 Guatemala has the second-greatest _____ between rich and poor in Latin America.

3 The reason the country is so successful at attracting _____ is that it has very low labour costs.

4 Western governments must improve _____ if they are to avoid future global financial crises.

5 Contraction of world trade in the inter-war depression had a severe effect on Britain's _____ .

6 The Mercosur Customs Union allows exceptions to internal _____ .

7 Local anti-NAFTA activists in Texas say _____ with Mexico has hurt local tomato growers.

8 Ali Riza Alaboyun is the deputy chairman of the Turkish commission charged with bringing traffic laws into _____ EU norms.

9 A new era of _____ emanating from the USA will severely damage the prospects of poorer countries hoping to export to the States.

10 Today, in Madrid, politicians from across the globe begin two days of dialogue aimed at addressing the _____ between nations and cultures worldwide.

11 The Arizona-Sonora Project encourages _____ and cooperation between the USA and Mexico.

2 Categorise the terms in exercise 1 into two groups as follows.

Economic convergence (where the economies of different countries are more inter-connected and moving closer together in the same direction)
Economic divergence (where economies are more independent and economic conditions of different countries are moving apart)

3 In your opinion, is your country becoming more or less integrated into the world economy in general and its regional economy in particular? Is this a good thing? Try to give examples to support your opinion.

Listening 1: The role and purpose of NAFTA

 2.28

1 Listen to Carlos Piñera talking about the objectives and goals of NAFTA and put a tick (✓) next to the points (1–6) that are mentioned.

1 increase governmental exchanges
2 increase economic integration
3 increase the number of jobs
4 improve welfare of people
5 create a duty-free trade zone
6 remove barriers to competition

2 Listen again and answer the questions below.

1 Complete the gaps in the list of aspects of regulatory cooperation that Carlos Piñera believes still need to be worked on.
   a more h_____ l_____ of products
   b better i_____ t_____ infrastructure
   c improved p_____ at c_____

2 What are the two areas of responsibility of the NAFTA Office of Mexico in Canada?

Listening 2: Benefits of NAFTA to Mexico

 2.29

1 Listen to the second part of the interview and answer the questions.

1 How has NAFTA created more employment opportunities in Mexico?
2 How has NAFTA created more opportunities for Mexican companies?
3 How much have Mexican exports increased to the USA and Canada?
4 What Mexican industries are benefiting from NAFTA?
5 What structural changes have occurred in the Mexican economy as a result of NAFTA?

2 Discuss the questions below about the structure of your local economy (or that of your country economy).

■ Which industries have grown rapidly and which have shrunk sharply?
■ What forces have been driving these changes?
■ What are your predictions for the future?

Listening 3: Defence of NAFTA

 2.30

1 Listen to the final part of the interview where Carlos Piñera defends NAFTA against criticism. Complete the table below with your notes. The first one has been done for you.

Subject	Details of problem	Defence of criticism
1 Shoe industry	history of problems	NAFTA not to blame: problem is low-cost Chinese imports
2 Chemical industry		
3 Textiles and agro-industry		
4 Corn farmers		
5 Political campaigns		

Output: Discuss the merits of free trade

Stage 1

Your country is about to sign a trade treaty with a neighbouring country. In the past, your country's economy has been heavily based on agriculture, but it is keen to modernise. The neighbouring country has a developed industrial base and has a GDP which is considerably higher than yours.

Work in pairs.

Student A turn to page 141 and read the information. Student B read the information below.

Student B

You are your country's Minister for Economic Development. You are very excited by the prospect of joining the treaty for the following reasons.

- You believe that the abolition of tariffs will increase inward investment in your infant industries.
- You will still have tariffs for countries outside of the treaty agreement and believe that this is adequate protection for your industries.
- You believe that more competition will lead to a stronger hi-tech sector which is more sustainable in the long term.
- The long-term goal is to make your economy more export-orientated. At present most of your exports are agricultural, but with your lower costs and a new trade partner you think the structure of your economy will change, creating a strong hi-tech sector.

Prepare to meet with the managing director of your country's leading producer of innovative products in the electronics sector. Think about what concerns he/she may have and develop your arguments for the treaty.

Stage 2

Have the meeting. Student A should begin.

12.3 Skills: Managing meetings

Learning outcomes
- Chair meetings effectively.
- Use functional language to aid effective communication in meetings.
- Deal with difficult colleagues.

Introduction

1 Have you ever been in a meeting, seminar or group discussion of some kind that you didn't enjoy? What was the problem?

2 Look at the list of guidelines for chairing a meeting. Discuss whether you agree or disagree with each of the points.

1 It is always important to have an agenda for a meeting.
2 The chair should always define the agenda at the start of the meeting.
3 There should always be strict time limits.
4 The chair should always be neutral and allow for both sides of the argument.
5 The chair should not be influenced by the personality of participants.
6 There should always be time to discuss matters not on the agenda at the end of the meeting.

Listening 1: Starting the meeting

2.31

1 Listen to the first part of a weekly meeting at a company that provides business training to other organisations. Are the following statements true or false?

1 Vanessa (the chair) always chairs these meetings.
2 The meeting will last for at least 45 minutes.
3 After the meeting they are going to have lunch.
4 Vanessa checks that everybody is happy with last week's meeting.
5 The points they need to discuss about the Customer First training are on the agenda.

2 Discuss the following questions.

1 How effective was Vanessa at starting the meeting?
2 How might the meeting have started differently if the meeting was not a weekly meeting, and was instead between people who haven't met regularly before?

Listening 2: Discussing a problem colleague

2.32

1 You are going to hear a later part of the meeting where Jack, who is one of the business trainers, brings up a problem with a colleague called Nick Hay. Listen and answer the following questions.

1 What feedback does Jack give about the morning and evening sessions?
2 What does Vanessa tell Lucy to write in the minutes?
3 Does Vanessa think that Nick's line manager should be told about the criticisms?
4 What criticism of Nick's character has Jack heard?
5 What is the criticism of Nick's material?
6 What does Vanessa think should be done <u>first</u> to address the problem with Nick?

2 Look at the questions below. Listen again and discuss the questions.

1 What do you think about Lucy and Vanessa's use of humour when Jack is trying to make a serious point?
2 Vanessa agrees with the criticism of Nick. Do you think that this is acceptable? Would you criticise a colleague in this way?
3 How do Vanessa and Jack react to Stefanie receiving a phone call in the meeting? What would you have done in the same situation?
4 How do you think Vanessa deals with the complaints about Nick in general?

1 Match the problems that frequently occur in meetings (1–7) with the solutions (a–g).

1	Subordinates are unmotivated.	**a**	Clarify what is meant.
2	The meeting runs late.	**b**	Brainstorm options and solutions.
3	A colleague is difficult to understand.	**c**	Direct people to the agenda.
4	You feel that there is a need to criticise a colleague.	**d**	Make criticism indirectly.
5	There is insufficient time to discuss the issues.	**e**	Encourage your staff.
6	The discussion keeps moving off topic.	**f**	Suggest a future meeting.
7	The group is finding it hard to come up with creative solutions.	**g**	Close the meeting.

2 Look at the following statements used by people chairing meetings and complete the gaps using phrases in the box below.

> why don't you   what I'm saying is   refer back   wrap it up
> absolutely great   choices open to us   I sometimes feel that

1 Just _____ to the agenda now.
2 I think it's _____ that they're thinking of this kind of thing.
3 No. _____ move the whole thing forward a week or back a week …
4 I'll just quickly _____ .
5 So, let's look at all the _____ .
6 _____ arrange a later time and come to a decision next week …
7 _____ some of the team members could be trying a little harder …

3 Match the statements (1–7) above to the solutions (a–g) in exercise 1.

4 Look at the problems below. Discuss what you would say in these situations if you were the chair of the meeting.

1 A colleague is very upset because he thinks that you have only given him a week to complete a report. You have actually given him two weeks.
2 A colleague wants to talk about the advertising budget, but it is not up for discussion in this meeting.
3 You have another appointment, but it is clear that the other four participants need to carry on discussing the situation.
4 You think that one of your colleagues is avoiding giving you information to cover up a mistake she has made.

Output: Overcoming problems in meetings

Stage 1

In small groups, take five minutes to brainstorm as many examples as you can of the following problems associated with meetings. Then brainstorm solutions to each one.

1 a bad chairperson
2 a difficult colleague
3 meetings are a waste of time

Stage 2

A meeting has been called to address communication issues in your team. There are three members in the team. Each person in the group should choose one of the three roles.

Chairperson

You find it difficult to keep your team members on topic. You think your colleagues are too uncooperative and that they often introduce topics that are not on the agenda. They always seem impatient to finish. You have called a meeting to try to address some of these problems. Think about what you are going to say, and how you are going to say it (assertively? calmly?).

Team member 1

You are frustrated because your team has too many meetings, and you have a lot of work to do outside of meetings. This means you find it difficult to keep to deadlines. Rather than having a meeting every day, you would like to have them less often. You also think the agenda should be sent out earlier by the Chairperson.

Team member 2

The Chairperson was promoted above you, and you think that he/she is really ineffective. Meetings don't stick to the agenda, and you don't think the appropriate issues are discussed (for example, you want more help with solutions to problems, but in meetings people often talk about why the problems are so difficult).

Stage 3

Give feedback to the Chairperson on his/her effectiveness in managing the meeting.

> ▶◀ **Watch Sequence 6 on the DVD to find out more about Trade, finance and the economy.**

Learning outcomes

- Learn language to describe financial and economic changes.
- Break down and group trends in graphs with financial information.
- Write a short report describing trends in stock prices.

Introduction

Financial and economic statistics (unemployment figures, cost of living, average salaries, interest rates, house prices, etc.) influence stock markets. Answer the following questions about your country and explain your answers.

- Which way have these statistics been heading recently?
- What are the predictions for the future?
- Do you think now is a good time to be investing in the stock market?

Language focus: Describing financial and economic changes

1 Read the following news headlines taken from the financial press. Mark them as either good news ☺ or bad news ☹ and whether the verb indicates an increase (↑) or decrease (↓). The first one has been done as an example.

1 House prices <u>slide</u> at fastest rate this year ↓ ☹
2 Standard of living to <u>plunge</u>, says Bank chief
3 Business confidence <u>bounces back</u> in January
4 Retail sales seen <u>rebounding</u> in January
5 Stocks <u>wobble</u> amid Middle East risks
6 Bank shares <u>slump</u>
7 Korea's household debt <u>surges</u> to record in Q2
8 German economy <u>shrinks</u> more than expected
9 Consumer confidence <u>dives</u>
10 Jobless figures in US <u>dip</u> by 20,000
11 Corporate bankruptcies <u>soar</u>
12 FreightCar America Q4 results <u>edge forward</u>

2 Match the underlined verbs in the headlines to their definitions (a–h) below.

a fall slightly
b recover (×2)
c fall sharply (×3)
d increase sharply (×2)
e increase slightly
f fall
g get smaller
h fluctuate and fall briefly

Writing skill 1: Describing a single trend line

1 Study the graph below and answer the questions.

1 What is the graph about?
2 How are the units of time measured on the horizontal axis?

NASDAQ-100 (^NDX)

2 When describing a graph showing changes over time in a report or a presentation, it is important to describe the <u>general</u> trends. Answer the questions below.

1 What would be the audience's likely reaction if you described the change in the movement of the NASDAQ for each of the 12 time periods shown?
2 Break this graph into six time periods to capture the main trends. Mark the breaks on the graph. Discuss your decision with a partner, and then check your answer in the text in exercise 3.

3 Complete the gaps in this description of the key trends in the graph.

From January to around August 2008, the Nasdaq index **1** f_____ considerably; it then **2** p_____ to a low of around 1,000 in November 2008. It remained low and continued to **3** w_____ for about five months until March 2009, when it **4** r_____ strongly, reaching a high of just over 2,000 at the end of the first quarter of 2010. The index **5** d_____ slightly at this point but then **6** b_____ back again, **7** s_____ to a new high of around 2,400 in the first quarter of 2011.

3 What are the noun equivalents to the verbs in the first seven headlines?

4 Use the notes below to help you construct single-sentence explanations for some of these headlines. The first one has been done for you as an example.

Example: *The main reason why house prices have slid so fast this year is soaring interest rates.*

1 House prices slide – change in interest rates
2 Standard of living set to plunge – inflation predictions
3 Business confidence bounced back – business leaders see new orders
4 Rebound in retail sales – consumers respond to tax changes
5 German economy shrinks – surprising change in export orders
6 Consumer confidence dives – figures released show change in unemployment levels

5 What causes could be behind the other headlines in exercise 1?

Writing skill 2: Describing multiple trend lines

1 Read the opening paragraph of a short report describing the graph below and complete the gaps.

This graph shows the 1 _____ in the stock price on the New York Stock Exchange of four 2 _____ companies (Royal Dutch Shell, Chevron, Exxon Mobil and BP) shown in blue, red, 3 _____ and 4 _____ respectively, over a two-year 5 _____ from March 2009 to March 2011.

2 Answer the following questions to check your understanding of the graph.

1 Which company's stock price increased the most? Which company's increased the least?
2 If you could 'turn back the clock' and buy shares in one of these companies in July 2010, which stock would you buy?

3 What are the possible causes behind the dramatic fall in BP's share price? Do you know what actually happened?

4 When describing multiple trend lines, you should avoid simply describing each line individually without reference to the others. This type of description will be long, boring and will not summarise the key information. Instead, you need to compare and contrast the trends by identifying and describing the similarities and differences between the trend lines. Discuss and answer the following questions, giving reasons for your answers.

1 Which stocks would you group together as being similar for the whole two-year period?
2 Which stocks would you group together for the period March to December 2009?
3 Which stocks would you group together for the period September 2010 to March 2011?
4 Which stock is the 'odd one out' for most of the period?

Output: Write a short report

Write the rest of the report for the graph below, describing the main trends and key information within the graph. Ensure that you group trend lines together to show clear similarities and differences between the four stocks. Write a minimum of 150 words and conclude with a short summary paragraph at the end.

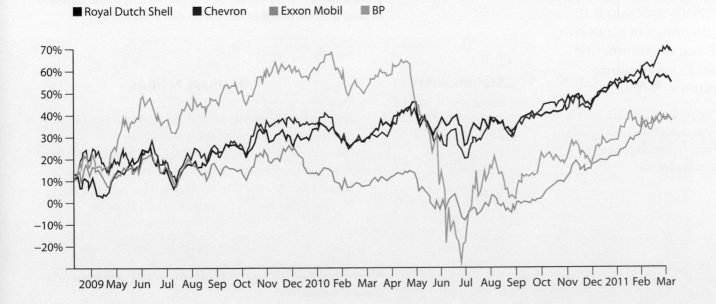

13 Sustainable development

13.1 Theory: The triple bottom line

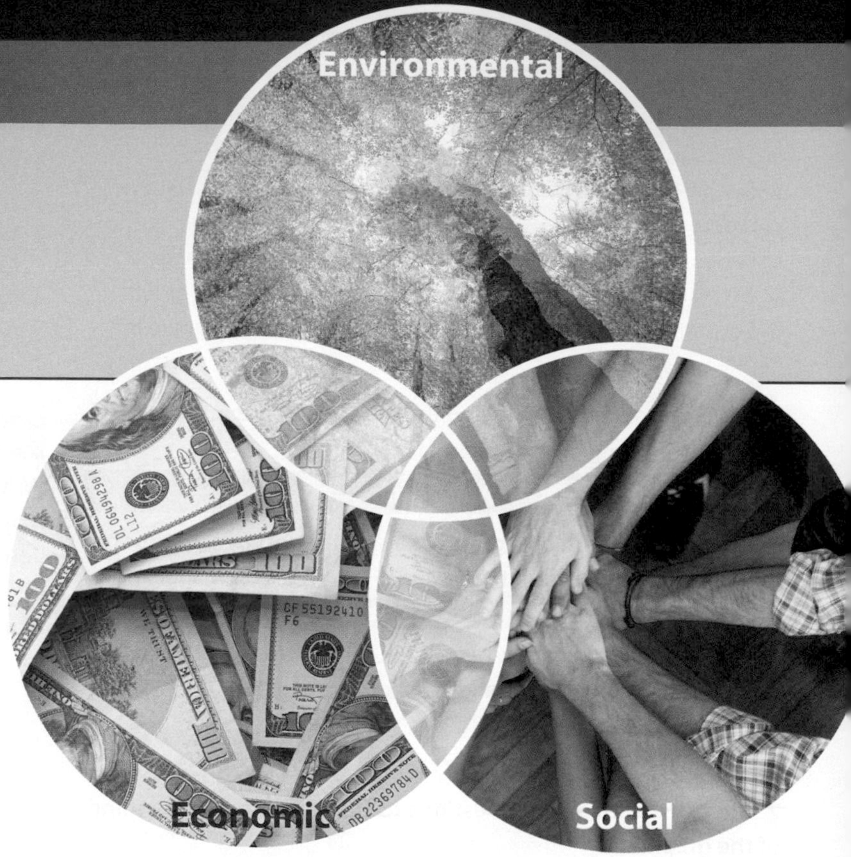

Learning outcomes
- Understand principles of the triple bottom line.
- Learn and use vocabulary to discuss sustainability.
- Evaluate impact of decisions on different stakeholders.

Environmental

Economic

Social

Introduction

1 How should companies measure their performance, in your view? Choose answer A or B and discuss the reasons for your choice.

A A company's performance should be measured exclusively by the 'bottom line', i.e. by how much profit it makes.

B A company's performance should be measured by the 'triple bottom line', which has three metrics:

- how much profit the company makes
- how socially responsible it is
- how environmentally responsible it is.

2 Read the quote below and discuss how sustainable the world's present business model is. Give examples to support your views.

> 66 Sustainability is the principle of ensuring that our actions today do not limit the range of economic, social and environmental options open to future generations. 99

John Elkington, leading authority on sustainable development and creator of the 'triple bottom line' theory of business sustainability

3 Business in the 21st century is characterised by multiple stakeholders. These are groups of people that have a strong interest in the company, and successful companies will want to address their needs. Match the business actions to the stakeholders in the diagram below. (Note some of the business actions address needs of more than one stakeholder.)

Stakeholders	Business actions
shareholders	Make profits
local community	Encourage educational visits from schools near the company
wider community	Switch to clean energy providers of electricity
employees	Monitor suppliers to ensure working conditions are acceptable
consumers	Run courses on 'stress management' for staff
future generations	Ensure promotions and advertising are ethical and honest
	Provide on-site nursery facilities for working parents

4 How desirable is it for companies to consider the needs of all these stakeholders?

Language focus: Topic verbs linked to sustainability

1 Complete the sentences below using the verbs in the box. You should use each verb only once and you may need to change the form of the verb.

| assign | advocate | eliminate | comprise | adapt | gauge |
| accommodate | drive | incorporate | secure |

1 We have _____ most of the feedback from the public into our report on the damage to the local area.

2 We have attempted to _____ the wildlife currently living in the area by leaving the wetlands untouched.

3 The company won't be able to _____ the success of their policies until they have put them into action.

4 The organisation's goals _____ of only profit-related outcomes.

5 We need to _____ someone to the post of CSR officer, if we are serious about making these changes.

6 The committee are looking to _____ funding from local businesses to pay for training in local schools.

7 Better counselling and redundancy pay may _____ the problem of ex-workers feeling poorly treated when they are laid off when we close the Doncaster factory.

8 The chairman strongly _____ a policy of involving the local farmers in the plans for developing the area.

9 The decision by the state's top environmental regulator to stop the power plant being built has been criticised for _____ investment out of the state.

10 It is quite hard for many organisations to _____ policies that they have had for many years to the new needs of the different stakeholders they serve.

Business view

Dr Timothy F. Slaper, Ph.D., is Director of Economic Analysis, Indiana Business Research Center, Indiana University Kelley School of Business.

Tanya J. Hall is Economic Research Analyst, Indiana Business Research Center, Indiana University Kelley School of Business.

Reading 1: Defining and calculating the triple bottom line

1 Read the first part of an article by Dr Timothy Slaper and Tanya Hall, which gives background information on the triple bottom line. Discuss the following questions.

1 Which of the three Ps mentioned in the text can be matched to each of the following dimensions?

environmental = p_____

social = p_____

financial = p_____

2 In what way does the TBL (triple bottom line) represent the fundamentals of sustainability?

The Triple Bottom Line Defined

Sustainability has been an often-mentioned goal of businesses, not-for-profit organizations and governments in the past decade, yet measuring the degree to which an organization is sustainable can be difficult.

The TBL is an accounting framework that incorporates three dimensions of performance: social, environmental and financial. This differs from traditional reporting frameworks as it includes ecological (or environmental) and social measures that can be difficult to assign appropriate means of measurement. The TBL dimensions are also commonly called the three Ps: people, planet and profits.

Well before Elkington introduced the sustainability concept as 'triple bottom line,' environmentalists wrestled with measures of, and frameworks for, sustainability. The TBL captures the essence of sustainability by measuring the impact of an organization's activities on the world.

The trick isn't defining TBL. The trick is measuring it.

3 Is it more difficult to measure the TBL or to define it? Why do you think that is?

2 Read the next section of text and answer the following questions.

1 What is the problem with measuring the TBL (the three Ps)?

2 What are the benefits of monetising all the dimensions of the TBL?

3 Why do some critics argue against monetising the dimensions?

4 What solution to the problem of measurement is put forward by the authors?

Calculating the Triple Bottom Line

The 3Ps do not have a common unit of measure. Profits are measured in dollars. What is social capital measured in? What about environmental or ecological health? Finding a common unit of measurement is one challenge.

Some advocate monetizing all the dimensions of the TBL, including social welfare or environmental damage. While that would have the benefit of having a common unit – dollars – many object to putting a dollar value on wetlands or endangered species on strictly philosophical grounds. Others question the method of finding the right price for lost wetlands or endangered species.

Another solution would be to calculate the TBL in terms of an index. In this way, one eliminates the incompatible units issue and, as long as there is a universally accepted accounting method, allows for comparisons between entities, e.g. comparing performance between companies, cities, development projects or some other benchmark. The benefit of an index is that it therefore ranks different organizations on the same scales.

3 In your opinion, how achievable and desirable is it for organisations to try to measure their social impact in this way?

Read the next section of the text. Are the following statements true or false?

1 There are strict guidelines used for calculating the TBL.
2 The general framework can be adapted for different types of organisations, but not for different projects.
3 The stakeholders have no say in setting the measures.
4 Economic variables are connected with the flow of money.
5 It's better if organisations have long-range trends available when measuring their environmental impact.
6 Measures put in place for a local project should be set at a national level.

What Measures Go into the Index?

There is no universal standard method for calculating the TBL. Neither is there a universally accepted standard for the measures that comprise each of the three TBL categories. This can be viewed as a strength because it allows a user to adapt the framework to the needs of different entities (businesses or not-for-profit organizations), different projects or policies (infrastructure investment or educational programs), or different geographic boundaries (a city, region or country).

Both a business and local government agency may gauge environmental sustainability in the same terms, say reducing the amount of solid waste that goes into landfills, but a local mass transit system might measure success in terms of passenger miles, while a for-profit bus company would measure success in terms of earnings per share. The TBL can accommodate these differences.

The level of the entity, type of project and the geographic scope will drive many of the decisions about what measures to include. That said, the set of measures will ultimately be determined by stakeholders and subject matter experts, and the ability to collect the necessary data.

Economic Measures
Economic variables ought to be variables that deal with the bottom line and the flow of money. It could look at income or expenditures, taxes, business climate factors, employment, and business diversity factors.

Environmental Measures
Environmental variables should represent measurements of natural resources and reflect potential influences to the viability of a project. It could incorporate air and water quality, energy consumption, natural resources, solid and toxic waste, and changes to land use. Ideally, having long-range trends available for each of the environmental variables would help organizations identify the impacts a project or policy would have on the area.

Social Measures
Social variables refer to social dimensions of a community or region and could include measurements of education, equity and access to social resources, health and well-being, quality of life, and social capital.

Data for many of these measures are collected at the state and national levels, but are also available at the local or community level. For local or community-based projects, the TBL measures of success are best determined locally. For example, a community may consider an important measure of success for an entrepreneurial development program to be the number of woman-owned companies formed over a five-year time period.

Source: *The Triple Bottom Line: What Is It and How Does It Work?* by Dr Timothy F. Slaper, Ph.D., and Tanya J. Hall

What are some of the tensions between the different measures of the TBL and between some of the stakeholders of an organisation concerned with sustainability issues? For example, between providing benefits for staff and making profits? Or between shareholders today and future generations tomorrow? Can these tensions be resolved, in your view?

Output: Using the triple bottom line to discuss impacts on stakeholders

Stage 1
Look at the following list of stakeholders in the production of a national daily newspaper. What social, economic and environmental measures would concern them?

- the owners of the newspaper
- the journalists
- other employees
- people who buy the newspaper
- suppliers in the local area
- future generations

Stage 2
One of your national daily newspapers is cutting its print run by 50% and planning to concentrate on electronic subscriptions. This will mean they will use 50% less paper. There will also be job cuts in the print room and it will have an impact on suppliers too. The move to more electronic formats may create new jobs, although the newspaper may decide to employ freelance journalists working remotely rather than full-time staff members.

Work in three groups and consider the different stakeholders.

Group A discuss the social impact of the changes.
Group B discuss the environmental impact of the changes.
Group C discuss the economic impact of the changes.

Stage 3
Present your ideas to the other groups.

Stage 4
Discuss who has the most to win and the most to lose from the newspaper's decision.

13.2 Practice: Masdar – the sustainable city

Learning outcomes
- Understand how sustainability futures are being created.
- Use the language of contrasts to persuade.
- Discuss the pros and cons of becoming a green city.

Solar power is one of the major sources of energy in Masdar City.

The wind tower circulates cooling air around the Masdar Institute of Technology without the need of an electric air-conditioning system.

Waste products are collected outside Masdar City for recycling.

Profile: Masdar City

Masdar City is located in Abu Dhabi. Established in 2006, it is a commercially driven enterprise that supports sustainable technologies, specifically those aimed at tackling climate change and building a more sustainable future. It is a key part of Abu Dhabi's goal of changing from an oil-based economy to one that is based on knowledge, innovation and cutting-edge technologies. Masdar's vision is 'To make Abu Dhabi the pre-eminent source of renewable energy knowledge, development and implementation, and set the world's benchmark for sustainable development'.

Introduction

1 Match the following three phrases to their definitions from the *Cambridge Advanced Learner's Dictionary*.

carbon footprint   greenhouse gas   carbon emissions

1 _____ *plural noun* CARBON DIOXIDE that planes, cars, factories, etc. produce which is harmful to the environment

2 _____ *noun* is the measurement of the amount of CARBON DIOXIDE that a person's activities produce

3 _____ *noun a* gas like CARBON DIOXIDE which acts as a shield trapping heat in the Earth's atmosphere. The resulting effect is thought to contribute to global warming.

2 Answer the questions below about your lifestyle.

How big is your footprint?

1 What kind of transport do you usually use to get to work or college?
- a bicycle
- b train
- c bus
- d car

2 How many people live in your household*?
- a more than 4
- b 3–4
- c 2
- d you live alone

3 How often do you trade in your old phone for a newer model?
- a every few years
- b every other year
- c about once a year
- d more than once a year

4 How often do you fly?
- a never
- b once a year
- c every six months
- d every month

5 How likely would you be to vote for politicians who put green issues before economic growth?
- a very likely
- b quite likely
- c possibly
- d unlikely

6 How often is your TV left in stand-by mode?
- a never
- b often
- c sometimes
- d always

7 How often do you eat meat?**
- a never
- b once a week
- c every 3–4 days
- d every day

* The more people who live in your household, the smaller your carbon footprint, as you will share heating and lighting and use of facilities.
** Farm animals are a major cause of greenhouse gases and this is an energy-intensive form of agriculture (you need 13 kilos of grain to produce 1 kilo of meat).

3 Check your results – 'a' answers give the smallest footprint; 'd' answers give the largest. Discuss your answers with a partner. Is your carbon footprint sustainable? Would you consider changing your lifestyle to reduce your footprint?

4 Read the profile of Masdar City and discuss the reasons why Abu Dhabi has decided to build this city.

Language focus 1: Green vocabulary

1 Much language related to sustainability, or being 'green', is concerned with the concepts of reducing waste and demand. Which words in the box can be used with 'green' or 'zero' to form word partnerships to talk about sustainability? Which can go with 'demand' and 'waste'?

Example: *green companies, consumer demand*

emissions   companies   markets   waste   consumer   carbon
water   energy   knowledge   reduce

2 Look at the photos on page 121 and discuss what you think Masdar City's attitude is to demand and waste.

3 How do you think your home town or city would measure in terms of being green?

Listening 1: Masdar City promotion Part 1

 2.33

You are going to hear part of a presentation on Masdar City, from the development company set up by the government of Abu Dhabi.

1 As you listen, complete the section headings in exercise 2 with titles from the box. The first one has been done for you.

Water, Waste and Electricity   Transport   Welcome to Masdar City
The Vision   The Design   Source of Wisdom

2 Listen again and answer the question for each section.

Section 1: Welcome to Masdar City
1 What is planned for the first phase of the project?

Section 2: _____
2 What is the advantage of having a fossil fuel-free city?

Section 3: _____
3 How does the street layout and dimension of the city change without fossil fuel vehicles?

Section 4: _____
4 What will the driverless electric vehicles carry?

3 If you were living and working (or studying) in Masdar City, what would you enjoy most about being in this city?

Listening 2: Masdar City promotion Part 2

 2.34

1 Read the statements below, which refer to two further sections from the presentation. Match each statement to one of the section titles in the box in Listening 1.

1 Conventional cities use 80% more electricity than Masdar City.
2 Most of the consumer waste will be recycled or used as an energy source.
3 All the city's energy will come from solar power.
4 Any unused electricity will be used by other consumers.
5 Electricity isn't the only thing that will flow in the city.
6 Abu Dhabi plans to keep the knowledge gained from Masdar within the country.
7 The Masdar Institute expects to encourage the growth of companies in the field of sustainability.

2 Listen to the second part of the presentation and decide if the statements above are true or false.

3 What type of renewable energy sources do you know of? How widespread is the use of renewable energy in your country?

4 Abu Dhabi is hoping to turn Masdar City into a hub where green businesses will also want to be concentrated. How important to the local economy are universities with strong engineering and science research departments? Can you think of examples from your own country where industry hubs are concentrated around particular universities?

Transferable skill: Challenging the consensus

1 Consensus views are opinions or positions that are reached by a group as a whole. For example, most people would agree that pollution of the sea should be stopped. Look at the following reasons why people decide to challenge consensus views. To what extent do you think these challenges are valid?

1 Consensus views are often created by a small number of people who are promoting their own interests as the common interest.
2 Consensus views limit debate and don't allow for a diversity of views.
3 Consensus views are often maintained through fear and so should be countered.
4 Consensus views are irritating!

2 Look at the quote below that challenges consensus views on global warming and discuss the question that follows.

" A majority of American citizens are now becoming sceptical of the claim that our carbon footprints, resulting from our use of fossil fuels, are going to lead to climatic calamities. But governments are not yet listening to the citizens. "

John Coleman, entrepreneur and founder of the Weather Channel

3 What is your view of why some people are sceptical about fossil fuels increasing their carbon footprint?

A They are right to be sceptical of the research findings.

B They are right to be sceptical of what governments say.

C They're looking for a way to justify their own unsustainable lifestyle.

4 What is your view of why business is now embracing the 'green movement' more and more?

A Companies are genuinely concerned about environmental issues.

B Cutting waste and using renewable energy is simply a way to save money.

C It's only done for appearance, in order to increase sales to environmentally conscious consumers.

5 Are you more challenging or more accepting of the consensus views around you at home, work and in your place of study? Explain why, giving examples.

Language focus 2: Using the language of contrasts to persuade

In order to make the message more persuasive, speakers and writers often use contrasts. There are several used in the Masdar City presentation in the Listening on page 122.

1 Match the two parts to make sentences using contrasts from the presentation.

1	The ultimate goal of its designers is the highest quality of life …	a	… lower temperatures so people can walk, interact and play.
2	To realise this vision for a city of the future, the master planners …	b	… with the lowest environmental impact.
3	This means more shade, and …	c	… be shared with the world.
4	The knowledge gained here will …	d	… have gone back in time.

2 When using a contrast, the emphasis needs to go on the contrasting words that relate to the theme.

> 66 One **small step** for man, one **giant leap** for mankind 99

Neil Armstrong, on becoming the first man on the moon

In pairs, practise saying the examples in exercise 1 with appropriate emphasis.

3 Complete the following sentences using a contrast that persuades.

1 The lower the level of emissions, …

2 Using green energy means fewer fossil fuels and …

3 The longer we continue to rely on fossil fuels, …

4 Designing greener cities means better public transport …

5 We want to ensure the lowest level of demand for energy and …

Output: Developing a sustainable city

Stage 1

Read the information below and discuss the pros and cons of the local government's plans.

You live in a city with a population of 150,000. Most of the employment is provided by the large food-processing factory that is located on the edge of the city and the small power station that runs on coal. The city centre also has a large shopping centre that attracts people from the surrounding area. There is a big car park adjacent to the shopping centre which offers free parking.

The local government want to make the city more sustainable. They have proposed the following vision for the city.

- The fossil fuel power station will be closed and replaced by a recycling plant.
- A large wind farm employing 30 percent fewer people than the existing power station will be located on the edge of the city near a residential area.
- Cars will be banned from the city centre and it will be made a pedestrianised zone.
- Public transport will be improved with trams running to the food-processing factory from the city centre. The tramlines will take up one lane of the existing highway.
- A new research centre will be built to look at new sustainable technologies. This will be funded by making cuts to the local business school's funding.

Stage 2

Work in two groups, A and B.

Group A

You represent local businesses. Prepare to discuss the new vision. Think about how the plans could affect your business – both positively and negatively.

Example: Restricting traffic in the town centre will make it more inconvenient for people to go shopping, thus damaging business there.

Group B

You represent the local government. Prepare to defend your vision to local businesses who are concerned about the future ideas for improving sustainability in the city. Think about how the plans will benefit the city and local businesses.

Example: Better public transport will mean that individuals will leave their cars at home, reducing traffic jams and improving traffic flow for business.

Stage 3

Have the meeting. You need to agree on a new vision for the city which is acceptable to both local government and business. Try to use some of the new vocabulary and expressions for persuading that you have learned in this unit.

13.3 Skills: Problem-solving

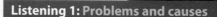

Learning outcomes
- Discuss interpersonal problems and their solutions.
- Give advice and make suggestions directly and indirectly.
- Analyse problems from different perspectives.

Introduction

1 Look at the pictures above. Do you ever do any of these things at work or at college? What kind of situation would prompt you to behave like that?

2 You are a manager. Working in pairs, discuss how serious it is if you have a member of staff who …

a … usually comes to work ten minutes late.

b … regularly misses internal work deadlines.

c … sometimes falls asleep at the desk after lunch.

d … takes company stationery home, and doesn't bring it back.

e … seems unwilling or unable to learn new procedures.

f … gossips about colleagues behind their backs.

g … shouts at difficult customers.

h … sometimes works very hard, but at other times is very lazy.

Place each problem on the scale below.

Not serious at all   Fairly serious   Very serious

3 For the most serious problem, discuss what you think you should do. Compare your answer with another pair.

Critical analysis

Problematic behaviour at work may be the responsibility of the worker, but the manager or institution may also be responsible for the problem. Choose one or two of the problems from the Introduction that the manager or institution could be responsible for. In what ways could the institution/manager be responsible, rather than the individual?

Listening 1: Problems and causes

2.35

Listen to a conversation between the director of a pharmaceutical company and his recently promoted team leader. They are discussing the performance of Magid, a new employee who works off-site. Answer the questions below.

1 The director and the team leader discuss why Magid is too slow. Which two of these reasons are mentioned?

a Magid is lazy.

b The team leader's expectations are too high.

c Magid is trying to be too careful.

2 Which of the causes is the most probable, according to the director? In general, do you think this is often the case?

Listening 2: Deadlines and timescales

2.36

1 Listen to the next part of the conversation and choose the best answer.

1 What does the director say about timescales?
  a Let the staff member suggest a deadline first.
  b The team leader should set the deadline and strictly enforce it.
  c The team leader should set the deadline, and then it can be negotiated.

2 What does the director say about working with people who have different work styles?
  a It's very interesting.   **c** It's very liberating.
  b It's very irritating.

2 Discuss the following questions.

1 Do you think the relationship between the director and the team leader is good? Why/Why not?

2 Why would a good relationship be important when discussing topics like problems with employees?

Intercultural analysis

This meeting took place in a British company, where most of the employees are British. However, the team leader in the meeting is Colombian. Discuss the following questions.

1 Do you think it is more difficult for foreign managers to succeed in business than it is for local managers? Why/Why not?
2 If you were a member of a multinational team, what do you think would be the advantages and disadvantages of working with other nationalities?

Language focus: Suggesting solutions and giving advice

In meetings, businesspeople often need to make suggestions or give advice. In the Listening extract, there are examples both of suggesting solutions in an indirect way and of giving advice more directly.

1 Look at the following extracts and decide which is indirect and which is more direct. Which words or phrases give you this information?

a So instead of saying, you know, 'Can you do this?' say 'Can you do this but have it back by six' or something.
b Because the one thing you could do is say, when you give him work to do, say 'Look, I need this done by this time.' And give him a deadline.

2 Read the extract below and notice how both direct and indirect forms are used.

Director: <u>Well, don't</u> say it like that. Don't let him dictate the timescale to you. <u>You say</u> to him 'I need it done by this date.' If he can't do it by that time, he should come back to you and say 'I can't do it by then because you've already told me to do this and this and this.' <u>And then you could say</u> 'Well, yes, you're right. You need to do those, so you can do the work I've just given you by next Tuesday.'

Team leader: Right.

Director: <u>OK?</u> So you dictate the timescale to him.

3 Complete the table to show what type of language is used at each stage.

Stage	Aim	Direct/Indirect
1 Well, don't …	Clarifying the problem	
2 You say …	Exploring the scenario and how to reach a solution	
3 And then you could say …	Exploring the scenario and how to reach a solution	
4 OK? …	Summing up the solution	

4 When is it more appropriate to use indirect suggestions than direct ones?

5 Look at the following examples of direct advice and change them into a more indirect style, using the prompts which follow each sentence.

1 Instead of doing it that way, do it this way.
  Have you thought about …
2 Don't let him dictate the terms to you.
  It might be a good idea …
3 You have to cater for all these different working styles.
  You could think about …
4 You can't expect him to do it all on the first day.
  You might need to …
5 Tell her she can't dress like that in the office.
  You could say …

6 Choose a problem from the Introduction and practise giving direct and indirect advice, using some of the language above.

Output: Discussing solutions to problems

Stage 1
Read the notes below about a problem employee and discuss what might be causing the problems and how they should be dealt with.

The problem
• The employee regularly leaves early.
• The employee is regularly stressed and shouts at colleagues.

The result
• The employee's productivity is down.
• Team morale is down mainly because colleagues are fed up with his/her attitude.

Other information
The employee has recently split up with his/her partner and is solely responsible for looking after his/her two school-aged children.

Stage 2
Work in pairs. Student A is the manager of the problem employee. Student B is a more experienced manager from the same organisation. Read your information and then have a meeting to try to reach an agreement on how to improve the situation.

Student A
Explain the situation and problems you are having with your employee to the other manager (Student B), then listen to his/her advice and try to find a solution together.

Student B
Listen to the other manager (Student A) explain his/her problems with an employee, then give advice and try to find a solution together. Try to give both direct and more indirect advice to explore possible solutions to the problem.

14 Social enterprise

14.1 Theory: Perspectives on social enterprise

Learning outcomes

- Understand different perspectives comparing companies to social enterprises.
- Learn common word partnerships in the field of business and society.
- Analyse a social enterprise's financial difficulties.

Lack of adequate housing

Lack of a convenient and reliable energy source

Youth crime

Deforestation

Poverty

Introduction

1 Look at the problems shown in these photos from different parts of the world. Discuss who you think is best able to successfully tackle these problems: governments, not-for-profit charity organisations or private-sector companies?

2 Read the definition of a 'social enterprise' from a UK government report.

> Social enterprises are businesses which exist to address social or environmental need. Rather than maximising profit for shareholders or owners, profits are reinvested into the community or back into the business.

Source: *Social enterprises: a strategy for success*

How do social enterprises blur the boundaries between the private and public sectors? Is this a strategy for success, in your opinion?

Language focus: Common word partnerships linking business and social issues

1 Look at the list of nouns below which commonly follow the word 'social' when discussing business issues linked to social issues. Use the words from this list to complete the sentences below. The first one has been done for you as an example.

entrepreneurs   good   change

problems   (**social**)   housing

need   responsibility

entrepreneurship

1 Joseph Wharton believed that the purpose of business was to improve people's lives by creating economic opportunities. He further believed that business leaders had to take the <u>social good</u> into account.

2 _____ are pioneers who are disrupting existing industries and business models to find solutions to poverty, hunger and environmental problems.

3 MBA courses on topics like _____ have exploded in the past few years.

4 GE was ranked in the top five US companies for its management quality and investment value but was only ranked number 72 for corporate _____ (CSR).

5 A site in Farnborough has been sold profitably, predominantly for the construction of _____ .

6 Rail companies received subsidies of £1.4 billion from the government last year for running services that do not make a profit but which meet a _____ .

7 Forces of modernisation, such as education and urbanisation, are producing _____ in the developing world.

8 The government is attempting to address _____ such as poverty and inequality.

2 Social responsibility is now a common feature of many private companies' business practices. It generally covers four main areas: care for employees, for the local community and for the environment, and a commitment to ethical business practices.

1 Why do you think private companies now pay more attention to issues of social responsibility?

2 What difference is there between corporate social responsibility of a private company and the aims of a social enterprise?

3 Choose all the words (a–e) that can be used in the gaps in the sentences below.

1 Large corporations are particularly interested in programmes to get their executives to adopt the behaviours and attitudes of entrepreneurs who create economic and social _____ .
a value **b** change **c** impact **d** need **e** purpose

2 The fund will invest in ventures that can grow into major operations and can deliver a high social _____ .
a mission **b** impact **c** value **d** change **e** responsibility

3 The XL Results Foundation is billed as 'the world's leading entrepreneur network', being entirely focused on helping people start businesses with a social _____ .
a objective **b** problem **c** change **d** purpose **e** mission

4 When venture capitalists hear about a for-profit company driven by a social _____ , their comment is still the same: 'You need to focus more on profits.'
a mission **b** entrepreneur **c** goals **d** impact
e entrepreneurship

Reading: Comparing social enterprises to profit-making companies

1 Skim read what Professor Jane Wei-Skillern and Dr Helen Haugh have to say about the comparison between social enterprises and private companies. Decide which of the following statements (A or B) best represents each person's position in these short extracts.

A There are both differences and similarities between companies and social enterprises.

B There are considerable differences between companies and social enterprises.

Business view

Dr Helen Haugh is Deputy Director of the MBA Programme and Senior Lecturer in Community Enterprise at the Cambridge Judge Business School, University of Cambridge.

Social enterprises are organisations that have been set up to achieve a social purpose. So they have at the heart of them a mission for trying to achieve social good. We use the term 'social' in a broad context to include environmental goals as well. The main thrust of the definition is that there is more to running the business than just generating profit. So social enterprise really tries to encapsulate the idea of a 'triple bottom line', that an organisation shouldn't be just trying to generate profit, but should generate some social good, and also manage its impact on the environment as well.

The enterprise perspective of social enterprise is very important as social enterprises are trying to find ways of generating income from opportunities. It is this aspect that they have in common with mainstream private-sector organisations. But what is distinctive about social enterprise is that many of them have their roots in the non-profit sector. They combine aspects of the for-profit sector (the idea of 'enterprise') with achieving social good (the idea of generating something that is of benefit to society).

Business view

Professor Jane Wei-Skillern is Lecturer in Organizational Behavior at the Stanford Graduate Business School, where she teaches an MBA elective on Social Entrepreneurship.

The key difference between private companies and social enterprises is that with social enterprise the primary focus is social value creation above and beyond shareholder return. By 'social value creation', I mean addressing an issue in society that is perhaps not readily addressed by market forces. Environmental protection, ecological conservation, or social needs are some examples.

I think that leaders in both companies and social enterprises can certainly share a lot of the same characteristics. However, I think that understanding of the context and the nature of the challenge that management faces, is very different. The nature of social sector work involves a higher degree of collaboration and coordination with other entities, whether it is funding agencies, government agencies or peer organisations who are also potential competitors. Management measurement of performance is also more difficult as you have to keep your eye on the larger social mission and not just the short-term metrics. Has the social enterprise grown its budget? Has it hired more staff? Have they opened new sites? Those are all signs of potential metrics of success, but organisations can deliver on all of those things but still fail miserably on their mission impact.

2 Categorise the following statements as representing the opinions of Professor Jane Wei-Skillern or Dr Helen Haugh, according to the texts. Label each statement as follows.

HH = Dr Helen Haugh   JWS = Professor Jane Wei-Skillern
B = Both   N = Neither

1 Social enterprises' goals and objectives exclude making a profit.
2 It's essential that social enterprises take an entrepreneurial outlook to exploit new revenue possibilities.
3 Many social enterprises are set up by entrepreneurs from the business sector.
4 Social enterprises are concerned with addressing social and environmental needs.
5 Unlike companies, managers in social enterprises need to undertake more joint action with other organisations.
6 Standard measurements of success in business don't necessarily translate to the social enterprise sector.

3 On page 127, Professor Jane Wei-Skillern refers to 'metrics of success'. What metrics do you think should be measured by a social enterprise dealing with one of the social and environmental problems shown in the photos in the Introduction?

Listening 1: Social entrepreneurs

 2.37

1 Listen to part of an interview with Professor Jane Wei-Skillern. Does she think that entrepreneurs in general make good leaders of social enterprises?

2 Listen again and answer the following questions.

1 What words are used to describe a typical business entrepreneur or business leader?
2 What are for-profit entrepreneurs focused on?
3 What kind of leaders are needed in the social enterprise sector?

Listening 2: Social enterprise goals

 2.38

1 Listen to part of an interview with Dr Helen Haugh. Does she think social goals are more important than economic goals?

2 Listen again and answer the following questions.

1 How is 'mission drift' defined?
2 What is it important to 'not lose sight of'?

Critical analysis

What views expressed in this lesson by Dr Helen Haugh and Professor Jane Wei-Skillern do you particularly agree or disagree with? Explain your reasons.

Output: Crisis meeting

You are going to take part in a crisis meeting of Centro, a social enterprise housing cooperative in Madrid. It is in a very difficult financial situation as a result of a 150,000 euro cut in its grant from the City Council. You need to decide how it can balance the need to increase income and reduce costs and at the same time maintain the organisation's social aims and objectives.

Stage 1

Read the brief description below of the organisation and a summary version of its projected income and costs for next year.

 **Centro**

Centro is a social housing enterprise set up over 20 years ago. Its mission is to help support local residents in one of the poorest parts of the city, where economic and social problems are severe. Here it owns an area of land about the size of three football pitches, where it has built a variety of structures to benefit local residents, including low-rent family accommodation for families on low incomes and a children's nursery. These facilities have been paid for from rents it receives from shops, restaurants and luxury apartments it has built on the same site for professionals who work in the nearby financial district.

Projected income and costs statement summary for next year	
Income	Euros per year
Rent from affordable housing (20 × 3-bedroom flats at 6,000 euros a year)	120,000
Rent from luxury apartments (12 × 1-bedroom flats at 30,000 euros a year)	360,000
Retail shop rentals	140,000
Terrace restaurant	80,000
Grant from City Council (reduced from 200,000 euros last year)	50,000
Misc (corporate events held in Centro's park)	20,000
Total income	**770,000**

Costs	
Building, gardens and park maintenance	160,000
Building insurance, security, professional fees	90,000
Senior Citizen Day Centre running costs	120,000
Children's nursery running costs	150,000
Unemployed Advice Centre running costs	140,000
Youth Club running costs	60,000
Interest on bank loans	250,000
HQ management and admin costs	200,000
Total costs	**1,070,000**
Balance	**-400,000**

Stage 2

Divide into small groups and discuss how to 'balance the books', as next year's income will need to match costs.

Group A read the information on page 141.
Group B read the information on page 144.

Stage 3

Meet with the other group and decide what you will do.

14.2 Practice: Trashy Bags – a social enterprise in action

Learning outcomes
- Understand how a social enterprise works in practice.
- Use linking words to build cohesion.
- Persuade an employer offering a work placement opportunity.

Profile: Trashy Bags

Trashy Bags is a social enterprise based in Accra, Ghana that makes recycled eco-friendly bags and gifts from plastic trash that people are paid to collect from the streets of the city. The plastic litter is cleaned and manually sorted by type and colour and finally turned into products. It makes over 350 different variations of 23 product lines. Its product list includes laptop bags, vanity cases, backpacks, sports holdalls, purses, hats, wallets, water bottle holders and shopping bags for everyday use. Trashy bags were presented as official gifts at the MTV Music Awards in Madrid recently. Trashy Bags was set up by Englishman, Stuart Gold, in 2007.

Introduction

Read the following questions and discuss your answers with a partner.

1 Look at the photos and read the profile of Trashy Bags. Would you consider buying their products?

2 Do you think a social enterprise like Trashy Bags would work in your country?

3 What do you think you might learn if you did a three-month work placement at Trashy Bags? Discuss this with reference to the following two areas.

- Personal development – learning about yourself and personal benefits
- Professional development – learning new skills, competences and knowledge

Transferable skill: Using a dictionary to decode a brand name

Read the definitions of 'trash', 'trash bag' and 'trashy' from the *Cambridge Advanced Learner's Dictionary* and a further slang definition of 'trashy' and answer the questions.

trash /træʃ/ noun 1 INFORMAL something that is of low quality: *I can't believe someone of his intelligence can read such trash! 2 US FOR* rubbish: *The trash really stinks – why don't you take it out?*

trash bag noun US FOR dustbin bag/liner

trashy /ˈtræʃi/ adj INFORMAL of low quality; with little or no value: *trashy programmes [on TV]*

trashy adjective SLANG used both positively and negatively to describe a provocative and controversial attitude or style of dress designed to shock: *Givenchy has this trashy deconstructed look for Spring that is super sexy. Think early 90s Madonna and Versace.*

1 How good a brand name do you think 'Trashy Bags' is?

2 Trashy Bags uses terms such as 'Trashy employees' and 'Trashy babies' to describe their staff and their baby clothes range. It's part of their branding strategy. Which of the following words best describes this strategy in your opinion?

shocking   appropriate   inappropriate   eye-catching   forceful   honest   ingenious   creative   disrespectful   provocative   offensive   direct   extreme   relevant

3 Discuss your answer. How effective is this kind of branding?

Reading: About Trashy Bags

1 Before reading an extract from the Trashy Bags company website, try to predict what the text is about by looking at the photos and answering the questions below.

1 What do you think the first section title 'Is there life after death?' refers to?

2 What do you think is 'The Problem' in the second section of the text?

3 What do you think is 'The Solution' in the third section of the text?

2 Read the text and check your answers to the questions above.

3 Look through the text to answer the following specific information questions.

1 What three kinds of plastic packaging litter are most common in West Africa?

2 What statistic shows the problem of plastic litter has got worse?

3 What problems does the plastic litter on the streets cause?

4 How environmentally friendly is the process of turning the plastic sachets into bags?

4 The text outlines five benefits (a–e) that result from the Trashy Bags operation. Which is the most important, in your view?

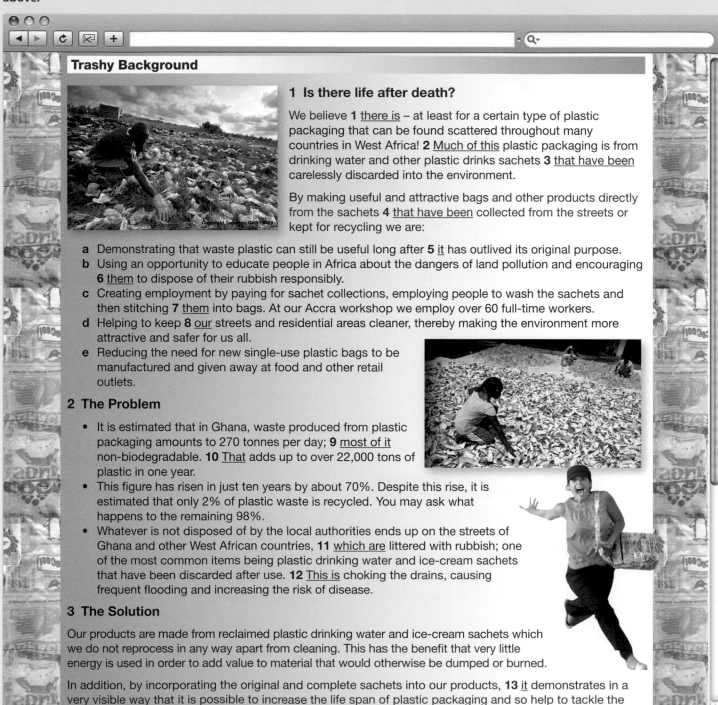

Trashy Background

1 Is there life after death?

We believe **1** <u>there is</u> – at least for a certain type of plastic packaging that can be found scattered throughout many countries in West Africa! **2** <u>Much of this</u> plastic packaging is from drinking water and other plastic drinks sachets **3** <u>that have been</u> carelessly discarded into the environment.

By making useful and attractive bags and other products directly from the sachets **4** <u>that have been</u> collected from the streets or kept for recycling we are:

a Demonstrating that waste plastic can still be useful long after **5** <u>it</u> has outlived its original purpose.

b Using an opportunity to educate people in Africa about the dangers of land pollution and encouraging **6** <u>them</u> to dispose of their rubbish responsibly.

c Creating employment by paying for sachet collections, employing people to wash the sachets and then stitching **7** <u>them</u> into bags. At our Accra workshop we employ over 60 full-time workers.

d Helping to keep **8** <u>our</u> streets and residential areas cleaner, thereby making the environment more attractive and safer for us all.

e Reducing the need for new single-use plastic bags to be manufactured and given away at food and other retail outlets.

2 The Problem

- It is estimated that in Ghana, waste produced from plastic packaging amounts to 270 tonnes per day; **9** <u>most of it</u> non-biodegradable. **10** <u>That</u> adds up to over 22,000 tons of plastic in one year.

- This figure has risen in just ten years by about 70%. Despite this rise, it is estimated that only 2% of plastic waste is recycled. You may ask what happens to the remaining 98%.

- Whatever is not disposed of by the local authorities ends up on the streets of Ghana and other West African countries, **11** <u>which are</u> littered with rubbish; one of the most common items being plastic drinking water and ice-cream sachets that have been discarded after use. **12** <u>This is</u> choking the drains, causing frequent flooding and increasing the risk of disease.

3 The Solution

Our products are made from reclaimed plastic drinking water and ice-cream sachets which we do not reprocess in any way apart from cleaning. This has the benefit that very little energy is used in order to add value to material that would otherwise be dumped or burned.

In addition, by incorporating the original and complete sachets into our products, **13** <u>it</u> demonstrates in a very visible way that it is possible to increase the life span of plastic packaging and so help to tackle the very serious problem of environmental pollution in Africa and elsewhere.

Source: Trashy Bags website www.trashybags.org

Language focus: Using referencing to build cohesion

1 Look at the underlined words and phrases in the text. What does each one refer to? Write your answers in the centre column of the table below. The first one has been done for you.

Example language	Refers to	Example of
1 there is	life after death	referring back
2 much of this		
3 that have been		
4 that have been		
5 it		
6 them		
7 them		
8 our		
9 most of it		
10 that		
11 which are		
12 this is		
13 it		

2 Complete the third column in the table by describing the function that the example language is illustrating.

- referring back (to something mentioned previously in the text)
- referring outside (to something which is outside the text but which is clear to the reader)
- adding information (using a relative pronoun to add information to a sentence)

3 The text description below of the Trashy Briefcase and Trashy Laptop Bag is too long and lacks cohesion. Rewrite it by cutting out unnecessary words and make it more cohesive.

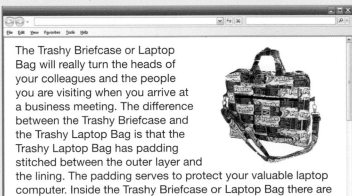

The Trashy Briefcase or Laptop Bag will really turn the heads of your colleagues and the people you are visiting when you arrive at a business meeting. The difference between the Trashy Briefcase and the Trashy Laptop Bag is that the Trashy Laptop Bag has padding stitched between the outer layer and the lining. The padding serves to protect your valuable laptop computer. Inside the Trashy Briefcase or Laptop Bag there are two divisions. The two divisions leave a central compartment so you can easily extract your laptop. The two divisions are especially useful at airport security. Both the Trashy Briefcase and Laptop Bag come in two sizes. The two products have a removable shoulder strap and two fixed handles.

4 Turn to page 190 to see the original marketing copy that appeared on the Trashy Bags website.

Output: Competing for a work placement opportunity

Trashy Bags runs a popular work placement scheme where people from abroad get the opportunity to work at their centre in Ghana. Some of these placements are designed for students and recent graduates. Others are designed for working professionals.

Stage 1

Divide into small groups.
Group A: Candidates applying together as a team
Group B: Trashy Bags' management team

Group A

Look at the 'criteria for selection' that Trashy Bags has set down in the table below and brainstorm a list of your individual strengths for each criterion. Question each other to explore what other abilities and experience you have that could also be useful to complete the criteria marked 'Other'.

Group B

In your group, discuss the details of what you are looking for from these teams for each of the criteria in the table below. Discuss and agree any other criteria that are relevant and note down the key details in the box marked 'Other'.

Criteria for selection	Group A What can your team offer?	Group B What are you looking for?
Commitment		
Adaptability		
Team players		
Relevant skills		
Other		

Stage 2

Each Group A should meet with a Group B and give a short, persuasive presentation (1–2 minutes) to convince them that their team is the best candidate for this work placement. One person from Group A will give this presentation. Try to make your arguments and ideas 'flow', using the language of cohesion. Group B should listen and check what they hear against the criteria they are looking for. After the presentation, ask Group A one or two questions and make a confidential note on how well Group A meets your criteria.

Stage 3

Repeat Stage 2, but this time Group A presents to another Group B. Make sure a different person in Group A gives the presentation this time round. After listening to several presentations, each Group B should inform the class of which Group A they have selected for the work placement. They should make a short presentation (1–2 minutes) explaining their choice. Try to make your arguments and ideas 'flow', using the language of cohesion.

14.3 Skills: Conference calls

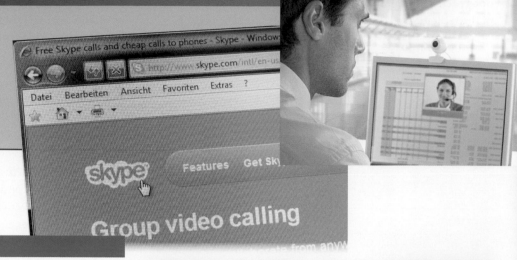

Learning outcomes
- Discuss protocol for conference calls.
- Practise ways of interrupting during a call.
- Conduct a conference call.

Introduction

1 What are the biggest differences between speaking to someone face-to-face compared to speaking to someone by phone or over the web?

2 What are the biggest differences between communicating with one person compared to communicating to a number of people, when you are not in a face-to-face situation?

3 Look at the following tips on managing a meeting at work involving a number of people. Which tips do you think are more important for conference calls than face-to-face meetings? Why?

1 Make sure that you have an agenda.
2 Start on time.
3 Define the objectives of the meeting.
4 Take a roll call of the people participating.
5 Establish ground rules for how to use the technology.
6 State your name when you speak.
7 Don't multi-task (use email, text, etc., during the meeting).
8 If you are the chair, make sure everybody has a chance to speak.
9 Be conscious of people in other time zones.
10 Always address questions to a specific person.

Listening 1: Opening the call

🎧 2.39

You are going to listen to a conference call with RESNA (Rehabilitation Engineering and Assistive Technology Society of North America). 'Assistive technology' is any product or service which is designed to enable disabled and older people to be independant.

1 Listen to the opening part of the call and answer the questions below.

1 Which of the following instructions are given to participants?
  a Use the mute button when you are listening.
  b If you hear music, put your phone on hold.
  c Do not move away from your phone during the call.

2 Which one of the following is the topic of the call?
  a the branding of RESNA's loan programme
  b the appointment of a new branding consultant

2 Look back at the tips in the Introduction. Which ones are covered here?

Listening 2: The reputation of the brand

🎧 2.40

1 Listen to the next part of the conference call and answer the following questions.

1 How many questions does Mary ask at the beginning?
2 What does Nancy suggest in order to answer Mary's questions?
3 Why can't Jane from Arizona answer the question?
4 What does Marion say about the reputation of the brand?

2 Look at the tips from the Introduction again and discuss the following questions.

1 Which tip does Mary ignore?
2 Which tip does Jane from Arizona ignore?

Language focus 1: Managing a conference call

1 Look at the audio script on page 165 and underline examples of the following functions. The Listening section they appear in is shown in brackets.

1 Explaining the procedure (Listening 1)
2 Handing over to another speaker (Listening 2)
3 Welcoming the participants (Listening 3)
4 Checking who is present (Listening 4)
5 Passing on your turn (Listening 2)

2 In conference calls, we cannot always see the other speakers, so we cannot communicate via body language. This means our tone of voice becomes even more important. Practise saying some of these phrases with friendly intonation.

3 Think of a conference call you may have in the future and practise the introduction using the audio script on page 165 to help you.

Language focus 2: Interrupting

🎧 2.41

1 All the expressions in Language focus 1 help maintain smooth communication. However, you may need to interrupt somebody or deal with interruptions. This is especially important when the participants can't see each other. Listen to the following short extracts and fill in the interrupting expressions.

Extract 1
A: Yes. Well, we've all …
B: _____? So, what I need to see …

Extract 2
A: Patrick was leaving in January and …
B: _____ – he paid you the …

Extract 3
A: Well, I think the best thing is …
B: _____ , Henry, because we've accepted …

2 Which of the examples seems the most aggressive when you listen? What makes it so aggressive? Does it seem aggressive when you read the text?

3 In pairs, choose a conversation topic on which you have an opinion (such as whether education should be free until university, or whether your country is a good place to do business). Practise interrupting each other, using the following framework.

A: So, I think that …
B: Sorry …, but …
A: Anyway, as I was saying …
B: Just …

Change roles.

Intercultural analysis

How accepting are people of being interrupted in your culture, in different situations? Give examples if possible.

Output: Conference call to discuss branding

Stage 1

You are going to participate in a conference call to discuss how your company is going to market its new footwear product. The soles of the sandals are made from recycled tyres, whilst the upper parts are made from plant fibres. The sandals are made in North Africa and sold in Europe. Your company is a social enterprise, which aims to make a profit from its commercial operations in order to invest in development programmes to support local communities in Morocco.

Work in groups of three and follow the instructions below.

Stage 2

CEO (chairing the meeting, during a business trip to Morocco): read the instructions on page 141.

External Marketing Consultant (at home in the UK): read the instructions on page 145.

Sales Director (on a business trip in Germany): read the instructions below.

Sales Director (Germany)

You think that a much larger number of customers will fall in love with your products if you focus as much on fashion and style as on the environmental and social message. You have noticed that customers are far less willing to buy 'green products' simply because they are 'greener' than they were in the past. They want more. Think of a name for your brand and ways to market it. What arguments will you use to persuade people to your way of thinking?

Stage 3

Hold the meeting. The CEO should start by going over any ground rules.

▶◀ **Watch Sequence 7 on the DVD to find out more about 21st century enterprise.**

Writing 7: Writing a covering letter for a CV

Learning outcomes
- Write a covering letter in a confident manner.
- Understand the key features and guidelines for a covering letter.
- Write a job response letter to accompany your CV.

Introduction

1 In English-speaking contexts, typically a covering letter accompanies your CV when you apply for a job. Look at the table below, which sets out the dos and don'ts for this type of writing. Match the sentence beginnings (1–8) with the correct endings (a–h)

1 Your covering letter should demonstrate	**a** show you can't be bothered to take the time to spell-check or proofread the letter.
2 Misspellings, grammatical errors or typos	**b** by writing to a particular named person.
3 Where possible, try to personalise your letter	**c** to demonstrate that you know something about them and can tailor your letter accordingly.
4 It's a good idea to do some research on the company	**d** how you're the right person for the job and how you can benefit the company.
5 Don't forget to include	**e** but don't overstep the line and be arrogant or clichéd.
6 Never write	**f** the job reference number in the subject line of your email (or first line of a letter).
7 Use confident and positive language	**g** between the job advert and your CV, highlighting your <u>relevant</u> skills, education and experience that match the <u>specific</u> requirements of the job advert.
8 Think of a covering letter as a bridge	**h** more than one single sheet of paper (around 300 words is a rough maximum length guideline).

2 What experience have you had of applying for jobs? Was a CV and covering letter part of the job application process?

3 Do you agree with all the tips in the table? Are any unsuitable for your organisation or country?

Language focus 1: Correcting common misspellings

1 What is the difference between a 'misspelling' and a 'typo'?

2 Find the ten misspellings and correct them.

1 accomodation **2** acknowlege **3** definate **4** responsability
5 dissappoint **6** seperate **7** liase **8** occasion
9 acheive **10** completely **11** enviroment **12** truely

Reading: Interpreting the job advertisement and planning the response

1 Read the job advertisement below, from a recruitment agency. What qualities are needed for this kind of job?

Customer Service Centre Manager

Location:	Nottingham/Derby
Salary:	£45,000 pa
Date posted:	02/06/2012 22:01
Job type:	Permanent
Contact:	Claire Williams
Ref:	Z123

I have the initiative to think up and implement new ways of working

About the role
Credible from the word go, you'll ensure the smooth running of customer service centre operations at either our Nottingham or Derby sites (300–350 staff in each), championing exceptional customer service. More than that, we'll look to you to devise, develop and deliver new customer relationship strategies, constantly improving our customer satisfaction ratings.

About you
There's no rulebook or script for you to follow – just your instincts. After all, your knowledge of call centre technology and industry developments is in-depth and up to the minute – as is your practical experience. Experience in a similar role is essential.

2 An interested candidate has made a list of what needs to be included in their covering letter. Highlight the parts of the job advertisement that each note refers to. The first one has been done for you in exercise 1.

1 I have the initiative to think up and implement new ways of working.

2 I am well informed about the technology and the industry.

3 I am results-orientated, focusing on keeping the clients happy.

4 I have leadership skills that show I can manage a large team.

5 I am passionate about delivering great customer service.

3 The candidate has failed to notice one key point in the job advert. Find it and write a note to add to the list above.

Writing skill: Content, structure, format and style of a covering letter

1 Read the sample covering letter below. Does Chris Smith include all the points she noted in response to the job advert? Find examples of these points in the letter.

Dear Claire,

[1]*I'm keen / I'm interested* to be considered for the Customer Service Manager role based in Nottingham or Derby[2] *as seen / I saw* on your website, ref: Z123.

I have three years' experience as a call centre team leader, [3]*managed / managing* 65 people for leading UK household insurer, Endsleigh. During this time I have:
- Decreased customer waiting times by 4% by [4]*intercepting / incentivising* quick call responses and a colour-coded display to inform [5]*team members / our guys* of customer waiting times.
- Cross-trained the team, [6]*who / which* has increased job satisfaction (reducing absenteeism and sickness) and eased holiday and off-site training cover.
- Championed implementation of new software as presented at the Annual Call Centre Technology Conference. Early indications [7]*is / are* that the software has increased productivity by 2%.

I [8]*would / will* relish the challenge of working for such a high-profile company and admire your [9]*commitment / commission* to customer service. I can [10]*assure / ensure* you that my experience, industry knowledge and track record to date make me a strong candidate for this role. Please [11]*read / find* my CV attached for further details.

I [12]*look / am looking* forward to hearing from you.

[13]*Kind regards / Yours faithfully*,

Chris Smith

---

2 There are three main sections to this letter: a short first section (pink) and third section (green), with a large second section (blue) sandwiched in the middle. This conforms to a standard structure. Which sections answer the following questions?

1 Who am I and why should you hire me?

2 Why am I writing?

3 Why do I want to work for you and why would I be an asset for your organisation?

Language focus 2: Correcting errors and writing with confidence

1 Read the letter again and choose the correct words in italics to complete it.

2 What three words or phrases in the letter demonstrate the candidate's enthusiasm? There is one example in each of the three sections.

3 The tables below show examples of 'overselling yourself' and 'underselling yourself'. Reorder the words in the second column of each table to make examples of strong, confident writing.

'Overselling yourself' by showing arrogance	Strong, confident writing
1 I am the best candidate for the job.	that make me / I have the right / a strong candidate / skills, experience and educational qualifications / for the job
2 You will definitely want to contact me to arrange an interview.	at any time / for an interview / convenient to you / I am available / over the coming weeks

'Underselling yourself'	Strong, confident writing
3 I was involved in a project where we had to conduct market research.	perceptions of the brand / a team project, / As part of / to find out customers' / I conducted market research
4 As a result of changing suppliers we were able to save a lot of money.	and managed to save / last year / our contracts with suppliers / I reviewed / the company over $120,000

Intercultural analysis

How appropriate is it to address a covering letter to someone using their first name (as in the example letter) in your industry, organisation or country culture?

Output: Write a CV covering letter

Find a job advert that you could realistically apply for, from a newspaper or online sources, and do the following.

Stage 1

Highlight the relevant key words in the job advert and reformulate them as notes to yourself to interpret what skills, experience and personality this organisation is really looking for. Compare your ideas with a partner.

Stage 2

Respond to this job advert with a CV covering letter using a simple three-paragraph structure and appropriate language and guidelines as presented in this unit.

Additional materials

Contents

1.1 Theory: An overview of market entry strategies

Output: Select an appropriate market entry strategy

Group A

Discuss the advantages and disadvantages of these two strategies for the school to fulfil its objective of attracting more international students. Think about levels of control, commitment of resources, risk exposure, profit opportunity and timescale. Take notes of the key points of your discussion, noting what changes you will have to make to existing operations in order to adopt either of these two strategies.

1 Set up own campus/premises abroad (Greenfield development).
2 Set up campus/premises abroad together with a local corporate training provider or private university (joint venture).

1.2 Practice: Entering the global market

Output: Selecting a franchise partner in a new country market

Angola
Local partner: Angolan lawyer who has come from a poor background to become a rich and successful corporate lawyer with an international law firm in Luanda. He is 46 years old with a big family. He enjoys a very active social life. His photo often appears in the country's main lifestyle magazine. He's looking for a career change and has been a member of Quintessentially for two years.
Characteristics of country market: A 27-year civil war ended in 2002. Angola is now one of Africa's major exporters of oil. Situated in Southern Africa, it joined OPEC in 2006. It has recently experienced some of the highest economic growth rates in the world, averaging 15% per annum, although over 40% of its population still live below the poverty line. Angola has a population of about 13 million with 4 million living in the capital city, Luanda. Portuguese is the main language spoken.

Serbia
Local partner: This young Serbian businesswoman in her mid-20s currently runs a successful computer software company which is part of a large business empire owned by her father. She is known to be bored with her job and looking for new exciting challenges. She is married to one of the country's most famous footballers. She speaks five languages including Russian, English and German. She has only recently become a member of Quintessentially.

Characteristics of country market: Serbia is a country of over 7 million people in South East Europe. Previously it had been the largest state within the Federation of Yugoslavia. A violent period of civil war led to the break-up of Yugoslavia at the end of the 20th century. The country is now rebuilding its economy and reintegrating into the international community. It is pursuing EU membership and implemented a Trade Agreement with the EU in 2010. The capital city, Belgrade, has a very lively nightclub scene and is home to over 1 million people. GNP per capita income is on a par with Brazil at $10,000 per annum.

Pakistan
Local partner: Educated in Pakistan and at Harvard Business School in the USA, this 50-year-old Pakistani businesswoman ran companies in the fashion business in the UK, the USA and Pakistan. She has recently sold a chain of fashionable boutique clothes shops she set up four years ago in the capital city, Islamabad. Quintessentially member for five years.
Characteristics of country market: Pakistan has a long border with India and Afghanistan and has the sixth-largest population in the world of over 180 million people. It has low levels of foreign investment and the level of poverty is high. Textiles account for most of the country's export earnings. Its main trading partners are the USA, the United Arab Emirates and Afghanistan. English is widely spoken by the upper classes and is the official language of government.

1.3 Skills: Brainstorming

Output: Brainstorming a new brand slogan

Group A

Facilitator's briefing notes

Brainstorming technique to be used: Lateral association

Time limit: 6 minutes

How to do it: Brainstorm everyone's lateral associations with this brand. Ask questions such as 'If this brand were a colour, what would it be?', 'If this brand were an animal/car/person what would it be?', etc. Write the colours/animals/names, etc. on a flipchart and the reason why these colours/animals, etc. were chosen. Write key phrases (not full sentences) on a flipchart sheet and put it up on the wall. Elect a 'scribe' if you feel you need some help.

2.1 Theory: Different approaches to international marketing

Output: Adapting advertising to fit different cultures

Group A

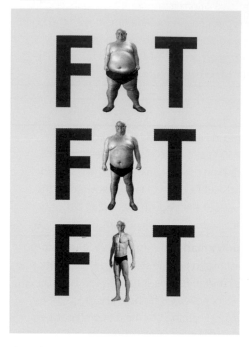

The advertisement is for an American gym. Discuss the following questions in your group.

- What do you think of the visual impact of the advertisement?
- What do you think is the message of the advertisement?
- Would advertising for a gym using an overweight person work in your country?
- What images do you usually associate with gyms and gym advertising?

2.2 Practice: Piaggio Vietnam

Output: Brand positioning

Group A

On the basis of your market research you believe that the company should adopt **a strategy for the new Piaggio brand that stays true to the core strengths and values of the company**. Your reasons for thinking this are set out below:

- Target market: The top end of the mass market. A scooter for people with a good level of disposable income.
- Key market concerns: Desire for high-quality scooter that is reliable and that looks and feels to be a premium product.
- Competition: Very strong and focused on keeping models affordable.
- Italian connection: This is essential. Vietnamese customer perception is 'Italy = quality'.
- Vespa connection: This is essential. It is not in the company DNA to focus on low cost. You see the Piaggio brand as a stepping stone to the Vespa brand.

Prepare a presentation by making recommendations for the marketing strategy regarding: positioning, promotion, branding, product and distribution (the dealer network). Make sure to prepare a good case by writing out two to four clear summary points of your discussion that you can memorise and deliver in the presentation, using the persuasive style presented in the Transferable skill section.

3.1 Theory: Five Forces Theory of Competition

Output: Analysis and presentation of an industry's competitive forces

Group A

In your group, discuss competitive rivalry for the industry you have chosen. You will need to make particular reference to the six influencing factors in Listening 2. Your discussion should cover the following bullet points – **for each point, you need to ask each other how the answers to the questions below affect competition within this industry.**

- How concentrated is this industry? Are the competitor companies the same size? Are there many of them? How monopolistic is this industry?
- How differentiated are the competitors' products/services in this industry? Can they easily be copied or not?
- How fast is the market growing? Is it confined to specific geographic markets?
- How easy is it to exit this industry and move into new industries? Has there been much evidence of this with the present industry competitors?
- How closely are customers tied into a company's product? How high are the switching costs for them to move to a competitor's product?
- How do companies' cost structures (especially the fixed cost element) impact on competition in this industry?

3.2 Practice: The UK budget hotel industry

Output: Presenting a hotel chain

Group A

Premier Inn

The chain – formerly Travel Inn then Premier Travel Inn and now Premier Inn – is the UK's biggest with more than 37,000 rooms in over 530 hotels, including high-profile locations such as County Hall on London's South Bank.

With an eye on the intense price competition from Travelodge, it emphasises the fact that it has rooms available at £50 per night or less (prices, you should note, are per room, not per person). Up to two children aged 15 or under can have a free breakfast when one adult has a full breakfast.

'Our guests have been enjoying staying with Premier Inn for more than 20 years,' the company says. 'They love the value we offer, our clean and comfortable rooms and the warm welcome they receive from our team members.'

4.2 Practice: Jack Ma and Alibaba

Group B

You are a company that manufactures high-quality pens. You sell the pens to luxury hotels and companies organising events, with their logo added. The hotels and companies give the pens away as gifts to selected clients and as a form of advertising. As China has a strong gift-giving business culture, hundreds of thousands of small and medium-sized businesses and an increasing number of foreign companies and hotels, you believe it will be an ideal market for your product.

The partner you are looking for:

- has links with the hotel industry and with local and foreign companies across China.
- has ideas of how you may be able to break into other markets in China.
- has excellent e-marketing skills who is able to exploit online channels to sell direct to local businesses.
- can work with local companies to finish the pens – adding the logos – in China, for your Chinese clients. (You plan to continue to manufacture from your home country as you have concerns about your product technology being copied by a local manufacturer.)

8.3 Skills: Dealing with Q&A

Output: Q&A session discussing staff redundancies

Group A
Senior Management

Stage 1: Setting up the Q&A

Discuss how you are going to manage the Q&A session at the end of this difficult presentation. In particular, be clear on what 'ground rules' you need to communicate to staff before beginning the Q&A.

Stage 2: Preparing for the Q&A

Anticipate difficult and hostile questions that you expect staff might ask you. Decide what strategies you will use to answer them. Summarise your discussion by completing the table below, then practise doing the Q&A as a 'dress rehearsal'.

Anticipated hostile/difficult questions	Strategies to be used in answering questions
1	
2	
3	
4	

Stage 3: Doing the Q&A

Get together with Group B (the staff) and have the Q&A session. As the senior managers, you should start the meeting by first setting up the Q&A and explaining the ground rules. The staff will ask you questions they prepared earlier. Answer them confidently, using relevant strategies.

6.3 Skills: Motivating staff

Output: Motivating a staff member

Manager

You are worried about a member of your staff. He/She used to be one of the best workers in your team and received good pay increases. However, over the past few months you have noticed the following problems:

- Sometimes comes late to work
- Does not always get involved in meetings, just sits silently, sometimes staring out of the window
- Has taken quite a few sick days

You have decided to call a meeting with the worker and try to improve the situation. Before the meeting, decide how you are going to motivate the employee and what you will say, ask and tell the employee.

9.1 Theory: Affordable innovation through reverse innovation

Output: Debate low-cost innovation solutions

Arguments	F/A
1 This is an example of top-down thinking by government administrators in countries with a state-funded health service.	
2 People in rich countries are no longer able or willing to pay for expensive medicines and treatment. This solution is demand-driven from the bottom up.	
3 The cost of the operation is only part of the equation. You also need to factor in travel costs and patient after-care services.	
4 There is always resistance to new radical ways of doing things at first, but then organisations (and people) generally act rationally.	
5 What is needed is an incremental approach to cost saving where costs are reduced step-by-step in a realistic way within the existing framework.	
6 A collaborative approach can help here where low-cost medical centres in the developing world can provide diagnostic services quickly and efficiently with online data transmission.	

7.2 Practice: Internationalising a company

Output: Developing an English policy for an international company

Management team

The CEO has given you responsibility for negotiating an agreement with the staff. Ideally, she wants all members of the company, including administrative staff, to have reached an upper-intermediate level within two years. She wants all written and spoken communication, including meeting minutes, documents, meetings, presentations and training seminars, to be in English. She wants the staff to pay for themselves, and staff who have not reached a sufficient level in two years should not have their contracts renewed. However, the CEO has said that achieving all these requirements may be too demanding, and she has therefore given you some flexibility to negotiate.

10.2 Practice: Dyson – a design-led company

Output: Explaining unusual inventions to potential investors

Group A Interchangeable High Heels

11.1 Theory: Government influence on the economic environment

Output: Assess impact of government and central bank action on a family household

Read the profile of the Chen family and discuss the following two points in your groups.

- Assess what impact the financial review and interest rate change will have on the Chen family.
- Make recommendations to the Chen family on what action to take to minimise any financial hardships now and plan for the future.

The Chen family

Mr Chen, 33, is a computer programmer with a major multinational software firm. He earns $70,000 a year. His wife Zara, 34, has a part-time job in the same company looking after network security; she earns $50,000 a year. Their little boy Nathan is four years old and will be going to school next year.

Family house

The Chens live in a nice area of their city with low levels of crime and good schools. They bought their house at the height of the boom 18 months ago for $600,000, with the help of their parents and a loan from the bank of $300,000. It's now worth about $450,000. Their bank presently charges them an interest rate of 3%. This is a variable rate tied to central bank rates; they are charged 1% over central bank rates.

Family savings

The Chens have savings of $50,000 in a savings account for 'a rainy day' and stock investments of $20,000 which they are hoping will be a long-term investment to pay for Nathan's university fees when he turns 18.

Family spending

Both Mr and Mrs Chen each have a number of credit cards that they normally pay off in full every month, although recently they haven't been doing so. The Chens have an active social life and like to go out two or three times a week to restaurants or bowling with friends.

11.3 Skills: Presenting charts and statistics

Transferable skill: Highlighting key data in a chart

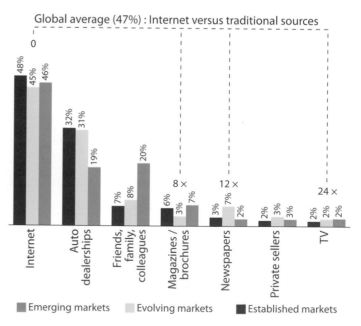

12.1 Theory: Free trade or protectionism?

Introduction

Hard-core protectionists (4–9 points)

You are anti-globalisation in the form that it exists at present and you might also be a firm believer in economic nationalism. You believe that free trade has been very damaging and that there have been few winners. The rich have got richer and the poor have got poorer.

In the middle (10–14 points)

You are either undecided or you have quite balanced views. You can see the advantages and disadvantages of trade liberalisation and globalisation. You are aware that you will have many benefits as a consumer with free trade; your choice of cars, phones, computers, clothes and other products and services will be much wider and you will pay less for them, compared to simply being offered products and services from your home country. However, you are also probably aware that local businesses and people at the bottom of the socio-economic scale can suffer from strong competition from abroad.

Hard-core free-traders (15–20 points)

You are a firm believer in free trade and globalisation. You think firms and individuals need to compete in a global marketplace and that tougher competition leads to the creation of strong, world-class companies. You believe that in the long term this is the best guarantee for job security for workers, offers the best choice to consumers, and provides the best returns for shareholders. Countries should specialise in what they do best. Protectionists don't appreciate that if they ban imports from abroad, their exports to those countries will also be banned, leading to job losses at home.

12.2 Practice: NAFTA and Mexico

Output: Discuss the merits of free trade

Student A

You are the managing director of your country's leading producer of innovative technologies in the electronics sector. You have the following concerns.

- This is an infant industry in your country and you believe it needs protecting.
- You are worried about better-quality imports coming in from the country you are signing a trade treaty with.
- You think that with freer movement of labour you will lose educated workers to the neighbouring country.
- You are also worried about cheaper imports coming into your country from other countries not in the treaty.

Prepare to present your case to the Minister of Economic Development and think how he/she may try to counter your concerns.

14.1 Theory: Perspectives on social enterprise

Output: Crisis meeting

Group A

You are in favour of making cuts to the services you provide. Whilst you understand their social value, you also recognise that if Centro doesn't balance its books it will have to close completely and its assets will be sold. If that happens, Centro will be providing no services at all to local residents! There is absolutely no room to make any more cuts to HQ costs or to move the loan to another bank. Your research also shows that the rents you are now charging for shops, restaurants and luxury apartments are market rents. It will be difficult to increase these rents, especially as the economic climate at the moment is not looking good.

14.3 Skills: Conference calls

Output: Conference call to discuss branding

Company CEO (Morocco)

You are chairing the meeting and want to hear different people's ideas on how to market the new brand. Look back at the tips in the Introduction and the functions in Language focus 1 to decide how you are going to manage the meeting.

1.1 Theory: An overview of market entry strategies

Output: Select an appropriate market entry strategy

Group B

Discuss the advantages and disadvantages of these two strategies for the school to fulfil its objective of attracting more international students. Think about levels of control, commitment of resources, risk exposure, profit opportunity and timescale. Take notes of the key points of your discussion, noting what changes you will have to make to existing operations in order to adopt either of these two strategies.

1 Sign deals with existing private universities and corporate training providers abroad to create 'associate' status campuses / training providers abroad (a form of licensing or franchising).
2 Take stands in international education trade fairs abroad (direct importing).

1.3 Skills: Brainstorming

Output: Brainstorming a new brand slogan

Group B

<u>Facilitator's briefing notes</u>

Brainstorming technique to be used: Provocation, also known as 'Shoot the boss'

Time limit: 6 minutes

How to do it: Get the people in your group to shout out some really inappropriate/ridiculous/stupid/crazy slogans for this brand. Encourage them to be extreme and provocative. For example, a crazy slogan for a coffee brand might be: 'Disgusting to the last drop'. Write key phrases (not full sentences) on a flipchart. After a few minutes, ask everyone to do some reverse thinking and reverse these crazy slogans. For example, 'Disgusting to the last drop' becomes 'Good to the last drop' – a famous advertising slogan for Maxwell House, a well-known coffee brand. Write the reversed slogans on the flipchart. Elect a 'scribe' if you feel you need some help.

2.1 Theory: Different approaches to international marketing

Output: Adapting advertising to fit different cultures

Group B

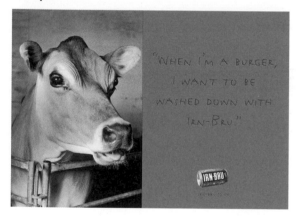

The advertisement is for the most popular soft drink in Scotland. Discuss the following questions in your group.

- What do you think of the visual impact of the advertisement?
- What do you think of the use of humour?
- The advertisement offended some vegetarians in the UK. Would this be a problem in your country?
- What type of advertising messages do soft drinks in your country try to get across?

2.2 Practice: Piaggio Vietnam

Output: Brand positioning

Group B

On the basis of your market research you believe that the company should adopt **a totally different strategy for the new Piaggio brand compared to the Vespa brand**. Your reasons for thinking this are set out below:

- Target market: The mass market. A scooter for city workers on low to medium incomes.
- Key target market concerns: Customers are highly price sensitive.
- Competition: Very strong and focused on keeping models affordable.
- Differentiation from Italy: This is critical. The scooter itself needs differentiation from Italian models – roads in Vietnam are in variable condition, the monsoon climate is also very different. Also promotion needs differentiating – Vietnamese customer perception is 'Italy = expensive'.
- Differentiation from Vespa: This is critical. Customers want a reliable workhorse, not a style icon.

Prepare a presentation by making recommendations for the marketing strategy regarding: positioning, promotion, branding, product and distribution (the dealer network). Make sure to prepare a good case by writing out two to four clear summary points of your discussion that you can memorise and deliver in the presentation, using the persuasive style presented in the Transferable skill section.

3.1 Theory: Five Forces Theory of Competition

Output: Analysis and presentation of an industry's competitive forces

Group B

In your group, discuss the supplier power and threat of new entrants for the industry you have chosen. Your discussion should cover the following bullet points – **for each point, you need to ask each other how the answers to the questions below affect competition within this industry.**

Supplier power

- Who are the different suppliers for this industry?
- How concentrated are these supplier groups? Are they all the same size? Are there many of them?
- How unique is the product or service from the key suppliers? How high are the switching costs for companies in the industry to move to another supplier?

Threat of new entrants

- Who are they? How fast are they growing? Where do they come from?
- What kind of threats might these new entrants pose in the future?
- How much know-how, technology and finance is needed to enter this industry?

4.2 Practice: Jack Ma and Alibaba

Group C

You are an office supply retailer with a network of shops across China. Your brand is well known. You sell a full range office supply products (everything from photocopy paper to office furniture) to small businesses and to individuals with home offices across mainland China. You have recently started to sell products from a number of foreign companies and this side of your business is expanding fast. You are now actively looking to supplement your product range with high-quality innovative products from abroad.

What you offer:

- The management are highly experienced and have been working in the company all their lives. Some speak good English, although none have studied abroad.
- An excellent distribution and sales network across the whole of China.
- Being a well-established company, you have good connections with local and regional governments where you operate. A number of these officials are personal friends of the directors.
- You are one of the best-known office supply companies in the country with a turnover of $300 million. Ten percent of your turnover comes from online sales through your website.

6.3 Skills: Motivating staff

Output: Motivating a staff member

Employee

Recently you have been having some problems at home, and have been having difficulty concentrating at work. You know you are a good worker, and have always received good pay increases. You are wondering about getting promotion in the future because you think you need a new challenge. Your boss has called a meeting, but you don't know what it's about. Try to raise the issue of your promotion.

Before the meeting, think about what you want to say, and how you want to say it.

7.2 Practice: Internationalising a company

Output: Developing an English policy for an international company

Staff team

You are quite worried that the CEO's plan might fail, because it is too demanding and you may not have sufficient support. You think that the use of English in your company should be staggered, with senior management using it first in their meetings. The following year middle management would be required to use it, and so on until after five years all management and administrative staff should have reached an intermediate level. However, you think that the use of written English documents could be introduced earlier if necessary. In meetings, you think English should only be used when there is someone present who doesn't speak your first language. You would also like to see at least some financial support provided for all employees. You also think that some incentives would be effective, such as bonuses for those staff who improve the most. You realise you will have to negotiate over these points, and not all of them may be achievable.

8.2 Practice: Offshore outsourcing provider's perspective

Output: Resolve misunderstandings between client and outsourcing provider

Group B

You work for Rock Solid Support. A number of problems have occurred with the passenger booking and information service you operate from your call centre for Star Air. These problems have a number of causes which you feel are largely outside your control. Read through the problems and brainstorm practical steps to resolve them.

Problem 1: Certain contract clauses between you and client are unclear

The contract states 'calls should be replied to promptly'. You interpret that to mean 'within 4 rings', and generally you feel you manage to fulfil this performance standard. However, Star Air is now starting to say that 'promptly' means 'within 2 rings'. This needs re-negotiating.

Problem 2: Communication channels with the client are one-way only

You receive huge amounts of customer service feedback from Star Air which is critical of your staff's level of English and service levels. You are trying to address the problems by seeking clarifications, better information and software fixes from Star Air but you are getting very little response.

Problem 3: Problems with software provided by client

Front-line staff are having problems inputting data for new travel arrangements as there are constant changes to Star Air's seat booking software. The result is that frontline staff have to refer calls to supervisors who have more technical expertise. This is not the primary role for supervisors though, and they are unhappy about doing this sort of work.

Problem 4: Difficulty in recruiting enough staff with right skills

Since the contract was signed, the competition to hire staff has intensified significantly. To get the right quality of people you need to pay much higher wages. Although you wouldn't want to admit it publicly, the low contract fees you receive to operate this service from Star Air mean that you don't assign your best people to this contract!

8.3 Skills: Dealing with Q&A

Output: Q&A session discussing staff redundancies

Group B
Staff

Stage 1: Anticipating the Q&A set-up

The senior staff are going to try to control the meeting by setting the 'ground rules' for the Q&A. Try to anticipate what these ground rules might be and work out strategies for how you can deal with them.

Stage 2: Preparing for the Q&A

Discuss the questions you want to ask. Select the most important ones and write them in the table below – make sure to use a variety of question types to keep the bosses 'on their toes'. Try to anticipate what strategies senior managers will use to deal with your questions and how you can effectively respond to this – note this down in the table. Practise doing the Q&A as a 'dress rehearsal'.

Questions	Strategies to be used in answering questions
1	
2	
3	
4	

Stage 3: Doing the Q&A

Get together with Group A (senior managers) and have the Q&A session. The senior managers will start the meeting by first setting up the Q&A and explaining the ground rules. As the staff, you will ask the questions you prepared earlier. Ask the questions confidently and be prepared to ask follow-up questions if necessary.

9.3 Skills: Dealing with criticism

Output: Making and taking criticism

Student A

You are the manager. Your employee spent a large amount of last year's advertising budget on TV advertising; however, your sales have not increased. You have a very direct style and think the employee should be made to feel bad about the situation. Think about what questions you will ask and what criticism you will make.

10.2 Practice: Dyson – a design-led company

Output: Explaining unusual inventions to potential investors

Group B Eye-Drop Applicator

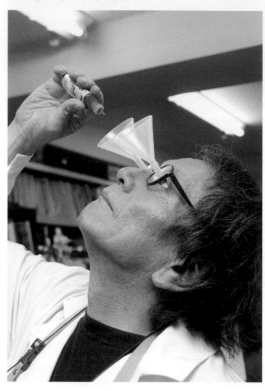

14.1 Theory: Perspectives on social enterprise

Output: Crisis meeting

Group B

You are in favour of finding any solution to this financial crisis that involves very little or even no cuts to the services, facilities and green spaces you provide the local community. Local residents have nothing else. You are a social enterprise, not a profit-making company and it's about time certain people realised what the true goals and objectives are! You feel strongly that you are not charging enough for the shops, restaurants and luxury apartments you own. You might accept some very limited cuts in HQ costs and you might be willing to accept some limited corporate sponsorship, but you don't want local residents to suffer and you don't want Centro to look too commercial.

14.3 Skills: Conference calls

Output: Conference call to discuss branding

External Marketing Consultant (UK)

You have some ideas on how to market the brand. You think that the positive social and environmental message of recycled clothes and shoes in particular needs to be strongly communicated both in the brand name and in the promotional message. This is what appeals to a key group of customers. Try to think of a name for the brand and ways to market it. How will you convince the others your ideas are the best?

1.1 Theory: An overview of market entry strategies

Output: Select an appropriate market entry strategy

Group C

Discuss the advantages and disadvantages of these two strategies for the school to fulfil its objective of attracting more international students. Think about levels of control, commitment of resources, risk exposure, profit opportunity and timescale. Take notes of the key points of your discussion, noting what changes you will have to make to existing operations in order to adopt either of these two strategies.

1 Provide training courses through online distance learning (direct exporting / electronic distribution using digital formats).

2 Buy a corporate training provider abroad (acquisition).

4.2 Practice: Jack Ma and Alibaba

Output: Starting business in China

Group D

You are a fast-growing company established three years ago. You are specialised in distribution of a range of office supplies (from paper clips to office desks) in Shanghai and the surrounding area. This is a market of over 30 million people, with average incomes 60% higher than the national average. You make all your sales online. Half the products you supply come from manufacturers located abroad. You are particularly interested in expanding this part of your business.

What you offer:

- A database of clients with $1 million of direct sales through your website and further $5 million through intermediary online channels such as Alibaba.com. As your website is also translated into English you do a sizeable proportion of your business with international companies located in the city.
- A small management team from Shanghai with an average age of 35. All speak English and have studied abroad, mainly in the UK and the USA. Most are qualified with MBAs.
- You have recently started to provide consultancy services to help foreign companies do business in China and are keen to expand this new line of business.

Audio scripts

1 Market entry strategies
1.1 Theory: An overview of market entry strategies

Listening: Defining different types of market entry strategies

 1.02

Dr Dennis De

Indirect exporting

Small and medium-sized companies can use export agents based in the exporter's home country, or use export houses to enter international markets. They buy from the supplier and sell to their customers in a different country. If most of the companies or the customers you want to address, let's say in Japan, don't know you, they don't know how reliable you are as a supplier. Or how good and reliable your products are. So if an export house already has good relationships with customers, it's very easy for foreign companies to use them. Companies use the service of export houses and export agents as a first entry step to get a feeling for the market.

Direct exporting

At some point, after testing the market through indirect exporting, you might look for a corporate partner in the target market you're exporting to. That could be a distributor or could also be another company; it's usually not a competitor, but a company that sells a certain variety of products and can nicely complement its product portfolio with your product. So they have their customers in the country already and you're basically surfing that.

Acquisition

Acquisition can be a very interesting way of entering a country because you're acquiring a presence in a country and a list of customers this company happens to have already. So that makes life easier for you. You might even have some production within the country; all of that is very helpful. The problem often is integrating your acquisition. You'll have some restructuring to do, and some integrating of this new business with your business. The other problem is one of paying the right price. What is the company really worth?

Greenfield development

If you do a Greenfield it's like planting a new garden; you can design everything afresh according to your plans. Completely new production facilities. There's a lot of freedom – you don't have all the difficulties and integration that you have with acquisition. So these are huge advantages. The disadvantage is that you don't have a customer base you start off with. So you're not buying into a given distribution or sales structure.

Joint venture

A joint venture involves two companies setting up a third together that they jointly own – the new joint venture company. In my experience it's not a useful strategy for companies to pursue, as roughly eighty percent of all joint ventures actually fail within the first five years. That's because the motivation behind setting up the JV is different for the two companies involved. Basically the local company, in China for example, wants to gain know-how and technology and offers access to its customers in China to the international company through a fifty-fifty joint venture. Eventually the local company will have understood and grabbed the know-how and doesn't need you any longer, because it has the access to its customers anyway.

Franchising

Franchising is a sales model – a distribution model. So you have a particular product, or a way to serve a product, like coffee for instance. Take Starbucks. This is the right to serve coffee in a certain way with certain mugs and a certain logo and in a certain fashion – a system. And you, as the franchisor can rent out this right, and charge the franchisee a percentage of their turnover for the right to run the franchise. The franchise model is going to give you a lot of control because when you rent out the right to sell your products using your brand you do so under certain conditions. You may want to stipulate the way the product is sold for instance, the way it's presented. You might even define the price at which it is sold.

1.2 Practice: Entering the global market

Listening 1: Quintessentially client profile

 1.03

Interviewer: Can you tell us something about who the typical Quintessentially member is?

Paul Drummond: The typical profile is about sixty percent male, forty percent female and between thirty-five and fifty-five, but obviously can be younger or older. They tend to be business people or entrepreneurs, and successful in their own right. Obviously we have celebrities in the entertainment business, models and so on, but typically it is your high net worth business traveller, or business executive.

Interviewer: And in terms of personality, lifestyle and aspirations?

Paul Drummond: The key determining factor is that members travel a lot. They are typically people who like the finer things in life and are sophisticated in that way, and like to do exciting and interesting things. They won't be reclusive millionaires.

Interviewer: What kind of unusual requests do members make?

Paul Drummond: The first thing I want to say is that the majority of what we do is very practical – assisting members when they are going from A to B to C to D. But in terms of unusual requests there have been many: for example, we closed the Sydney Harbour Bridge so a member could propose to his partner at the top of it.

Listening 2: Characteristics of new country markets and local partners

 1.04

Interviewer: What are some of the issues you consider when deciding on entering a new country market?

Paul Drummond: We look to see whether there's a good base of high net worth individuals who could potentially be members. Is there a vibrant restaurant scene, a nightclub scene, events party scene?

Interviewer: How do you choose a local partner?

Paul Drummond: Typically we're approached through our existing membership network. Somebody has joined up, really liked the service and then gone 'Well, you're in New York and you're in London – why aren't you in Kuwait, or Saudi Arabia?' And then we have gone and met with them, got to know more about them and then worked out if there is a business opportunity for them and for us in their city.

Interviewer: How important are first impressions when you actually meet that potential partner for the first time?

Paul Drummond: Oh, I think they're very, very important, because it is fundamentally a people business. So if your first impressions aren't spot on, or aren't positive anyway, then you need to think again. I mean, it's not a hundred percent as I'm sure you know, but this business is driven by the dynamism of the individuals in it. And so we take it as read that potential partners are well connected, sophisticated and well positioned within, you know, whatever country it is. What I'm always looking for is people who are entrepreneurial. People who have lots of energy and are driven to succeed. What we don't really want are people who are attracted by the brand for the brand's sake.

Listening 3: Quintessentially's market entry strategy

 1.05

Interviewer: What is Quintessentially's preferred method of entry into a new international market?

Paul Drummond: Our preferred one is through a franchise model. We've got our own offices which we own a hundred percent of, and we operate a kind of hub and spokes structure. So in each of the regions of the world we have a wholly owned office. So America is New York, London is Europe, Dubai is Middle East and Africa, and Hong Kong is the Far East. And then off that we typically run franchises which are managed by the hub office. There are a number of reasons for that – one is, obviously, the partner takes the capital costs involved in setting up the office. And I don't think we would have expanded as quickly as we have without that. But it's not just about the cost side of things. It's actually very important for the cultural side too. What do I know about the local society and contacts in, for example, South Korea and Seoul? Well, now a lot more, but before it was very little.

Interviewer: What kind of control of your international operations does Quintessentially head office feel is desirable?

Paul Drummond: We are a brand and service business, so it's important that the brand is projected in a consistent way across the world. And it's important that when a member goes to Athens or to São Paulo, that they are treated the same, at the same high level. And so control is a key factor – I mean, it's a cliché, but 'you are only as strong as your weakest link', and if a member has a horrific experience in, er Seoul or Tokyo, even if they mostly spend their time in London or New York, then they're going to remember that experience.

1.3 Skills: Brainstorming

Listening 1: Principles of running a classic brainstorming session

 1.06

Manager: One of the best ways of generating ideas is brainstorming. Everybody used to brainstorming? It's really easy, very easy. What you do, you have your group together, and you have a facilitator, somebody that presents the problem, and you also have somebody that's going to be the scribe. Their job is just writing – on a whiteboard, or a flipchart. You sit round and you tell them that they can say anything they like, no holds barred, and nobody's going to criticise anything they say. The problem is presented, and they think about it for a minute, and then they say anything that comes into their head. And I mean anything. And the scribe just writes it up, as fast as he can. The idea is that it's quantity that breeds quality. Because the more ideas you get, the better your problem-solving is likely to be. If you only get a few ideas, you've only got a few things to look at. Whereas the more ideas you get, the more chances you've got of getting something that's really good. But you don't at any stage say, 'What did you say that for?' – you know, something like that, you just don't do that sort of thing. You allow people to say what they like, write it down. Also you have to set a time limit because people get tired, it takes a lot of energy to do this, and concentrate on it. So you set your time limit, right we'll have say twenty minutes, half an hour at the most, then you stop and look at it, and say 'Anybody want to add anything else?' When you've finished, you just tear off all your flipcharts, and put them up round the room so people can read them. You then move on to the selective phase where you start to narrow …

 1.07

The audio script is in the unit (see page 16).

1.08 1.09 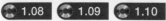 1.10

1

1 Anyone else got anything to add here?
2 Mandy, what do you think about that?
3 That's a great idea!
4 What about building on Paul's idea to …

4

1 We're going to start by looking at …
2 How about going with Ian's idea to …
3 Let's go with this idea of …
4 Maybe we should go with Dave's idea of …

5

1 I'm lovin' it
2 Because you're worth it
3 Just do it

2 Standardisation and differentiation
2.2 Practice: Piaggio Vietnam

Listening 1: Brand strategy

 1.11

Interviewer: How can you take a brand which is so closely related to Italian culture and internationalise it, or make it relevant to Vietnamese consumers?

Costantino Sambuy: We're entering the Vietnamese market with the Vespa brand which is an extremely strong brand, that remains the same all over the world. Our values are linked with heritage, with design, with Italy, with glamour. Whoever buys a Vespa is buying an Italian dream. So we're positioning this brand in exactly the same way as we would do in England, or in America. The second phase of the penetration of the Vietnamese market is going to be different, because in that phase we are going to enter with another brand: the Piaggio brand with a series of plastic scooters, the Vespa on the other hand is made of metal. So with Vespa we are entering the local market at three times the price of a typical competitor scooter. With Piaggio the price will be ten to twenty percent higher than the local market. So at the moment the first entry is very much at the top of the pyramid … actually, we are creating the top of the pyramid because the market doesn't exist, and then the second phase we are going to go closer to the mass market but still at the top end of this. With the Piaggio brand, our product will need to be incredibly adapted to the local market. The basic concept though remains the same in Vietnam. We are not going to go to the bottom end of the mass market with a product that we may be technically able to make but is a product that we have never made before. It's not that we don't know how to make it, but it is not really our core market. We're not a low-quality brand. It's not in our core DNA.

 1.12

Interviewer: How is the promotion and advertising strategy for Vespa different in Vietnam compared to your home market in Italy?

Costantino Sambuy: It's similar, but in Vietnam there is much more emphasis on Italy. An Italian icon. In Italy you don't say it's an Italian icon, it's obvious, it's irrelevant. So here in Vietnam we very much underline the Italian heritage. And secondly we make the positioning a bit more extreme. So we make it, in this case, much more glamorous, much more fashionable than it is in Italy. Our dealer network in Vietnam has this standardised branding too. It's very professionally organised. In Europe, whenever we go to our motorcycle dealer, to a scooter dealer, you will see them with different methods, different colours, different branding. Here, in Vietnam, dealers are all the same, in uniforms, following the same instructions. You find a similar concept in Europe, but only in flagship stores. So today we have seventy points of sale around the country which are all exactly the same, always the premium image that we require, always the product displayed how we require it.

Interviewer: Right. What about celebrities? Who do you use to promote the brand image?

Costantino Sambuy: Historically, Vespa has positioned itself strongly in the cinema business, starting with 'Roman Holiday' onwards. And so there is some activity happening on a global scale. But we tend to use local celebrities, because they are more relevant to the everyday people who buy our product. Even though we do use the big Hollywood stars such as DiCaprio. But we still try to associate with the local market.

Listening 3: Product strategy

 1.13

Interviewer: If I've got an Italian Vespa LX, made in your factory in Italy, and the Vietnamese Vespa LX made in your factory in Vietnam, are they identical?

Costantino Sambuy: The two Vespas are exactly the same for … I would say ninety-eight percent of the components. There are only two modifications we make for the ergonomics of the Asian customer. The seat is slightly lower, and the handbrakes are slightly closer to the handlebar because the hands are slightly smaller. So we just had to adapt to the local customer. From a product standpoint it is the same, the engine is the same, the suspension is the same because the customer usage of the product is the same. This is not a workhorse, this is something you want to be seen with around town with your friends. It's something you want to be brightly coloured, you want a fantastic colour on it, and the same thing would happen in Italy. So the positioning is the same, the product is the same. And actually, if we changed something, we would not sell it! To give an example: we added a very fashionable colour, a fuchsia, a strong pink, thinking that that would be a great colour, and widely appreciated. People went online and saw that this product was not distributed in Italy, therefore it was not originally from Italy, and therefore they didn't buy it. This was a huge failure. So as soon as we start innovating locally, we force it locally, it doesn't work. So that really taught us a lesson.

1.14

1 Our values are linked with heritage, with design, with Italy, with glamour.
2 So we make it, in this case, much more glamorous, much more fashionable than it is in Italy.
3 From a product standpoint it is the same, the engine is the same, the suspension is the same because the customer usage of the product is the same.

2.3 Skills: Managing time

Listening 1: Lecture on time management

 1.15

Randy Pausch: Let's talk first about goals, priority and planning. Any time anything crosses your life you've got to ask, this thing I'm thinking about doing – why am I doing it? Almost no one that I know starts with the core principle of 'There is this thing on my "to-do" list, why is it there? What is the goal? Why will I succeed at doing it?' And here's my favourite. 'What will happen if I don't do it?'

The other thing to remember is that experience comes with time and it's really, really valuable and there are no short cuts to getting it. So good judgement comes from experience, and experience comes from bad judgement. So if things aren't going well, that probably means you're learning a lot and it'll go better later.

Planning is very important: one of the time management clichés is 'Failing to plan is planning to fail'. And planning has to be done at multiple levels. I have a plan every morning when I wake up and I say what do I need to get done today, what do I need to get done this week, what do I need to get done each semester. And that doesn't mean you are locked into it. People say 'Yeah, but things are so fluid, you know I am going to have to change the plan', and I'm like 'Yes. You are going to have to change the plan'. But you can't change it unless you have it. So have a plan, acknowledge that you are going to change it, but have it so you have the basis to start with.

The last thing about 'to-do' lists, or getting yourself going, is if you've got a bunch of things to do, do the ugliest thing first.

Listening 2: IT company team meeting

 1.16

Jennifer: I'm not sure how popular this is going to be, I was thinking of, and this will include myself, well, being more strict with deadlines.
William: It would have helped me quite a lot because that last project took me ages.
Jennifer: Well, that's what I was thinking.
William: But I do set my own deadlines, but then they just change.
Jennifer: Yeah. Well, that's what I was thinking 'cause I do the same. When nobody's actually checking up on you it's very easy just to move a few weeks.
William: You just move it. And I do the same with revision. I've got really lazy on that. It depends how good people think they are at giving themselves their own deadlines. But I mean it might help me. I think it might help me to do exams, for instance.

Steve: There is a slight problem with that, because, say it was happening in June and you set yourself a deadline, in the preceding weeks there happened to be like a lot of maybe illnesses or holidays coming up.
William: Yeah. That's the other thing.
Steve: If you're on your own you can't always predict how busy you are.
Jennifer: No, absolutely. But what I'm saying is, we have deadlines and then if you say, you came to the week before you knew your deadline was up and then you said to me that I'm not going to meet this deadline because, you know, last week three people were off sick or I've been on my own all week or something. Then we could sit down and work out a … a new deadline so that, you know, that we could agree on. 'Cause at the minute we're just sort of going indefinitely on and on and on. Without any cut-off point.

Writing 1: Writing notes for presentations

 1.17

Slide 1 – Creating DRTV

Andrew Guy: Thank you for inviting me along to talk about using TV adverts to further the aims of your organisation. I'm going to start by telling you a bit about the background to creating a TV advert.

Slide 2 – Principles of DRTV

Andrew Guy: So, let's talk a little bit about the basic principles of DRTV. There are two key parts to DRTV. One is an emotional connection with the subject-matter. You have to get people to care before they start thinking about your cause and before they will start donating money. The first thing you have to do is appeal to people's emotions and then you give them the reasons to support you.

 1.18

Slide 3 – Reasons

Andrew Guy: So what reasons do you need to give people to get them to respond? The first thing to say is that in your TV advert you have to give someone a very, very simple idea of why they should respond. And it has to be compelling. It has to be immediate. There has to be a reason why people should want to care now, and involved in there should be persuasive, engaging words. Be very, very wary of the clever idea that some agencies might pitch. DRTV is not a sophisticated format, it doesn't lend itself to clever, creative ideas that some of the big agencies might like to pitch. It has to be very simple. It has to be based around something that everyone can understand in a short space of time. It has to be simple.

Slide 4 – Reasons

Andrew Guy: The length of the advert is absolutely critical, and in some ways the more you say, the more you sell, and so we tend to recommend that ninety seconds is ideal. Sixty seconds is possible, but a thirty-second advert is far too short. Within that ninety seconds you should include lots of captions, lots of voice-over. We want to see the telephone number and we want to see it big at the bottom of the screen. And we want to hear as much as possible about the need and the solution that your organisation's providing. And as I said in the previous slide, don't be clever. Keep it simple. And most important of all, make it clear from the very beginning of the advert that you are expecting a response – you want them to give you their money.

Competition within industries

3.1 Theory: Five Forces Theory of Competition

Listening 1: General description of the 'Five Forces' diagram

 1.19

Interviewer: Porter's Five Forces model explains a firm's competitiveness. He's saying that the state of competition in an industry depends upon five basic competitive forces. Can you talk us through the model?

Alex Muresan: The five forces that we have are three which Porter considers to be from horizontal competition – the threat of new entrants, competitive rivalry among existing competitors and the threat of substitute products or services. And the other two forces are what Porter calls vertical competitions. These are the bargaining power of suppliers and bargaining power of buyers. All these …

Interviewer: Can I just interrupt you a second? What does he mean by 'horizontal competition' and 'vertical competition'?

Alex Muresan: Well, when you think of the supply chain. – if you visualise it vertically from suppliers all the way to buyers – you've got the suppliers, which would be your manufacturers. You've got some intermediates there, like wholesalers. Then you'll have potentially the retailers in your supply chain and then the customers, the buyers. So if you position it vertically, this is your vertical chain. The horizontal level is those people who compete on the same level with you; they're supplying the same or substitute products to the market that you target. So it would be similar businesses to yours, competitors of yours, but on the same level in the supply chain.

Interviewer: Right.

Alex Muresan: Now any change in these forces normally requires the business to reassess the market place, given the overall change in industry information. So the arrows show there is an influence on the part of these factors onto your organisation.

Listening 2: Analysis of competitive rivalry

1.20

Alex Muresan: For most industries, the intensity of competitive rivalry is the major determinant of competitiveness and this depends on a number of factors as well. One of them is the concentration of the industry. What Porter means by this is that, for example, an industry with many competitors of equal size will lead to more intense rivalry – the pressure on companies to compete will be higher, as they are more likely to have similar strengths and weaknesses. Another factor is the rate of market growth. If you have slow growth you will have greater rivalry. High-growth markets, less rivalry.

Interviewer: Because in low-growth markets, they'll be competing …

Alex Muresan: For the same customers. Yes. And usually in slow-growth markets, for example, you'll be struggling to target the same customers as everybody else. Another factor would be the structure of costs and this is to do with the costs incurred by organisations, in that particular industry or sector. When an organisation incurs high fixed costs, for example, the pressure will be price cutting to fill capacity which will increase competitive pressures. Then there is another factor called a degree of differentiation and its …

Interviewer: This is still competitive rivalry?

Alex Muresan: Yes. It's another factor that influences competitive rivalry. There are a number of them. Some products cannot be copied easily; they are highly differentiated and some are strongly branded, which differentiates them even more. In this kind of case, customers see the difference between different products, and so have a reason for buying a particular product. This kind of environment is associated with less intense rivalry. The opposite is true where more intense competitive pressures in an industry occur and customers see products from different companies as very similar. In this situation, they tend to buy the product with the lowest price.

Interviewer: Right.

Alex Muresan: Then we have switching costs. When switching costs are high – because the product is specialised and the customer has invested a lot of resources in learning how to use it – rivalry is reduced. So customers tend to stick with the product that they have invested the most money, effort and time in.

Finally, you have exit barriers. When exit barriers to leaving a market are high, the rivalry will be more intense than when they are low. So companies won't quickly or easily exit industries if they don't see opportunities elsewhere.

3.3 Skills: Making a sales pitch

Listening: Sales presentation

1.21

Speaker: Imagine the scenario … You've got a great business. Things are moving forward. You're generating more income. Employing more people. The only thing is, all of these good things lead to more administrative tasks, more paperwork, more communication channels and more people to share information with – giving you an ever-increasing need to organise and tie together strands of expanding information before they fly out of control.

All of this takes your precious time away from doing what you do best – making your business flourish. And you don't want to stop that whilst it's in full flight.

So you put things off – 'it's on my "to-do list". But the longer you leave it, the more chaotic things get as you struggle to keep on top of it all – information might not be on-hand when you need it, and sales leads could start slipping through the net.

Sound familiar?

It's the growing pains of any successful business. But Bizantra means it doesn't have to be this way. Bizantra offers you a complete, low-cost suite of all the essential applications you need to organise and grow your business efficiently.

Bizantra means you don't have to rely on clunky, expensive and complicated software aimed at big corporations. Bizantra is a simple, intuitive and cost-effective alternative. And when you come to look back at this exciting stage of your company's growth, you'll recognise it as a time when you really started to step up your business game.

Exercise 2

 1.22

1 You've got a great business.
2 … more administrative tasks, more paperwork, more communication channels.
3 Sound familiar?
4 It's the growing pains of any successful business. But Bizantra means it doesn't have to be this way.
5 Bizantra is a simple, intuitive and cost-effective alternative.

Language focus 1: Presentation techniques of persuasion

 1.23

Bizantra is an integrated suite of all the essential, latest-technology business tools for the smarter, smaller business. It gives you everything a growing business needs, all in one place and for just a small subscription fee.

Bizantra makes collaborating easy. Use as many of Bizantra's Shared Spaces as you need to connect with your team, whether they're across the office or on the other side of the world. Share documents, discussions, tasks and contacts with whomever you want, wherever they are.

Whether you're on or offline, at your PC or on the web, with Bizantra you'll have access to your whole business, whenever you need it.

Create opportunities and strengthen customer relationships with our powerful Contact Management and Email Marketing. Store contacts, track discussions and prioritise your sales efforts in one place, then set up email marketing campaigns in minutes.

Stay on top of increasing staff demands with Bizantra HR. Easily manages record keeping, absence tracking and compliance to help make informed staffing decisions, fast.

Designed for smaller businesses, our easy-to-use Finance application gives you an at-a-glance summary of all your finances so you can manage them easily. Giving you more time to focus on what makes your business tick.

Bizantra does all that and much more. And it comes with rock-solid security, so you know that, even if your PC fails you, Bizantra won't.

Bizantra is integrated, efficient and simple. You don't need technical expertise; you just sign up, download and away you go. And with a no-commitment, great-value price, you'll wonder how you did business without it.

Why not see for yourself? Sign up for a free 60-day trial now.

Language focus 2: Pausing and stressing words in presentations

 1.24

Exercise 3

1 … You've got a great business. Things are moving forward. You're generating more income. Employing more people.
2 … You've got a great business. Things are moving forward. You're generating more income. Employing more people.

4 Entrepreneurship
4.1 Theory: Fostering entrepreneurship

Listening 1: New research on risk

 1.25

Interviewer: Can you tell us a little bit about what the new risk research tells us? And why it is important for the business community?

Dr Shai Vyakarnam: We saw this as an opportunity, between the Centre for Entrepreneurial Learning and the Department of Psychiatry, to look at entrepreneurship in a slightly different way. We thought it would be fun to apply some of the tests that the psychiatrists normally do to our entrepreneurs, and compare them with so-called successful normal managers.

Interviewer: And were the results very different?

Dr Shai Vyakarnam: The tests were conducted between hot and cold decision-making. The cold parts are the calculating parts – the mitigating of risk, and analysing situations. And in those cases there's no difference actually between entrepreneurs and other successful people. But the difference arose really in the so-called hot decision-making. The impulsivity tests. The test of gambling. The test of taking risks. And the differences are really stark.

Interviewer: So entrepreneurs are risk-takers. Does that mean they don't quite fit into management models of today?

Dr Shai Vyakarnam: Well, that's quite possible. There's certainly this group of serial entrepreneurs, the risk-takers. They've started more than two companies. Some over fifty. And I guess if we're looking at their approach to impulsive behaviours, it goes contrary to the flow of management generally, which is all about business planning, budgeting and so on. And so the impulsiveness of the entrepreneur combined with the planning skills traditionally connected with management roles would be the ideal combination. Entrepreneurs, if they are impulsive, wouldn't fit ideally into the management role.

Listening 2: Young entrepreneurs

1.26

Interviewer: Young people take more risks so if you want to be an entrepreneur, you ought to start your business when you're young?

Dr Shai Vyakarnam: Yes. That's a really interesting point because the data is showing us that a 51-year-old entrepreneur, serial entrepreneur, has a very similar risk profile to most 17- to 27-year-olds. Whereas managers have a similar risk profile to people of their same age across the population as a whole. So certainly if the younger people are more open to taking risk – have a higher appetite for it, then we should give advice which goes contrary to what they normally get. We normally tell graduates 'Go get a proper job. Get some experience. Earn some money. Learn the skills. And then go start a company if you want to.' Whereas what we should be saying is 'Have a go to begin with when you are young, when the risks don't seem so great. Learn about entrepreneurship. Maybe learn your own attitude towards risk. Go and find somebody who has done it before and try to learn from them'. A bit like an apprentice. Go and learn from many of them. Get networking. Stretch your boundaries. Do things that are new and different, away from your routines. Try to get a feeling for what it is to take a risk – not just the scholarly view of risk, but actually deep down in your gut, what it feels like.

Language focus 2: Giving friendly advice

 1.27

3

1 Go and learn from many of them. Get networking.
2 Go and learn from many of them. Get networking.

4.3 Skills: Collaborative and aggressive negotiation strategies

Listening 1: Discussing effective negotiating

 1.28

Salesperson: But I love it when it gets to negotiation stage, 'cause you know they want to buy. If they start to negotiate, they want you.
Sales manager: Absolutely.
Salesperson: If it really comes down to it and someone says 'Look we want to deal with your company. We want you to be our supplier but you're five thousand higher than the competition and I can't justify it to my group financial director.'
Sales manager: Yeah.
Salesperson: What I tend to do when people start mentioning the word 'discount', the way I tend to do it is I tend to throw it back at them: 'Well, fine. We can probably do something but, you know, what are you going to do for me?' Because it's a two-way street. I can't go back to my manager and say 'I've given them a ten percent discount because I felt like it.' And then they say 'Oh, what we'll do is we'll upgrade the lease from level 2 to level 4.'
Sales manager: Uh-huh.
Salesperson: And then I'd say 'Well, okay. If you can commit this level of business to me, this is what you're going to pay now and I'll shift this cost to the back end of the deal and you don't have to pay it till the end of the year.' So that's the way I tend to work.
Sales manager: Yeah.
Salesperson: I suppose with more junior salespeople they're afraid – you know, they think 'Oh, I've got to give a discount, you know, because otherwise I won't get the deal.'
Sales manager: Hmm.
Salesperson: And I think if you hold your own as a quality supplier, people have respect for it.

Sales manager: Absolutely. If you need to offer some discount then go for the win–win. You know you want something back. We'll give discounts on two-, three-, five-year contracts. Get someone to take the contract out for two years, we'll give a five percent discount. Fine. You've tied them in for two years.

Listening 2: A price negotiation

 1.29

Manufacturer: Would you bend a little and leave it at the same price? James? Just say yes or no.
Supplier: I'm hesitant to do it as we've held our prices for a long time and we try to be competitive. I know we have a laugh and a joke and we do try and be competitive and it's …
Manufacturer: I tell you where you can give us something, James.
Supplier: Yeah?
Manufacturer: You know where the service contract was a hundred and twenty? And you've made it a hundred and twenty-six?
Supplier: Yeah.
Manufacturer: It would look nice as a round figure. A hundred and twenty-five.
Supplier: Yes. I can definitely work that one.
Manufacturer: To be fair, it would look even better at a hundred and fifteen.
Supplier: But it's a round figure. We're happy with a hundred and twenty-five.

5 Crisis management
5.2 Practice: Successfully dealing with a crisis

Listening 1: In search of funding

 1.30

Interviewer: When the company suffered a serious crisis and lost seven million euros, how did you manage to survive?
Brendan Dow: Well, since the crisis we have survived successfully having raised a substantial amount of further capital, to progress our commercialisation. At the time of the crisis the company hadn't yet delivered its first product. Throughout the crisis it was really critical to continue progress towards developing and then releasing the product, as the investment horizon of investors that were coming in was much shorter than those that had previously invested.
Interviewer: Right.
Brendan Dow: The Board was of the opinion that, having reached a critical stage of commercialisation, maybe the State, or even the Federal Government, might support the company during the crisis. And, predictably in hindsight, the government sat on its hands. So one of the lessons there is save yourself, because nobody else will. The next thing we did was approach our commercialisation partners, the big utility companies like Gaz de France, E.ON in the UK, Nuon in Holland …
Interviewer: Huge companies.
Brendan Dow: And we thought that, given their size, they would continue to support us, with a relatively small amount of capital

required to <u>see us through</u>. At the same time we would give them a generous share of the future upside. I guess, when we look back, none of the utilities could move quickly enough. I mean, a crisis happens quickly, the utilities move slowly, and we already have a disconnect. So we looked at a careful selection of existing investors and we approached them in December for additional equity, but unfortunately we weren't able to raise money here either. We re-approached existing investors, but this time with a new cornerstone investor in place. Someone who had <u>come out of the woodwork</u>, and we convinced him that this might be a good investment for him. He'd looked at a number of other fuel cell investments globally. <u>He had done his homework</u> on it and was happy to invest.

Listening 2: Lessons learned

 1.31

Interviewer: What lessons do you think the company has learned as a result of going through this crisis event?

Brendan Dow: That cash is key. So, whilst we thought we were investing our money and using an external adviser to do that, at the end of the day we would have been better off just leaving it in cash, or some sort of government bond. And not putting it in the hands of someone else who thought they could do a better job. I think one of the main lessons we learned was you shouldn't expect that a white knight just comes out of the blue. White knights are unlikely to emerge in a crisis. You know, people often think well, there's a crisis, so there must be something wrong. There wasn't anything fundamentally wrong with the technology, or the company, or our strategy, it was just something fundamentally wrong with what had happened to the cash that was going to fund our way forward. Another lesson we learned was when you are looking for new capital in a crisis, you need to operate on many fronts. You can't rely on a single investor or shareholder, or target. You need to have many in play at a particular point in time. We learned to communicate with employees, because what we didn't want was to lose key employees in the crisis, and make a bad situation worse. So we brought them into our trust. In a crisis I think you have just got to convince people that if they save the company, then we are all going to be better off – rather than just everybody saving themselves.

Listening 3: Leading out of a crisis

 1.32

Interviewer: How did it feel personally to be running a company in the middle of a crisis?

Brendan Dow: Well, it felt like you were under siege. You put in a lot more hours, particularly after hours. I mean, travel for me became quite onerous – between October and February I was in Europe on six occasions. So I probably spent about three out of the four months overseas, so that was always difficult. So you feel as though you've lost control of the situation. But I think it's important – I mean, the things that I did was really focus on keeping your body language positive. Keep smiling. Stand up straight. All the basic things that you

don't think of when you feel really down; the shoulders go down, and the head goes down, and all that sort of stuff. Well, really focus on keeping your head up, your shoulders up, keep smiling, talk about what is happening, the future, the breakthroughs in the technology. Those sorts of things.

Interviewer: So confidence as well as cash is key.

Brendan Dow: You need to demonstrate confidence. One of the reasons for doing the travel was also to face the investors, so they could make sure that they could see that you were still … you know, there was a process going on. Go and see suppliers and tell them they are going to get paid, because the last thing you want is them to stop supplying you, because they know you're in a bit of trouble.

5.3 Skills: Dealing with conflict

Language focus 1: Conflictual turn-taking

 1.33

Exercise 1

1

David: … And the rent's stupid.

John: Not as stupid as I was trying to make it.

2

David: So what else can we get out of you other than this?

John: Absolutely nothing.

3

John: Well, if you have an extreme problem with it then I can, er …

David: I have got an extreme problem with it, yeah.

Listening 1: Opening the meeting

1.34

David: Nice to meet you, John.

John: And you, David.

David: Dive in. Grab a chair.

John: Thank you.

David: Right now, John, I have to say I'm a little bit in the dark here.

John: OK. I'll give you the story then, shall I?

David: Please.

John: From the beginning, you know both the restaurants you operate are owned by us and we supply drinks to these restaurants.

David: Mm.

John: So you rent two properties at the moment with our basic range of drinks package. Now, you have received very good discounts on this range since you started renting the restaurants from us.

David: Mm.

John: So that was all fine. That agreement was put in place for a period of about five years. When you started renting the properties, which was just over five years ago, we guaranteed the discounts on the drinks until the end of this calendar year. We said that we would honour that agreement, then after that we probably wouldn't. Right. So this is the 'probably wouldn't' bit.

David: Right.

John: So what we've done is put into operation a scheme to give you discounts on …

David: But not ones that I'll notice.

John: … most of your range. No, no, no. You'll notice it. I'll talk you through it. It's all fairly logical. It's not rocket science – because we're a supplier, we're not keen on you selling other people's products.

Listening 2: Disagreements

 1.35

David: I've got to try and figure out what we can do about this, 'cause that contract is giving us no opportunity whatsoever to get any benefit from increased volume.

John: No. It's supposed to be protecting you, though.

David: The wholesale price is – well, it's not protecting us at all, because in real terms the percentage of the discount's gone down. And will continue to go down every year. So soon, the discounts will be meaningless.

John: Yeah.

David: And the rent's stupid.

John: Not as stupid as I was trying to make it.

David: It's ridiculous already. The amount you were trying to make it was absolutely beyond any business sense whatsoever. So what else can we get out of you other than this?

John: Absolutely nothing.

Listening 3: Closing stages

 1.36

John: Well, if you have an extreme problem with it then I can, er …

David: I have got an extreme problem with it, yeah. Specially for hundred and fifty quid. It's absolute madness.

John: You didn't let me finish the sentence. If you've got an extreme problem with the legal fees then we can pay them.

David: Good. You can say that about the rent.

John: No.

David: Mm. OK. Well, thank you for your time, John.

John: OK. So you're clear where we're sort of coming from.

David: Yes. Clear.

John: Yeah.

David: John, I don't envy you. You must be welcomed up and down the country.

John: Well, yeah. Most people are kinder than you are, but there you go.

6 Leadership

6.2 Practice: Nikki King – a business leader

Listening 1: The qualities of leaders and managers

 1.37

Interviewer: What do you think are the attributes of a good leader, and do you think leaders are born or made?

Nikki King: I think passion and vision make a good leader. I think good leaders have to have a vision. They have to know where they are going in two years, five years, ten years. And then they can't deviate from that, so they have to be passionate about that vision.

Interviewer: OK.

Nikki King: And I think the one thing that denotes a good leader is somebody who is pretty consistent. I don't think, generally, people like leaders that run off in thousands of different directions.

Interviewer: Yeah, right.

Nikki King: So I think that's two attributes of a good leader. I think, to a degree, they are born. I don't think you can make a good leader.

Interviewer: Right.

Nikki King: Good leaders are inspirational in the way they behave. You know, you can have two sorts of general, can't you? The one that sits and plans an attack, and just hopes somebody else does it, which is generally probably a good manager.

Interviewer: OK.

Nikki King: But a good leader says, 'Come on, I'm jumping over this. I don't know what is on the other side of this, we might all die, but come with me anyway for the fun of it', and people go.

Listening 2: Leadership in different sectors

 1.38

Interviewer: How does leading and managing in the private sector and in, say, social enterprises – or NPOs, charities – compare?

Nikki King: Oh, it's completely different. In the voluntary sector, you're dealing with volunteers and not people who work for you. So you have to be much more persuasive and far less … not necessarily dictatorial, but you can't actually tell people what to do, and you have to be very, very careful on that one.

Interviewer: Yes.

Nikki King: You also have to really analyse why people are doing it, because people tend to work for the voluntary sector for many different reasons. It might be because they are just generally all-round good eggs who really want to help, or because they want their OBEs, or because they want some sort of kudos, or it looks good on their CV. And so you have to analyse it before you actually motivate them, which is very different to having somebody working for you.

Interviewer: Yeah.

Nikki King: In the local government sector, there is so much red tape that you don't have as a leader of your own business. So, you know, tremendous amount of committees for the sake of it, rules and regulations around health and safety and HR, and all these other things that we don't generally have so much of in the private sector.

Interviewer: Are there any other differences?

Nikki King: The major difference is that, unlike the private sector, the public sector and charities are not commercial at all.

Interviewer: Yes.

Nikki King: Which really works against them. So to actually bring somebody in with a commercial mind would normally have a very beneficial effect on both.

Listening 3: Advice for business leaders

 1.39

Interviewer: What advice do you have for people wanting to be good leaders?

Nikki King: First of all be honest, be yourself. You can't keep up a pretence of being somebody else for your whole life. If you are a woman, don't try and manage like a man or be a male leader, because you are a woman, and behave like one because it's very unattractive otherwise.

Interviewer: Yeah.

Nikki King: Practise what you preach. Don't say one thing and do something else.

Interviewer: OK.

Nikki King: And really, really … that's back to the vision and passion. Set your vision, do it with passion, and don't be deviated, and just keep going. And that's all I can say about it really.

6.3 Skills: Motivating staff

Listening 1: Describing transactional and transformational motivation

 1.40

David Prasher: The reason this motivation thing is so interesting at the moment is I think what many businesses are going through, especially media businesses like ours, is transformation. And in the old business model, which everybody understood, leadership and management were fairly transactional. Which is 'I am the boss. You work for me. I have done your job before. There's only a limited set of outcomes, and, you know, experience tells us what they are. Therefore, if you do this you will succeed.'

Interviewer: Yeah.

David Prasher: And I think that leadership and management now have to change from transactional to transformational, which is 'We have a vision. The world is changing. We're asking you to work in new ways. We think we know the outcome, but we're not all one hundred percent sure. And we don't all know what it takes to get there.'

Interviewer: Right.

David Prasher: Technology is driving rapid change, and therefore that leadership and motivation can't be transactional. And so the language needs to move from transactional language – which is telling, doing, pointing – to transformational, which is about consulting, joining, togetherness.

Listening 2: Motivating different types of people

 1.41

David Prasher: We try to define our staff in one of four different ways – coasters, or problem children, or strivers, or stars – based on a group that has motivation going across the X axis.

Interviewer: Say those four again? Coasters?

David Prasher: Coasters, problem child, star, or striver. So, if you want me to define those, that would create a quadrant, because you would have 'ability' going up the Y axis, with high ability at the top, low ability at the bottom.

Interviewer: The 'motivation' going across the X axis. Right?

David Prasher: Yes, low on the left, high on the right. And, therefore, if you are top left you're a coaster. If you are bottom left you're a problem child, because you have got low motivation and/or low

ability. If you are top right you are a star: high ability, high motivation. And if you are bottom right you are a striver.

Interviewer: OK.

David Prasher: So, the way that you motivate those people, and coach those people – and I think a lot of motivation comes from coaching nowadays – is different. So, for a star, the job is to keep them motivated. You probably have a higher frequency of contact. Give them real praise. Give them projects, and just harness their talents really. Whereas if you've got a problem child, there's far more of a building job required with a problem child, to move them up the scale. You might do more telling with those people.

Interviewer: Right.

David Prasher: You give them a detailed sort of plan of action. Concentrate on their skills. So, you know, they'll feel motivated if they think that you are improving their skill set.

 1.42

The audio script is in the unit (see page 61).

7 International communication
7.1 Theory: Culture in international business

Listening 1: International organisations and their cultures

 1.43

Interviewer: You talk about three types of companies – what are they?

Fons Trompenaars: Let me start with 'globalisation', when everything is universal and you think only about 'one size fits all'. It's very cynical when American firms come to Europe and Asia and say 'Oh gee, that's the way we do things around here.' And you don't have any freedom to do things differently.

Interviewer: OK.

Fons Trompenaars: The opposite is what we call the 'multi-local organisation – an organisation that has, for example, a shared brand. But the local offices have complete autonomy. They have different approaches in different nations. A good example is Walt Disney's amusement parks. In the parks you see the major themes are the same, in Japan, in Paris, in Florida, but there are slight differentiations to make it more attractive to the local audience.

Interviewer: Yes.

Fons Trompenaars: Now, how do you recognise a trans-national firm and what are good examples? A trans-national firm is a firm that is always keen on learning locally, then taking the best practices which they globalise. So a trans-national team – even McDonald's nowadays – says 'Gee, what is the fastest-growing market? Oh, it seems to be Paris. How come? Oh, it is because of the architecture of the restaurant.' So what we have seen suddenly is that McDonald's took the French architect to Manhattan to refurnish their restaurants. So, you take local best practices which you then globalise. The second characteristic is the top management is very often very multi cultural. At one stage Applied Materials, a company based in California, had seven people in the management team with nine different nationalities, because two had a double passport. Now that kind of management team is very often a sign of a trans-national type of organisation. And interestingly enough they don't very often have one centre. They have multi centres, which is the third characteristic.

Interviewer: Right. Yes.

Fons Trompenaars: So there's not this dominant 'Here is Chicago or London calling'. The final characteristic is it's very often a value-driven organisation. But the values are very often sophisticated. Let's take PepsiCo International. They have values like 'We strive for teams that consist of creative individuals.' Reconciling individuals and the group. Values like 'We give direct feedback with diplomacy.' So that's the trans-national firm, that copes with cultural differences in a much more sophisticated way.

Listening 2: Merging companies with different cultures

 1.44

Interviewer: Research shows that acquisitions or mergers often fail. Can this be explained from a cultural perspective?

Fons Trompenaars: For sure. A lot of research also shows that between fifty and … eighty percent of the failed mergers are caused by misunderstandings on the human side. Now, I very often, also with our little consulting firm, help companies to integrate and in fact it is fifty percent of our business, so we do a lot of merger and acquisition work. And I am saying this because what we find is we clean up the mess of the technical type of consultants, because they just look at the better IT system. How many people can we kick out? The organisational structure, all the hard stuff. On the cultural side, I would say be careful because culture is nearly always taken as an excuse for mergers which technically fail. In other words the CEO is awful and they say 'Yeah. I don't know what it is so let's call it culture.'

Interviewer: Right.

Fons Trompenaars: However, the beauty of taking culture seriously in a merger acquisition is helping people talk to each other. We say even if you don't reconcile all the cultural dilemmas, at least you have a better dialogue between the cultures, which will help the business in the long run. So it can help, but let's not over-exaggerate.

7.3 Skills: Conducting successful intercultural communication

Language focus: Collaborative turn-taking

 1.45

2

Extract 1
Speaker: Helen, run us through this if you would.

Extract 2
Speaker: Deborah said not being vigilant on the standards, which in other words means not always following the sequence which is described.

Extract 3
Speaker 1: So, if you have considered another Yokohama bridge you might consider this, er …

Speaker 2: Oklahoma?

Speaker 1: No, Yokohama.

Speaker 2: Yokohama Bay Bridge. Okay.

Extract 4
Speaker: Thanks, Dan. Our goal today was to explain the growth opportunities available to Kodak and to make a strong case for the higher valuation we think Kodak deserves. To sum up: Kodak plans to achieve an annual top-line growth rate of eight to twelve percent by the end of our annual planning period.

Extract 5
Speaker 1: If we go and do this it, it, it doesn't work. Is that correct?

Speaker 2: That's correct.

Extract 6
Speaker 1: It's actually, erm, an internet TV site as well.

Speaker 2: Oh, is it?

Speaker 1: Yeah.

Speaker 2: Oh, right.

Speaker 1: Mm.

Speaker 2: Okay. I see. So what's the business it's been doing?

Listening: Expert advice

 1.46

Speaker 1: Hiro Tanaka
Hiro Tanaka: Very often I find Japanese people's interaction to be very monotonous, including their facial expression. So sometimes I encourage them to smile, and it works very well. A person may know their job very well, and be intelligent, but when that person smiles, the personality comes out. I think smiling helps a lot.

Speaker 2: Nikki King
Nikki King: Well, the first tip is always to study the history of a country before you start, because I don't believe you can understand the country's culture until you understand its history. You understand its DNA, what made it what it is. I think that's really, really important. I think you must try and learn the language, even to a small degree. And I think the other thing is to watch very carefully, and listen to the way people are dealing with you, because it's quite a good pointer on the way you should be dealing with them.

Speaker 3: Charlie Peppiatt
Interviewer: Is it true when people meet somebody for the first time they'll use the kind of pre-meeting chat time, the small talk preceding the meeting, quite strategically in order to gauge the other person's English. Is that right?

Charlie Peppiatt: Yes, I think rather than people finding out about people's background and interests, which might be the typical context for a meeting amongst native speakers, you find that people spend the first few minutes just feeling out the ability with which they can communicate with each other in English.

8 International outsourcing

8.2 Practice: Offshore outsourcing provider's perspective

Listening 1: Benefits of offshore outsourcing

 2.02

Interviewer: What benefits are companies looking for when they outsource offshore?

Gigi Virata: Basically they are looking for skills: human resources and a mix of other skills. Some of them are looking for a certain number of new recruits in order to scale up their business – sometimes in the thousands. Or they are looking for a certain depth of skills that are getting harder to come by in their home base.

Interviewer: Can you give us some examples of that?

Gigi Virata: Well, you might have back-office needs: maybe two to three thousand accountants just doing simple transactional work, like payroll processing or accounts receivable. That can be a challenge in, for example, a smaller city in the United States – and so they come to the Philippines or India where they can find these people easily and quickly. So part of the benefit is that they have the people and services available here. And there are, of course, cost savings doing it in low-cost countries like India and the Philippines.

Listening 2: Why companies choose the Philippines

 2.03

Interviewer: Why should companies choose the Philippines in particular as an outsourcing destination?

Gigi Virata: We are the third-largest English-speaking country in the world. We have a hundred million people now, and we produce about four hundred thousand university graduates a year. And of those graduates about seventy percent speak English, and that's primarily why we have so many North American and UK companies working with us here. We have not had as much business from the non-English speaking countries. For companies from non-English speaking countries we do more work in IT, but we are not as big as India is in IT.

Interviewer: What about call centre operations?

Gigi Virata: Well, for voice services, companies tell us that we are a little bit better than India. Our accent seems easier to understand, for Americans or westerners, than most Indian accents. And then – well, you know, you could say India was an English colony, but the Philippines really embraced western culture. We were an American colony for fifty years and we took everything, Hollywood, basketball and all that stuff. It seems that that is something the customers really appreciate. People feel more comfortable talking with our call centre agents. It's really all about customer satisfaction.

Listening 3: Challenges facing the industry

 2.04

Interviewer: What do you see as the main challenges and problems facing the offshore outsourcing industry? Is it a bright future?

Gigi Virata: Our problem is a good one, but still it's a big challenge.

We do have a lot of raw talent. There are people in the Philippines that would be very suited to work in our industry, but not everyone is applying to work with us. Also those who do want to work with us, not all of them have the skills. Either they haven't been practising their English – they've been learning it in school but they haven't been using it – or they're not up to speed with their computer skills.

Interviewer: I see.

Gigi Virata: So far what the companies are telling us is that, out of a hundred candidates who come to be interviewed, they are lucky to hire ten suitable ones. But we find that the next twenty to thirty applicants would only require maybe two weeks of intensive English practice to become hireable. So there are two things that, as an association and as an industry, we look at. First, how do we make the whole recruitment, hiring and training process more efficient? The other is, we want to change some negative perceptions of the industry that some people here have – that it's bad for your health, the work is too hard, and that kind of thing. So we need to have more awareness campaigns and to talk to parents, students and teachers to show the different kinds of careers that can be had in this industry. So that's another thing we have to tackle. That's a challenge.

Language focus: Taking different stances to intensify or tone down the message

 2.05

1 I'm just writing to ask if you could …
2 It's not a big seller really.
3 It's really easy to do.
4 You could actually smell all the smoke coming up …
5 It was quite an experience!

8.3 Skills: Dealing with Q&A

Listening 1: Managing a Q&A session

 2.06

Leo Dillon: It's now time to begin our discussion period, our question and answer comment period, if you like, and before we open this part of the meeting for discussion, I want to review a few ground rules. We look forward to trying to answer to the best of our ability all your questions as fully as we can. We do, however, reserve the right to pass on any issues that might involve confidential information. And we really do not plan, because we can't effectively do it, to deal with personal issues related to the individual shareholder, although if you have personal issues, please write to us and we will try to deal with them. If you wish to ask a question or make a comment, go to the nearest microphone in the aisle and they will take your name and draw you to my attention. I have a little monitor here of which microphones are trying to get attention.

Language focus 1: Inviting questions from the audience

 2.07

1 Are there any questions about how we're going to proceed?
2 I'd be happy to take questions at the end of the talk.
3 If you have any questions, please raise your hand.

4 So, any questions anybody? Please fire away.

5 Right, are there any questions before we start?

6 I'll move straight over to Graham and open it up for any questions from the floor.

Listening 2: Dealing with different question types

 2.08

1

Shareholder 1: Good morning. I have a simple question. I would like to know the future of the motor racing sponsorship.

Leo Dillon: We think that motor racing – which is one of the, if not the, fastest-growing sports in the United States – is one of our best sponsorships, and we are happy to be associated with it. It's hard to measure what real money you get out of these things, but it's a very brand-loyal audience and we plan to continue with motor racing, and maybe move forward from the middle of the pack. Thank you.

2

Shareholder 2: Good morning, Mr Dillon. Given the consolidation that is taking place in the commercial printing industry, what impact do you see on that vis-à-vis Zelig products in the years going forward? And on the cost side, speaking of folding cartons, has there been any thought given to outsourcing the manufacture of Zelig's little red boxes, and the collection and disposal of solid waste?

Leo Dillon: There are many questions there. On the outsourcing issue, we give consideration to outsourcing everything that we don't think is strategic. In some cases we find we can do it much better than anybody on the outside and we don't outsource those. So we look at that. I know we are looking at outsourcing some of the packaging efforts. Is Bill here? Do you want to comment?

3

Shareholder 3: Zelig changes their products and organisations to keep up with the times. It's time the old wage bands and the culture of the human resources and legal departments change also, to get in step with the Zelig values in our new value-based high-performance culture.

Leo Dillon: Your question was what?

Shareholder 3: Just a statement.

Leo Dillon: A statement. OK, thank you. We do make mistakes from time to time. I would be the first to admit that. When you have a hundred thousand people all over the world and you are changing a lot of the culture and the structure, we make some mistakes. But by and large, I am very, very proud of the people in our HR and legal functions, who have to manage through these very difficult times.

4

Shareholder 4: How do you plan to raise the morale of the few employees who are left to do the work of many, and who are fearing the loss of their jobs tomorrow?

Leo Dillon: That's a very serious issue, and one that we don't take lightly. First of all, when you have gone through as much restructuring as we have over many years, it has a damaging effect on morale. The good news is that, as people begin to see some progress, things change. You can do a lot of things to help, but there is nothing like business success today to build morale.

5

Shareholder 5: I would ask you what you're going to do about your management problem, because it's been written up in the national papers. I know of it personally. I have written you personally and offered to share comments with you, and you have not felt free to come back and find out about any of the incidents at all.

Leo Dillon: I haven't seen these recent articles you refer to in the national papers that talk about this management team. The articles I have seen and what I have gotten from my associates who are the analysts on Wall Street, is that they believe this may be the best team Zelig has ever had in its history. They are making the changes. Unfortunately, I know that some people, like yourself, have lost their jobs and we all feel bad about it. We don't like that. I don't know a person on this management team that likes to lay off good people. A lot of good people like you have lost their jobs. That is not a fun thing to do. Unfortunately, it is necessary to do to get our cost structure in line, in order to be competitive so that the remaining thirty-five to forty thousand people in Zelig have a viable future. Thank you.

9 Affordable innovation

9.2 Practice: GE Healthcare – low-cost reverse innovation in practice

Listening 1: GE Healthcare in China

 2.09

Five years ago, GE pioneered an ultra low-cost, portable ultrasound machine in China which cost fifteen thousand dollars; contrast that with the premium ultrasound machines that are sold in the US for three hundred and fifty thousand dollars. Where do you need a portable machine in China? Ninety percent of China is in rural China. In rural China you don't have hospitals, so you can't ask the patient to go to the hospital – the hospital has to come to the patient. That means that the machine has to be portable. You can put it in your backpack and go to these remote villages. It has to be ultra low-cost because of customer affordability. The low-cost, affordable ultrasound machine which was originally innovated for the Chinese market is now creating market for General Electric all over the world including the United States. In fact, the portable ultrasound machine today, five years later, is a three hundred million-dollar global business for GE.

Let me just describe one application of this in the US. Imagine there is an accident on a highway; an ambulance is going there. You can't put the big three hundred and fifty thousand-dollar machine in an ambulance, but you can put the portable ultrasound machine – which looks like a laptop computer – in an ambulance. This is the kind of new market innovation from poor countries that can be re-created in rich countries.

2.10

You may wonder how come reverse innovation has become such an important strategic priority for companies today. It is really because of the great recession which has fundamentally reset this world. And one way it has reset the world is growth has shifted from developed countries to developing countries.

There was a time, fifteen years ago, when General Electric used to prepare its global strategy. It used to have a strategy for the US, for Western Europe and for Japan and then a strategy for the rest of the world. Today, when GE prepares its global strategy, it has a strategy for the so-called BRIC countries: Brazil, Russia, India, China. And resource-rich countries like the Middle East, Canada, Australia. And the rest of the world. And 'the rest of the world' includes the US, Western Europe and Japan. That is the kind of fundamental change we are seeing.

Multinationals had taken the total population of this world of seven billion and divided them into two. There are two billion rich customers who can afford to buy the products we make in the US, and the five billion poor we have left for charity to take care of, government to take care of, NGOs to take care of. That's an outmoded way of thinking. We need to bring the five billion poor into the consumer base. And they cannot consume the same products the two billion rich are consuming.

9.3 Skills: Dealing with criticism

Language focus: Recognising and reacting to criticism

 2.11

Exercise 2

The audio script is in the unit (see page 88).

 2.12

Exercise 6

1

Speaker A: I have no idea why you didn't consult me before agreeing to the contract.
Speaker B: The reason I did it was because they wanted a decision today and I didn't want to lose the contract.

2

Speaker A: Your mistake has cost us an absolute fortune.
Speaker B: I know I've made a mistake and I'll be more careful in future.

3

Speaker A: That is the stupidest idea that I've ever heard.
Speaker B: I'm not prepared to accept that.

4

Speaker A: I can't believe it. I never had these problems with my old supplier.
Speaker B: I hear what you're saying and understand the problem.

5

Speaker A: It's all your fault. What are you going to do about it?
Speaker B: Let me have a think and I'll get back to you.

 2.13

Sally: What feedback have we had? How worthwhile has it been? It says here you spent just over two thousand pounds. What have we got for our money?
Mark: We got quite a few leads. I mean, the leads followed up haven't produced anything in the way of actual sales.
Sally: So.
Mark: So, you know, you could argue there's not been a return yet.
Sally: OK.
Mark: This was really the first year that we've entered into the marketplace and started to push the product. Over a period of time it will come, but I don't think advertising on its own is ever going to be the answer, is it? I think you've got to follow up with attending these exhibitions, with mailshots and trying to contact the customers as a result, which we just haven't had the resources to. But just as a straight answer to what we've done up to now I can say no, we haven't had a return on our two thousand pounds.
Sally: You haven't sold one subscription?
Mark: No.
Sally: I don't know what that exhibition cost you but it probably cost a lot more than two thousand pounds, because I know it cost us nearly a thousand pounds just to get the magazines over there. So our bill was probably nearly three and a half to four thousand pounds.
Mark: Yeah.
Sally: Just for that one exhibition. And it's like anything else. I think everybody at the exhibition said 'Yeah, it's been a good exhibition this. We've got a half a dozen good names.' And you will probably not see any business from that exhibition for maybe eighteen months, two years.
Mark: No.
Sally: I think exhibitions are very expensive, but there again it's getting in front of the people. And that's the thing, isn't it?

10 Design and invention

10.1 Theory: Design in business

Listening 1: Design and people

 2.14

Interviewer: When you talk about design, you mention 'people' again and again. Why is that?
Dr Clare Brass: Well, designers are people-focused. It's a people-centred activity. And I think this is what sets it apart from many other disciplines. I think there are many disciplines that could be said to be problem-solving disciplines, but design has an almost natural tendency to start with the user, start with a person. So when engineers solve a problem, they start with a technical problem which they aim to solve. However, when a designer starts to address a problem, they often worry less about how to solve it, and they think more about who they're solving it for, and then they worry about solving the technical aspects later on. Take Apple, for example. There is nothing quite like Apple for having really taken design

thinking and created successful products on the market. There are plenty of MP3 players on the market, they all basically use a similar technology, but what Apple have been able to do with the iPod is create a delightfulness through that interaction with the product. In this case, design provides the interface which allows a person to access a whole system behind the product, in a way which is both functional, but also delightful.

Listening 2: New ways of thinking

 2.15

Interviewer: There's an old business saying: 'If you do what you've always done, you'll get what you've always got.' How does design help business people break out of this way of thinking?

Dr Clare Brass: Well, I think the key here is about not focusing on an object. So, if you set out to design a toaster, for example, you'll get a toaster. So you might have it in an infinite number of different colours, or you might have buttons that look different, but basically you'll get a toaster. So the way we train Innovation Design Engineering students, and the way that many designers work, is not to look at the design as a noun, but to look at design as a verb. So you might end up with something completely different – because you no longer are constraining yourself to look at the object. You're looking at everything that's surrounding the object. So, if we just stick with a very simple example of toast, if you're designing toasting then you might take into consideration the whole system around toasting, everything else, all the other aspects that might come into play. So you might be thinking about how do you spread butter on toast, or how do you slice the bread. Or you might be thinking about how do you open the bag of sliced bread, or where do you keep the bag of sliced bread. So you begin to think about all the things that are connected with toasting, and the design trick is to join them up according to the user's need.

Interviewer: Right. And how do you find out about the user's need?

Dr Clare Brass: Well, the only way you can really find out about user's needs is by going and finding users. So, if you want to innovate, what you need to do is go and look people in the eyes and talk to them. When you really go out and talk to people it brings your ideas to life. And what you notice is there are lots of things people do which we all know about, we've seen them before, but we've never really noticed, we've never really looked properly. And those insights can lead to you doing something in a different way.

10.2 Practice: Dyson – a design-led company

Listening: James Dyson talks about design and invention

 2.16

James Dyson: There's a myth about inventors that all you need is one good idea and you'll make your fortune. But the fact of the matter is you don't have ideas like that. You start with a problem that you're having to solve and you start building prototypes, hundreds of them, perhaps even thousands of them. And very often the original idea or the original problem doesn't look anything like the

final solution. So the important thing is this journey from prototype to prototype and during that process, of course, you get hundreds or thousands of failures. And the failure is the starting point because when something fails you understand why it fails, and then you start to think of ideas as to ways to overcome that failure. I mean, the cyclones for my vacuum cleaner took over 5,000 prototypes. That's 5,000 failures before I cracked it. So the moral of the tale is keep on failing. It works.

10.3 Skills: Communicating negative information in a positive light

Listening 1: Talking about the customers

 2.17

Sales director: There's an astonishing number of businesses out there which used to be our customers and have churned. That may have been because they didn't pay. They may have churned because they chose to, but there's an opportunity there perhaps to go back in and reconnect with them, because the network will be on their doorstep so there'll be no connection problems, and there must be some of those thousands of churned customers who might want to reconsider us again. You know, they will be tough doors to knock on but they might want to come back to us … And of course, existing customers are an easier win. Teamwork, as I said – we aren't going to achieve this on our own, no one individual is going to make that target next year, and we all need time in front of the customer.

Listening 2: Talking about marketing support

 2.18

Sales director: In terms of support for the sales guys, we'll be helping them as much as we can. So we're arming the guys with the capability, hopefully to go out there and up their activity levels. We've got to get out there in front of the customer. We're expecting support from Marketing. I was talking to someone in Marketing the other day; they've had to cut people too. So they're thin on the ground but we're looking for their support this coming year with specific product focus.

Front Line is the tool that we're going to use for monitoring all sales activity and sales opportunities. It's crucial that all the guys understand Front Line. Everyone uses Front Line in one way or another, and that will be a key tool for us in the coming year. But the point is – can we go along and do what we did this year, next year? I think you probably all know the answer. So we've got to make some step changes, and some of the challenges we're facing today are how to grow the business more quickly in a very strange environment, with a lack of capital, with fewer people. Everyone's lost people, so it's a huge challenge for us all.

Writing 5: Writing for meetings – notes, minutes and agenda

Writing skill 1: Taking meeting notes and interpreting an agenda

 2.19

David Sinclair: Let's press on quickly because I'm sure we've all got plenty of other things to get on with. Apologies for absence. I have apologies from Paula Summers, who apparently is in Paris sightseeing for a week. That's a joke, by the way. Paula's setting up our stand at the Trade Fair over there. Any other apologies?

Elizabeth Willis: I don't know about the Health and Safety people?

Emile Lahar: Are we expecting them?

David Sinclair: No, they're not coming in on this one. Shall we press on with the next item? Everyone OK about those minutes? OK. Any matters arising? Peter.

Peter Chen: Can I make a suggestion? Well, it crossed my mind that a few of the headings on this agenda here are actually duplicated by the 'User-First' interdepartmental meeting we had with IT and Estates Management last week, which covered some of these things, so do we want to cover them again in this meeting?

Elizabeth Willis: You're right, 'Liaison with IT' and 'Equipment survey' were definitely covered.

David Sinclair: OK, if everyone's in agreement let's bin these two. I followed an entirely conventional format for the agenda here. So, where was I? Right, yes, we're going to jump all the way to item 6.

Elizabeth Willis: Can we just come back to matters arising coming out of those 'User-First' meetings a moment? I think we ought to circulate the minutes of those meetings, to the whole group.

David Sinclair: Good, yes. They've been done; they haven't been circulated, but they're available. But if everybody would like them? Who would like them? Well, I can get them. I'll get on to that. So …

Language focus: Structure and style of meeting minutes

 2.20

1 **Dina Ahmed:** OK, I'll investigate the incident about that injury the other day when that guy from the bank tripped over the PC leads in Caroline's office.

2 **Alfonso Garcia:** No problem, I'll ask the guys in marketing to give us the revised sales figures for last month.

3 **Steve Knox:** If that's what everyone wants, I can send round copies of the course outlines for those two areas.

4 **Magda Zboina:** OK, let's do it. Let's get that leaflet going out in a mega mailing to all our clients in Spain, Italy and France.

11 The economic environment

11.1 Theory: Government influence on the economic environment

Listening 1: Government and central bank objectives

 2.21

Interviewer: Why do governments seek to manage their economies, and what are they trying to achieve?

Dr Tatiana Damjanovic: Well, usually governments try to achieve the welfare of their citizens through an appropriate mix of taxation and spending that is broadly acceptable to the people living in that country. In general, the poor will be in favour of higher taxation and higher spending and the rich in favour of far less taxation and spending.

Interviewer: What are the main tools that governments and central banks can use to effect changes in the economy? And how do they work in theory?

Dr Tatiana Damjanovic: The purpose of the central banks and the purpose of the government can be different. In general though, the objective of the central bank is to ensure a stable economic and financial environment. The basis of this involves issuing and maintaining a stable national currency that people have trust in; a currency that holds its value and can be used as a reliable means of payment for goods and services.

Listening 2: The impact of government spending

2.22

Interviewer: In a time of economic crisis, some economists recommend government spending should be cut, whilst others say it should be increased. Which approach do you favour personally?

Dr Tatiana Damjanovic: In times of crisis, governments usually collect lower revenue because there are businesses that make losses and so governments cannot collect so much corporate tax. People become unemployed, so governments cannot collect so much income tax. And because people are unemployed they spend less, so VAT collection is also lower. So in times of crisis, government revenues fall, sometimes significantly. So this is why governments actually do not have enough resources to pay for their expenditure programmes, and it's why some people think that governments should reduce expenditure in times of crisis.

Interviewer: OK.

Dr Tatiana Damjanovic: However, government expenditure in times of crisis has a much higher value than in time of prosperity. It's really a time when people require their unemployment benefits for example, and business is more dependent on government orders for their goods and services. It's a way for the government to stimulate the economy that is slowing down too much.

Listening 3: Taxation

2.23

Interviewer: How effective is government economic management in different countries in the world?

Dr Tatiana Damjanovic: There are definitely huge differences in fiscal policies. There are different levels of taxation. For example, income tax can be more than sixty percent in some Scandinavian countries, and it can be zero percent in countries such as the United Arab Emirates. In Russia it's thirteen percent. VAT also varies considerably between one country and another, in most of Europe it's about twenty percent but in Korea, for example, it's very low – around ten percent.

Interviewer: What do you think are the main reasons for this?

Dr Tatiana Damjanovic: It's relatively easy for the Arab Emirates, because their governments have such large oil revenues that they don't need to collect taxes. In Scandinavian countries I think they actually are able to tax so much because tax discipline is very good. So there's no issue about tax evasion – the issue in Sweden is much smaller than in India, for example, or in Russia. Actually, there are some empirical studies which say that higher levels of taxation result in higher levels of tax evasion. It's partly why Russia has such low income tax, because even if they try to charge higher tax rates …
Interviewer: … people will declare lower and get away with it.
Dr Tatiana Damjanovic: Exactly.

11.3 Skills: Presenting charts and statistics

Listening: Analyse a chart in a slide presentation

🎧 2.24

Josh Crandall: So, let's begin by looking at what the trigger points are or the triggers are that force people to purchase a new car. In established markets it shouldn't be much of a surprise that the primary reason that people are purchasing a new car is that their former vehicle is no longer functional. And that's the main, the primary, trigger for twenty-three percent of respondents from the established markets.

Whereas in emerging markets we find that people didn't previously own a vehicle. So, these data confirm what we would expect to see in emerging markets versus the established markets.

In the evolving markets, the yellow bars, we see that the desire for a second car as well as a change in circumstances are driving … twenty-seven percent of the purchases of new cars in these markets. And what we mean by changing circumstance …

Language focus: Structuring and describing a chart

🎧 2.25

Now, what's the first source of information people use to research different brands of car? Where do you go first? And it is surprising to me to see the strength of the Internet here. Forty-seven percent of all new car buyers surveyed said that they use the Internet first for their auto research. This is significantly higher than auto dealerships, and other traditional media sources really fall off the cliff. So, when we compare the use of the Internet to other media, it's pretty striking. Given the difference we can't really make these comparisons by point differences, but we have to look at this in terms of multiples. So, the Internet is eight times more popular as the first means of research than car magazines and brochures; twelve times more popular than newspapers; and twenty-four times more popular than TV as the first 'go to source' for research in the auto purchase process. Finally, it is interesting to note the reliance on friends and family in emerging markets – it is actually comparable to the use of dealerships, and as the auto industry matures in these markets it will be important to monitor how this trend evolves over time.

12 International trade
12.1 Theroy: Freetrade or Protectionism?

Language focus: Emphasising key points through inversion

🎧 2.26 🎧 2.27

The audio script is in the unit (see page 110).

12.2 Practice: NAFTA and Mexico

Listening 1: The role and purpose of NAFTA

🎧 2.28

Interviewer: Can you briefly explain what NAFTA is and what is the role and purpose of the NAFTA Office of Mexico in Canada?
Carlos Piñera: Well, as you know, NAFTA is a free trade agreement signed by Mexico, Canada and the United States, which came into force in 1994, and became the largest free trade area in the world. NAFTA has principles and obligations to govern the exchange of goods and services, but its main objective is to generate a greater economic integration between the economies of North America, and to create jobs and improve the welfare of the population in North America. NAFTA has now fulfilled its objective of creating a duty-free trade zone, but there are other aspects that we still have to work on to ensure barriers to competition are removed. For instance, we need to have more regulatory cooperation such as more harmonised labelling of products, better integrated transport infrastructure, improved procedures at customs and so on.
Interviewer: So, how does the NAFTA Office of Mexico in Canada fit into all this?
Carlos Piñera: Well, we're responsible for the monitoring and compliance of the commitments we have to make under the NAFTA agreement and we are also responsible for the promotion of trade and investment between Mexico and Canada. Our office develops strategic information in order to identify business opportunities for Mexican companies in the Canadian market.

Listening 2: Benefits of NAFTA to Mexico

🎧 2.29

Interviewer: What are the main opportunities that NAFTA provides to Mexico and Mexican companies?
Carlos Piñera: Let me tell you that before Mexico signed NAFTA in the early nineties, we were implementing a policy of openness and modernisation of our industry. And at that time NAFTA was conceived as an important tool to support this process, and make our industry more competitive. We also saw another possibility coming out of NAFTA, that Mexico would become more attractive for inward investment with the consequent generation of greater employment opportunities. NAFTA has also created more opportunities for Mexican companies by making them more competitive and encouraging them to expand into international markets. For instance, since NAFTA came into force, Mexican exports have increased five-fold to the US and Canada and now stand at almost three hundred billion dollars.

NAFTA also has made positive interventions in some industry sectors, for instance auto parts and the automotive industry, in order that Mexico participates actively in the supply chains, reducing costs and facilitating access to the latest technology in these sectors. We are also now implementing a policy deriving from the NAFTA agreement where we are also promoting the integration of the space sector, which is really important for us.

In general, though, NAFTA has been a modernising factor in the Mexican economy that has generated a structural change in the economy of Mexico. Let me give you some data to underline this point: in 1990 oil exports accounted for seventy percent of total exports – exports were totally dominated by oil. Today, oil exports represent only fifteen percent of the total, while the manufacturing sector is sixty percent of total exports. In terms of the foreign trade component of GDP, it was eight percent in 1992, but the latest figures that we have now show that it's shot up to sixty percent of GDP. These are dramatic changes that show how we have transformed our industry and made it more open and more export-orientated.

Listening 3: Defence of NAFTA

 2.30

Interviewer: What adverse effects has NAFTA had on Mexico and Mexican companies?

Carlos Piñera: Well, opponents of NAFTA will point to the shoe-making industry in Mexico, for example. It has had a lot of problems for a long time, but that's not exactly to do with NAFTA – the competition here is Chinese. They are producing shoes at a really low cost. But when we're talking about industries in Mexico we have to look in detail at the different segments of that industry. For instance, when we are talking about the chemical industry, there are segments of that industry where we are really exporting well, and have really efficient businesses. But there are other segments of this industry where the opposite is true. It's the same for some agro-industries and the textile sector; some of these segments are totally export-orientated, but others are not interested … they are having problems adapting to new technologies, etc.

Let me tell you, when you sign up for an opening process, the competition forces companies to be more efficient. Mexican companies now have to deal with this new competition. When NAFTA was negotiated, not all sectors of the economy were opened up to free trade immediately. Certain industry sectors such as textiles and agriculture were initially protected but then were opened up in stages, allowing them to adapt gradually to the new competitive conditions.

Interviewer: Right.

Carlos Piñera: An important example is in the case of corn. The United States is a big producer of corn, the basic element in the Mexican diet. Politically it was a really sensitive sector and so we established a long period of protection for our farmers that was only phased out in 2008. I can tell you now, with the figures for this industry, that the situation for our farmers is much better than it was before NAFTA.

Interviewer: Right.

Carlos Piñera: So usually when we are talking about the negative effects of NAFTA, it comes mainly from political campaigns. People saying 'NAFTA is a threat to local economies and local companies', that kind of thing. I have seen a lot of these political campaigns painting NAFTA as the enemy, and once they get elected they forget about this kind of thinking, and they say that NAFTA is exactly the opposite!

12.3 Skills: Managing meetings

Listening 1: Starting the meeting

 2.31

Vanessa: OK, so it's my turn to chair this particular meeting with the rotation of the chair. So, we want to try and get through this in at the most forty-five minutes so that we can get to lunch. Is there anything arising from last week's minutes? I think these are OK from my point of view. What about other people?

Jack: Yeah. They look OK to me.

Vanessa: OK. So any matters arising from the Customer First training or is it all on the agenda? Right then. Let's go straight to the first point.

Listening 2: Discussing a problem colleague

 2.32

Vanessa: OK, so the next point on the meeting is the business skills course you ran in Brighton. Do you have any feedback on that?

Jack: The afternoon and evening went very well again.

Lucy: Did you get a round of applause again?

Jack: Er, no. I didn't this time. But I got a number of mentions about Nick Hay.

Vanessa: And how much better you are?

Jack: Yes.

Vanessa: Put that down in the minutes, Lucy.

Lucy: I'm not writing that down.

Jack: But seriously, criticism of Nick has come independently from two people over the last couple of days.

Sarah: Are you feeding that back at all to his line manager?

Jack: No.

Sarah: You're not?

Vanessa: I think you shouldn't, we've got to be a bit more proactive with this sort of stuff rather than just complaining to the trainer's manager. What was the nature of the criticism?

Jack: Well, he comes across as very self-important.

Vanessa: Yeah. Well, he did that when I met him. And I don't know how many years ago that was.

Jack: It turns people off. He just gives a PowerPoint presentation. There are no notes.

Stefanie: We're in a meeting. Is it urgent? The staff meeting I mentioned in the morning. I'll call you back.

Vanessa: Well, do they do evaluations on the courses?

Jack: I think that's the next step.

Vanessa: I think people would be prepared to say, you know, 'I don't think the materials are helpful'. There's usually a question on the evaluation form and participants should be receiving these. We have to make sure that people are filling the evaluation forms in before I take this problem with Nick any further.

13 Sustainable development
13.2 Practice: Masdar – the sustainable city

🔊 2.33

1 On February the 8th, 2008, the government of Abu Dhabi launched an ambitious plan to create what aims to be the world's first sustainable city, Masdar City. The Arabic word 'masdar' means 'the source'. This is fitting, because the aim is that Masdar City will become home to the world's leading businesses, academics and researchers, involved in the fields of renewable energy and sustainable technologies. Construction is already under way, and the first phase includes some of the city's most iconic buildings.

2 This is viewed by many as one of the world's most exciting developments. Seventeen kilometres south-east from the centre of Abu Dhabi in the United Arab Emirates, a vision for all future cities is taking shape. Masdar City aims to be zero waste, zero carbon and a fossil fuel-free city. The elimination of fossil fuel ultimately means that the air is clean, and the pedestrian-only streets provide a level of intimacy and charm for all to enjoy. The ultimate goal of its designers is the highest quality of life, with the lowest environmental impact. To realise this vision for a city of the future, the master planners have gone back in time.

3 The city's architects have drawn inspiration from traditional Arabian cities. Every aspect of the city is being designed to reduce energy demand. The city's north-east orientation reduces exposure to the hot desert sun. Parks and green spaces create breezy green oases. – Water features evaporate and cool the surrounding air. Without fossil fuel vehicles, Masdar City can be smaller and feature narrow streets. This means more shade and lower temperatures so people can walk, interact and play.

4 It also means Masdar City will feature the first large-scale zero-emission transportation system. A subway of personalised driverless electric vehicles that carry people and freight. In addition, a ground-level light rail system and a subterranean metro high-speed train keep the Masdar citizens well connected. You will never be further than two hundred and fifty metres from public transport.

Listening 2: Masdar City promotion Part 2

🔊 2.34

5 The city's design aims to reduce electricity and water demand as much as possible. Smart buildings and appliances will monitor consumption, and reduce demand further still. Masdar City can use around 80% less water than a conventional city. All of the consumer waste is either recycled or turned into energy. Waste water is processed and used to illuminate the city's landscape.

The city will draw one hundred percent of its electricity from renewable sources, such as solar, geo-thermal and even waste. The energy that Masdar City doesn't use gets exported onto the local power grid. But electricity isn't the only thing that will flow from Masdar City.

6 Masdar City is working with the government and schools of Abu Dhabi to raise awareness and engage communities in environmentally friendly behaviour. And soon the knowledge gained here will be shared with the world. The Masdar Institute has been built as part of phase one: it is the world's first university dedicated to studying sustainability and renewable technologies, and a hub around which green companies can flourish.

13.3 Skills: Problem-solving

Listening 1: Problems and causes

🔊 2.35

Director: How's Magid getting on?

Team leader: Er, well, really slow. I don't know why. I just feel the things that he has to do take too much time. I don't know if he's … if he's lazy, or maybe I pressure him too much or, you know, I'm pushing too much or …

Director: Yeah, well, that's … that's part of it. I mean, there could be a couple of reasons. One is because he's not ready.

Team leader: OK.

Director: Well, he's learning, yeah?

Team leader: Yeah.

Director: One reason could be that he's not doing any work. And we don't know because he's not working in the office.

Team leader: Yeah.

Director: And the third reason and probably the most likely reason is that you're thinking, like any person who's managing would think, 'I could have done that in half a day. Why's it taking him two days?'

Team leader: Uh-huh.

Director: But you know, you have to eventually let the people do it themselves … because if you don't give them a chance, if you do it all yourself, you just end up being really overworked.

Team leader: Yeah, yeah.

Listening 2: Deadlines and timescales

🔊 2.36

Team leader: You know, Magid is very helpful and willing. But I'm not happy at the moment with the things that he has done.

Director: Right.

Team leader: Do you know, I think 'Hmm. He's probably not taking the time seriously.'

Director: Right.

Team leader: You know. He has to finish everything on time.

Director: Right. So have you mailed him to say that? Because one thing you could do is say, when you give him work to do, say 'Look, I need this done by this time.' And give him a deadline. Yeah? So instead of saying, you know, 'Can you do this?', say 'Can you do this but have it back by six' or something.

Team leader: What I'm doing is I'm saying 'OK, so I need to do this, this, this and this.'

Director: Yeah.

Team leader: 'When do you think we're going to finish these things?'

Director: Right.

Team leader: He says 'OK, so I think I'll finish on Thursday.'

Director: Well, don't say it like that. Don't let him dictate the timescale to you. You say to him 'I need it done by this date.' If he can't do it by that time, he should come back to you and say 'I can't do it by then because you've already told me to do this and this and this.' And then you could say 'Well, yes, you're right. You need to do those, so you can do the work I've just given you by next Tuesday.'

Team leader: Right.

Director: OK? So you dictate the timescale to him. When you're managing people, you have to cater for all these sorts of different work styles. And sometimes it's very annoying.

14 Social enterprise
14.1 Theory: Perspectives on social enterprise

 2.37

Professor Jane Wei-Skillern: I think society's view of an entrepreneur is as a charismatic, hard-driving, celebrity type, and this way of thinking has been transferred to the social sector, sometimes at the cost of mission impact. For-profit entrepreneurs look to advance their organisations and build shareholder value. In the social sector, we need people who are committed to working towards the mission – in many cases even at the cost of advancing their own organisations or their own individual interests toward the larger cause. In the business world, being more organisational or ego-focused is acceptable, and we admire those types of leaders. These norms have also influenced current views of leadership in the social sector. However, to achieve large-scale and sustainable social impact, I believe that we need leaders that are less focused on individual and organisational-level success and instead work with and through others toward system, not just organisational-level, change.

Listening 2: Social enterprise goals

 2.38

Dr Helen Haugh: What we really want within a social enterprise is to treat the social goals as equally important as the economic and environmental goals. And one of the dangers is to sort of get what you might call 'mission drift'. This is when the economic goals become more important than the social goals. And if that happens then you are losing what is distinctive about social enterprises, which is about using your tried and tested techniques from the private sector to improve the performance of the social enterprise, but not losing sight of the social purpose of the organisation.

14.3 Skills: Conference calls

Listening 1: Opening the call

 2.39

Operator: Welcome to today's RESNA conference call. As a reminder, today's conference will be open and interactive and all lines will be open for the duration. We ask that you use a mute button when not speaking to cut down on the background noise. Also if you need to

step away from today's call, please do not place your line on hold as doing so may feed music into the conference. At this time, I would like to turn the conference over to Ms Nancy Meidenbauer. Please go ahead, ma'am.

Nancy Meidenbauer: Thank you so much, and welcome everyone to the RESNA conference on creating a brand for our financial loan programmes. We're lucky to have with us again Mary Virtue of Cornerstone Consultants and she's going to be working with us on our branding of our loan programme, the benefits of the brand, how to create one and also how to protect a brand. Before we begin, what we'd like to do is have a … to find out who's all on the call. We'd like to have a roll call, so I'd like people to identify themselves and what state they're from.

Jane Fortune: Jane Fortune from Arizona.

Marion Black: Marion Black from Michigan.

Justin Corey: Justin Corey, Pennsylvania.

Listening 2: The reputation of the brand

 2.40

Mary Virtue: So, I'm now going to open this up a little bit to get some sense from all of you. What do you know about your reputation, your brand? I think it's helpful to start with a baseline of where we are, so the question is – what do you know about what your reputation is right now?

Nancy Meidenbauer: I think maybe we have to call on these people. We'll start right at the beginning. Jane from Arizona.

Jane Fortune: Yes. Actually, I apologise. I got distracted by a different phone call so why don't you just go on to the next person.

Nancy Meidenbauer: Marion in Michigan.

Marion Black: Could you repeat the question?

Mary Virtue: Sure, sure. What I'm trying to find out is what do you know about your reputation right now? Is it positive? Are there places where it's negative? What is your sense of that?

Marion Black: I really don't have a sense of it. I think it's positive because we get a lot of applications and people seem to hear about us from friends or family or people that they know, so I guess it's positive since people spread the word for us.

Mary Virtue: Yeah.

Marion Black: But I don't know how to track it actually. I wouldn't know how to … how to get a sense of it …

Mary Virtue: Yes.

Language focus 2: Interrupting

2.41

1
A: Yes. Well, we've all …
B: Can I interrupt you? So, what I need to see …

2
A: Patrick was leaving in January and …
B: Just let me stop you there – he paid you the …

3
A: Well, I think the best thing is …
B: You might want to shut up Henry, because we've accepted …

Answer key

1 Market entry strategies

1.1 Theory: An overview of market entry strategies

Listening: Defining different types of market entry strategies

2

1 e **2** a **3** b **4** f **5** c **6** d

3

1 Indirect exporting – Advantages: Export houses are easy for foreign companies to use. Useful as a first entry step to get a feeling of a new market.

2 Direct exporting – Advantages: Using a company that already produces other complementary products allows you to access their client base.

3 Acquisition – Advantages: You acquire a presence in the country with a ready list of customers. Disadvantages: Problems integrating your acquisition into your own existing business. Acquisition will require some restructuring. Problem of valuation – difficult to know how much the company is really worth.

4 Greenfield development – Advantages: You can design everything afresh. You don't have difficulties of integration associated with acquisition. Disadvantages: No customer base and no distribution and sales structure and network.

5 Joint venture – Disadvantages: 80% failure rate in first five years. Local company will eventually grab your know-how and technology and then end the partnership.

6 Franchising – Advantages: Gives franchisor a lot of control – for example, you can stipulate the price and the way the product is sold.

Critical analysis

Suggested answer

The company can share the risks and costs with a partner.

Language focus: Market entry terms and concepts

1

1 electronic distribution **2** overseas production
3 risk exposure **4** exit strategy **5** profit opportunity
6 control **7** commitment

2 Overseas production would be included in: joint ventures, acquisition, franchising (each franchisee is a service delivery centre in that new market), Greenfield site development (new production facilities abroad).

Reading: Entry strategy overview

1

1 false **2** false **3** false **4** true **5** true **6** false **7** false
8 true

1.2 Practice: Entering the global market

Listening 1: Quintessentially client profile

1 60/40 male/female
2 35–55 (but can be younger or older)
3 business people and entrepreneurs, also celebrities and models
4 travel a lot, like the finer things in life, do exciting and interesting things
5 closed Sydney Harbour Bridge for a marriage proposal

Intercultural analysis

Suggested answer

Wealthy people are more internationally mobile than other sections of the population; they may well have studied overseas and have friends, contacts and interests abroad. As such there is a high probability that the lifestyle, aspirations and tastes of the rich in one country will be internationalised. This means in practice that luxury lifestyle companies can offer more standardised services. Cultural differences will still be apparent, but there will be less need for high levels of differentiation of products and services.

Listening 2: Characteristics of new country markets and local partners

2

1 high net worth individuals **2** vibrant restaurant scene
3 existing membership network **4** very important **5** think again
6 well positioned **7** entrepreneurial **8** the brand's sake

3

1 Having liquid assets generally means they have money to spend on enjoying the type of lifestyle that companies such as Quintessentially promote. Wealthy people with property assets but minimal cash are unlikely to sell their assets to finance a lifestyle of spending on services promoted by Quintessentially.

Listening 3: Quintessentially's market entry strategy

1 Diagram A shows a company with branches that are answerable to the head office, but there is less hierarchy and, we can assume, more autonomy to make decisions locally. Diagram B shows a company with a line of hierarchy where everything is controlled by the head office.

2

1 franchise model

2 Diagram A

3 The partner pays the capital costs to set up the office, which also allows for fast expansion; a local partner knows and understands the local culture and market.

4 It allows the company to provide a consistent high standard of service.

Transferable skill: Using a diagram to take notes

1 The wheels in Diagram A are the regional markets: Europe, Far East, Middle East and Africa, America. The hubs (centres) of the wheels are the four hub cities for these markets: London, Hong Kong, Dubai, New York.

2

1 The ends of the spokes represent the franchise offices. The hub cities are wholly owned branches of Quintessentially. These wholly owned offices manage the franchises for that particular region.

2 'Hub and spokes' is both a metaphor and a visual representation of an international organisational structure. It refers to a wheel where the hub is clearly the centre of operations, to which the individual spokes are attached.

Language focus: Adding emphasis to explanations

1 These sentences begin with the word 'What' or a noun phrase such as 'The key determining factor is ...', 'The first thing I want to say is ...'. The first part of the sentence finishes with a form of the verb 'to be'. Both parts of the sentence contain a verb. These types of constructions are known as *cleft sentences*.

2 *Suggested answers*

the main advantage is ..., the big disadvantage is ..., our biggest concern is ..., the biggest task facing us is ..., the main reason is ..., the thing is ..., What is important here is ..., What we need is ...

3 *Suggested answers*

1 What is important to remember is (that) joint ventures often fail.

2 The benefit of the franchise model is (that) it allows Quintessentially to standardise quality.

4 *Suggested answers*

1 ... to decide if you can do business with this person.

2 ... recruiting senior managers with strategic vision.

3 ... that they understand the local market.

4 ... to get good PR coverage in local markets.

5 ... failing to find the right local partner.

1.3 Skills: Brainstorming

Introduction

1

4, 2, 5, 1, 3

Listening 1: Principles of running a classic brainstorming session

1 Guidelines mentioned: 1, 4, 5, 7, 8, 10, 11

2

1 Guideline 8

2 In the selective phase, people select information that best solves the problem posed at the beginning of the brainstorming session. Whilst the emphasis in the first phase is on generating a large quantity of ideas, the emphasis in the second, selective phase is on quality. The selective phase is more controlled, and creative and lateral thinking tend not to be used.

Listening 2: A problematic brainstorming session

1 The aim is to list the reasons why they need to be consistent when dealing with customer enquiries.

2 There is no problem posed which the participants need to solve. Instead, they are given the solution and told to come up with reasons to support it. In addition, the manager 'leads' participants to the answer that he wants – the reference to following the company standard and customer feedback. Classic brainstorming sessions allow for creative thinking.

Language focus: Using fluent pronunciation features to move discussions forward

2 Mandy, what do‿you think‿about that?

3 That's‿a great‿idea!

4 What‿about building‿on Paul's‿idea to ...

2 The rule is that we link two words together when the end of the first word finishes with a consonant or consonant cluster (e.g. /ŋk/ in 'think') and the start of the second word begins with a vowel (e.g. /ə/ in 'about').

3

1 We're going to start by looking at ...

2 How about going with Ian's idea to ...

3 Let's go with this idea of ...

4 Maybe we should go with Dave's idea of ...

5

1 McDonald's

2 L'Oréal

3 Nike

6

1 McDonald's: I'm lovin' it (aymlovinit)

2 L'Oréal cosmetics: Because you're worth it (becuzyaworthit)

3 Nike: Just do it (jusdoit)

2 Standardisation and differentiation

2.1 Theory: Different approaches to international marketing

Introduction

1

1 Unlike in Italy, in the USA both children and adults generally eat cereal and toast for breakfast. Biscuits would be considered an unhealthy option for breakfast; they are acceptable for a mid-morning or afternoon snack.

2 Nearly 100% of all washing machines sold in the UK are front-opening models, as they are generally located in the kitchen under a worktop/counter.

3 The company thought that the word 'embarazar' ('to make pregnant') meant 'to embarrass', so the ad read: 'It won't leak in your pocket and make you pregnant'.

4 For many Asians, white flowers represent bad luck and even death.

Language focus 1: International marketing terminology

1 g **2** h **3** d **4** f **5** c **6** a **7** b **8** e

Reading: Two perspectives on international marketing strategies

1

1 B **2** A

2

Student A – Text A

1 Competitive capabilities and competitive position in the marketplace

2 They don't sell any beef products such as hamburgers or Big Macs.

3 Globalisation strategy and differentiation strategy

4 Companies whose products are not culturally specific and whose promotions are easily understood

5 Very uncommon

Student B – Text B

1 For economies of scale benefits, i.e. lower production costs per unit.

2 They think that these are universal, i.e. they communicate across cultures.

3 Not universal; they reflect the value system of the home country.

4 Speak to consumers in each country in a way they understand.

5 Cultural segmentation, i.e. produce different promotions for different segments according to differences in the customers' culture.

Language focus 2: International marketing word formations and word partnerships

1

a standardise **b** standardised/standard **c** differentiate
d different/differentiated **e** adapt **f** adaptable
g environmental **h** globalise **i** global **j** segment
k segmented **l** minimise **m** minimal

2

1 standardised/differentiated **2** minimise **3** global
4 environment **5** segment/segmentation
6 adaptation/differentiation

3 *Suggested answers*

1 ... product adaptation to the needs of local markets.

2 ... then it makes more and more sense to plan strategy around global market segments across countries. Not simple market segments within countries.

3 ... how influential the socio-cultural environment is on customers' buying behaviour.

4 ... ensure that their tax obligations are minimised.

5 ... promote closer integration between member states then companies are more likely to take a standardised approach to their regional marketing strategy.

2.2 Practice: Piaggio Vietnam

Language focus 1: Describing brands and products

1

1 historical importance **2** identity **3** representative
4 comfortable and efficient **5** functional **6** brands and products

Listening 1: Brand strategy

1

1 the values are (Italian) heritage, design and glamour; customers are 'buying an Italian dream'

2 exactly the same

3 They will introduce the Piaggio brand.

4 It will be 10–20% higher.

5 top end of the mass market

6 They're not a low-quality brand. It's not in their core DNA.

Listening 2: Promotion strategy

1

Promotion: In Vietnam the strategy is to emphasise the connection to Italy (obvious and irrelevant to Italians), plus more extreme positioning as a glamorous, fashionable brand in Vietnam.

Dealer network: In Vietnam, there is more standardised branding and service and it is more professionally organised. In Europe, the network is not standardised apart from at flagship stores.

Celebrities: Hollywood stars such as DiCaprio are used across global markets, but local celebrities are very important. Local Vietnamese celebrities need to be seen on Vespas in Vietnam.

Listening 3: Product strategy

1 true **2** false **3** true **4** false **5** false

Critical analysis

Suggested answers

1 It associates Vespa with the glamour of Hollywood and its star actors. As the film is also set in Rome, it reinforces the connection between Italy and the brand for a non-Italian audience.

2 In general, product placement works by connecting a company's products and brands to the association the public has of that particular movie or actor.

Language focus 2: Describing products, brands and markets

1

1 branded

2 mass (you can say 'mass market brand' but not 'mass brand')

3 emerging

4 competition (but you can say 'competitive market')

5 innovation (you can say 'brand innovation' but not 'innovation brand')

6 retailer (but you can say 'retail product')

3

1 core product   **2** niche market   **3** premium-priced
4 fastest-growing segments   **5** well-known brand

Transferable skill: Using repetition for persuasive effect

2 *Suggested answers*

a The Piaggio scooter will be far superior to the competition; in terms of product quality, in terms of service levels, and in terms of reliability.

b The Piaggio brand will be very different from the Vespa brand; it will have a different image, a different price and be aimed at a very different target market.

2.3 Skills: Managing time

Introduction

4 A good time manager will prioritise and put tasks in all four boxes; a bad time manager will probably group all tasks in box 1.

Language focus: Time management language

1

1 f   **2** a   **3** g   **4** c   **5** i   **6** j   **7** h   **8** d   **9** e   **10** b

2 To fail to keep a track of time, to suffer from procrastination, and to miss a deadline are all bad for time management.

4 *Suggested answers*

It means if you don't plan properly, you will not achieve your goals. Planning can be inappropriate when it may hinder spontaneous thought or action and lead to inflexibility.

Listening 1: Lecture on time management

2 *Suggested answers*

Goals, priorities and planning

Ask why you are doing this.

Ask what will happen if I don't do it.

Experience

Experience teaches us how to do things better – we learn from our mistakes.

Planning

Plan at multiple levels – day, week, semester, etc.

Build flexibility into your plan.

'to-do' lists

Do the most difficult / least attractive thing first.

Intercultural analysis

2 *Suggested answers*

Person X (from the punctual culture) will probably arrive on time for the meeting and expect Person Y (the person from the more flexible culture) to also be there. If Person Y isn't there, Person X may become angry or frustrated at having to wait, and see this as a lack of respect. Person Y, arriving late, will perhaps find Person X's attitude as inflexible and even shocking.

Listening 2: IT company team meeting

1 false   **2** true   **3** true

Critical analysis

Suggested answers

1 Generally, yes. The team seem to be fairly open and honest about the need to have stricter deadlines, but also about the realities of their workplace and the need for some flexibility.

2 She does not seem very strict, but she obviously thinks this is important. She seems to be trying to involve the team members in the improvement process.

Writing 1: Writing notes for presentations

Language focus: Preparing slide presentation notes

3 All the guidelines are used except 2 and 9.

Writing skill: Creating bullet points on slides and adding notes

1 *Suggested answers*

Slide 3:

1 Simple, compelling proposition

2 Reason to respond now

3 Persuasive, engaging words

4 Clever, demanding ideas rarely work

Slide 4:

1 Length of advert critical

2 Include lots of captions and voice-overs

3 Show needs and solutions

4 Make it clear you need response from beginning

2

Slide 3 = 4th   Slide 4 = 1st and 4th

3 *Suggested answers*

Slide 3 – 4th bullet point: big advertising agencies

Slide 4 – 1st bullet point: 90/60/30 secs

Slide 4 – 4th bullet point: telephone number bottom of screen

Critical analysis

Text-only presentation – Advantage: it is quick to prepare and is especially appropriate for regular weekly internal presentations within the company or organisation. Disadvantage: having no visual images means that slides are less engaging and consequently it is more difficult to maintain an audience's interest.

Image-only slides – Advantage: the right image can easily illustrate an idea and inspire an audience. Disadvantage: for inexperienced presenters there are no text prompts to help them talk through the slide.

Combination of text and image – Advantage: clear explicit linking of words and images helps audience to absorb information yet still provides text prompts to help more inexperienced speakers. Disadvantage: slides can get crowded with too much information.

3 Competition within industries

3.1 Theory: Five Forces Theory of Competition

Listening 1: General description of the 'Five Forces' diagram

1

1 new entrants   2 competitive rivalry   3 substitute
4 buyers/suppliers   5 suppliers/buyers

2

1 Horizontal competition is competition from firms at the same level; vertical competition is competition from the buyers and suppliers in the supply chain. Note that while the diagram shows buyers and suppliers on a horizontal axis, they are said to be in vertical competition as they are not on the same level.

2 Horizontal competition – new entrants, substitutes, competitive rivalry amongst existing competitors
Vertical competition – buyers and suppliers

3 Firms should reassess the market place.

Listening 2: Analysis of competitive rivalry

2

1 more   2 less   3 more   4 less   5 more   6 less   7 more

3 *Suggested answers*

1 … they have similar strengths and weaknesses.
2 … the same customers.
3 … fill capacity.
4 … tend to buy the product with the lowest price.
5 … a lot of resources learning how to use the product.
6 … they don't see opportunities elsewhere / exit barriers are high.

Language focus 1: Changing comparisons

1 The first sentence shows a standard comparison for specific, fixed circumstances. The second sentence moves the emphasis to 'more competitors' to highlight the important information.

2 *Suggested answers*

2 … the more likely they will buy on quality considerations and therefore the less competitive the industry will be.
3 … the more new companies will enter into the industry and consequently the more competitive the industry will be.
4 … the more likely customers will switch to substitutes and as a result the higher the competition in the industry is likely to be.

Language focus 2: Phrases of competition with dependent prepositions

1

1 on, with   2 of, of   3 on   4 of, in, upon/on   5 of, in

2

threat **of** new entrants/substitutes
rivalry **among** existing competitors
bargaining power **of** suppliers/buyers

3 *Suggested answers*

There would be a cost in terms of time and effort: learning how the new operating system works. There would also be a financial cost

as most operating systems cost money. Some peripherals, such as printers and mobile phones, might only work with the old operating system and so would also need to be replaced.

3.2 Practice: The UK budget hotel industry

Language focus 1: Effectively conveying information with noun phrases

1

1 the no-frills airlines
2 one thing the recession has taught businesses
3 a major beneficiary of any decisions
4 confident predictions about the coming year
5 the UK budget hotel chains
6 conspicuous value for money

2

a 2   **b** 6   **c** 1   **d** 4   **e** 5   **f** 3

3 *Suggested answers*

Main idea: Companies that offer great value for money, like cheap airlines and budget hotels, can do well even in difficult financial times.
Suggested title: Low prices push up profits

Transferable skill: Effective reading using skimming and scanning

1

1 skimming   2 skimming   3 neither   4 scanning   5 scanning

2

1 scanning (answer: Frank Barrett)
2 skimming (answer: A journalistic style)
2 skimming (answer: Budget hotels)
4 scanning (answer: Yes – the UK)

3 They both save time, but there is a danger that you may miss key information or get the wrong overall impression.

Reading: Newspaper article on budget hotels

1 a

2 2

3

	cheap airlines	budget hotels	supermarkets
'no frills' style	Yes	Yes	Not stated
invite early booking	Yes	Yes	
self check-in	Yes	Yes	
monitor prices of rival chains	Not stated	Yes	Yes
offer budget and luxury ranges	Not stated	Not stated	Not stated
conduct price-cutting	Not stated	Yes	Yes
offer a 'price check' programme	Not stated	Yes	Not stated

Language focus 2: Recognising persuasive language

1 1, 2 and 4

2

1 In the budget hotel <u>war</u>, it seems everyone's <u>a winner</u>.

2 They <u>love</u> the value we offer, our clean and <u>comfortable</u> rooms and <u>the warm welcome</u> they receive from our team members.

4 <u>The ferocious competition</u> can only mean ever more <u>attractive</u> prices.

3

1 **1** b **2** c **3** d **4** a

2 **1** Catch our smile: happiness (and humour in the meaning of 'catch' – usually the collocation is 'catch a plane')

2 Motion and emotion: a feeling of attachment to the car

3 Save today, save tomorrow: caring about money but also about the environment

4 Stay smart: stay in a stylish hotel / make a clever choice about accommodation

3.3 Skills: Making a sales pitch

Listening: Sales presentation

1

1 B **2** C

2

1 great **2** paperwork, communication **3** familiar

4 doesn't have to be **5** intuitive, cost-effective

3

1 b **2** d **3** e **4** a **5** c

Language focus 1: Presentation techniques of persuasion

2

1 smaller **2** wherever **3** prioritise **4** to help make

5 gives you **6** Bizantra won't **7** simple **8** great-value

9 see for yourself

3 The presentation describes Bizantra's product service features and benefits. Unlike the first presentation, it is not divided into two clearly identifiable parts; the structure moves between features and benefits throughout the presentation.

4

Contrast a problem with a solution:

… even if your PC fails you, Bizantra won't.

Use a positive adjective to show enthusiasm:

great-value

Group three adjectives together to give a higher impact:

Bizantra is integrated, efficient and simple.

Repeat the same language structure to make a powerful impact:

… whomever you want, wherever they are.
Store contacts, track discussions and store your sales effort in one place.

5

1 Why not see for yourself?

2 the smarter, smaller business

3 Easily manages record keeping, absence tracking and compliance to help make informed staffing decisions, fast.
our easy-to-use Finance application gives you an at-a-glance summary of all your finances

Language focus 2: Pausing and stressing words in presentations

1 <u>Bizantra</u>| is an integrated <u>suite</u>| of all the <u>essential</u>| <u>latest-technology</u>| <u>business tools</u>| for the <u>smarter</u>| <u>smaller business</u>.| It gives you <u>everything</u>| a growing business <u>needs</u>,| all in one <u>place</u>| and for just a <u>small</u>| subscription <u>fee</u>.

2 The pauses are located immediately after the stressed words. The exception is for common word partnerships, such as 'latest-technology', 'business tools' and 'small(er) business'. These partnerships generally have both words stressed, but there is no pause after the first word as this would split the partnership down the middle.

3

1 A **2** C

4 Entrepreneurship

4.1 Theory: Fostering entrepreneurship

Language focus 1: The language of risk

1

1 for **2** of **3** to/towards

2

1 mitigate risk, spread risk, minimise risk

2 take risks

3 understand risk, tolerate risk, calculate risk, control risk

3

1 reputational risk

2 operational risk (plus possible financial risk)

3 reputational risk (plus possible financial risk)

4 financial risk

Listening 1: New research on risk

2

1 B **2** A **3** C

Transferable skill: Conveying meaning visually

1 *Suggested answer*

The image of the light bulb shows an entrepreneur as idea generator. The image of the hands holding flowers shows an entrepreneur as someone who grows, nurtures, creates and produces. The image of the rodeo shows an entrepreneur as risk-taker.

Listening 2: Young entrepreneurs

2 Dr Shai Vyakarnam agrees with the statement. His reasoning is that young people have a similar risk profile to serial entrepreneurs.

Language focus 2: Giving friendly advice

1

1 get **2** Get **3** Earn **4** go **5** Learn **6** Go **7** Go
8 Get **9** Stretch **10** Do

3

1 The phrases are said as commands or orders. The word stress is as follows: <u>Go</u> and learn from many of them. <u>Get</u> networking.

2 The phrases are said as a form of friendly advice. The word stress is as follows: Go and <u>learn</u> from many of them. Get <u>networking</u>.

4.2 Practice: Jack Ma and Alibaba

Reading: The rise of Jack Ma

1

Paragraph 1: The achievements of Jack Ma
Paragraph 2: The philosophy of Jack Ma
Paragraph 3: Different companies connected to Alibaba.com
Paragraph 4: How the Internet has grown in China
Paragraph 5: How the Internet is used in China

2

1 primary business tool **2** mental discipline
3 Yahoo! and Softbank **4** the Chinese government
5 competitive and profitable

3

1 weighting **2** world('s) stage **3** counter-intuitive
4 conventional wisdom **5** formulate
6 an online payment service platform **7** a steep curve
8 government backed **9** overturned
10 internet filtering technologies

Critical analysis

1 Doing things differently from the general view of what is the 'right thing to do' is perhaps a higher-risk strategy. However, it also ensures that thinking is original and creative, which leads to radical innovation.

Language focus: Quantifying data

1 *Suggested answers*

1 a huge number of **2** over 50% of **3** 80% of

2 Internet users: 1, 2, 3, 4, 6, 7, 9, 10   Internet traffic: 1, 4, 5, 6, 8, 10

3

1 The population of those countries varies from around 30 million to 225 million. / The number of people of those countries varies from around 30 million to 225 million.

2 Global Ports Inc. only handles a small quantity of freight in Europe.

3 Only a small number of people work over 12 hours a day. / Only a small fraction of the workforce work over 12 hours a day.

4 The great majority of UK tourists go to France, but a significant number also go to Spain.

5 With the new booking system, the number of visitors is now controllable.

4.3 Skills: Collaborative and aggressive negotiation strategies

Language focus 1: Negotiating strategies

1

a collaborative, e.g. compromising
b aggressive, e.g. threatening

2

Collaborative	Aggressive
promises	commands
recommendations	warnings
commitments	blank refusals
open information exchanges	threats
shared secrets	

3

1 d **2** g **3** c **4** a **5** e **6** f **7** b

4 In the corpus, the examples in the left-hand column are extremely rare or non-existent. This is because they can sound very aggressive. In every case, expressions in the right-hand column are far more typical.

5 *Suggested answer*

This relates to the quote at the top of the page. If you want to maintain a long-term relationship, then probably a collaborative approach will mean the relationship is better. However, if the situation is extremely serious then a more aggressive approach may achieve your goal.

Listening 1: Discussing effective negotiating

1 b **2** b **3** a

Listening 2: A price negotiation

1 d **2** a **3** b **4** c

Language focus 2: Collaborative negotiating language

1

1 g **2** f **3** c **4** a **5** b **6** e **7** d **8** h

2

1 8h **2** 3c **3** 4a **4** 7d **5** 6e **6** 2f **7** 5b **8** 1g

Writing 2: Business plan and executive summary

Writing skill 1: Outline structure for a business plan

1

1 d **2** e **3** h **4** a **5** f **6** g **7** b **8** c

Language focus: Key features of an executive summary

1

1 d **2** e **3** b **4** f **5** c **6** a

2

1 Paragraph 1
2 Paragraph 2 (from beginning of paragraph to 'monthly basis')
3 Paragraph 2 (from 'According to the Association of Canadian ...' to 'two years)
4 Paragraph 2 (last sentence)
5 Paragraph 3 (from beginning of paragraph to 'excellent prices')
6 Paragraph 4
7 Paragraph 4 (from 'all three competitors' to 'awareness campaign')
8 Paragraph 5
9 Paragraph 6 (sentence 1)
10 Paragraph 6 (sentence 2)

5 Crisis management

5.1 Theory: Dealing with crisis events

Introduction

1

1 A   2 A   3 B   4 A (and possibly B)   5 A (and possibly B)
6 B   7 A   8 A   9 B (and possibly A)   10 A

Reading 1: 'Black Swan' metaphor

1

B and C

2

1 impossible   2 huge   3 mistakenly
3 He means that it is always easier to see what to do after the event has already happened.

Reading 2: Dealing with unknown crisis events

1

1 true   2 false   3 false   4 false   5 true   6 false   7 false
8 false

2

1 paramount   2 an absolute must   3 tunnel vision
4 figuring out   5 give breathing room   6 day-to-day business
7 cascading effect   8 plummet

Language focus: Comparison of strategy and tactics

1 tactics: B   strategy: A
2 The word 'tactics' sometimes has negative associations. There is a sense that tactics can be opportunistic – taking unfair advantage of opportunities that present themselves in that moment. The word can also have positive associations too, as seen from the partnerships with 'useful', and 'effective'. The word 'strategy', on the other hand, has more positive connotations, being associated with something that is solid and properly thought out with due care and attention. Strategy is generally seen as a plan that is in operation for a long duration of time, whereas tactics are planned for a relatively short period of time – a specific meeting or crisis event, etc.

3

1 e   2 d   3 a   4 b   5 c

5

1 a good strategy   2 good tactics
Planning to be market leader of your industry sector from being the number 4 in the sector is a medium- to long-term plan and will be wide-ranging, involving all aspects of the company's business in this sector. These are characteristics of strategic planning. A plan to achieve a successful outcome in the next stage of negotiations is tactical as it refers to only one part of the negotiations. The organisation might well have a negotiating strategy, but how it is implemented in a particular stage of negotiations will be tactical.

6

1 tactical   2 tactics   3 strategy

5.2 Practice: Successfully dealing with a crisis

Introduction

1

1 The probable loss of a financial investment of €7 million – a loss caused by the global financial crisis.
2 Product and technology development – the money was needed to fund this.
3 It wasn't; at this point the technology was at the product development stage i.e. it hadn't yet been commercialised, with products available for sale.

Language focus: Contrast financial terms 'investment', 'capital' and 'equity'

1

1 b i   2 c iii   3 a ii

2

1 investment horizon   2 equity stake   3 raise capital

3

1 investment   2 investments   3 equity   4 investment
5 capital

4

1 The company spent €12.4 million on a new factory in Germany; this shows evidence of expansion and continued progress.
2 The company sold some of its investments. The company needs to fund its activities from its investments.
3 The company offers shares in itself to staff and Directors to align their interests with the interests of the company and incentivise performance and staff loyalty.
4 The company received monthly reports on how much its investments are worth and whether they have increased or decreased in value. The company needs to carefully balance the money it needs to fund its everyday activities with available cash.
5 The company successfully raised £36 million finance in London when it listed on the London Stock Exchange. This money would be essential to fund the next phase of product development. The successful raising of capital indicates that investors had confidence in the company at that time.

Listening 1: In search of funding

1 He mentions 2, 3, 5 and 7.

2 They tried to raise money from existing investors together with a new investor.

3 *Suggested answer*

The investors coming in were investing on a shorter horizon than was needed. The State and Federal Government were approached, but didn't support the company. They also approached the big utility companies that they were working with, as it was only a small amount of money they needed – however, the companies were slow to respond and the crisis happened quickly. They also looked at their current investors, but they couldn't help. In the end they approached an individual who was happy to invest.

4

1 they took no action when action was required

2 enable us to overcome the present difficulties

3 appeared after being hidden for a long time

4 he had done research

Listening 2: Lessons learned

3

1 key   **2** someone else   **3** unlikely to emerge

4 a single investor   **5** trust

Listening 3: Leading out of a crisis

1 *Suggested answers*

1 He felt as if he was under siege and as though he had lost control of the situation.

2 He put in more hours and he did a lot more overseas travel to Europe.

3 Use positive body language – keep smiling, stand up straight, keep your head up, keep your shoulders up.

4 Talk about the future, the breakthroughs in the technology; tell suppliers they are going to get paid.

5 investors and suppliers

2 *Suggested answer*

Stress reduction techniques include slow breathing at the moment of critical stress, doing sport or being physically active.

Transferable skill: Confident and insecure body language

1 *Suggested answers*

The following answers are typical for a western culture such as the UK or the USA, and may be different for your culture.

Body language type	Communicates confidence	Communicates insecurity
eye contact	consistent eye contact (but avoiding staring)	darting eyes or looking down a lot
facial expression	natural smile	forced smile
gestures	keep hands still or make slow movements with hands	hand wringing, hands in constant motion
the way you stand or sit	stand straight with head up and shoulders slightly back; keep your hands out of your pockets	head down, shoulders down, crossed arms
the way you greet someone	firm but not 'iron grip' handshake and don't hold on too long	limp handshake

2 *Suggested answers*

1 Culture A may think culture B is weak or passive. Culture B may think Culture A is aggressive.

2 Culture A may think culture B is dishonest or embarrassed. Culture B may think again that culture A is very aggressive, and perhaps angry.

3 Culture A may think culture B is very unfriendly and cold, whereas culture B might think that culture A is behaving strangely, or is far too friendly.

5.3 Skills: Dealing with conflict

Introduction

2

1 e   **2** a   **3** f   **4** d   **5** c   **6** b

Language focus 1: Conflictual turn-taking

1

1 throwing back the criticism   **2** direct refusal   **3** interrupting

2 *Suggested answers*

Making predictions here is possible because usually people respond in similar ways, and the language also gives us hints. David's comment in 1 is a criticism, therefore we can predict John will try to react directly to the criticism. Comment 2 involves a request, therefore accepting or refusing it is very likely. In 3, we can see that John has not finished his message, which suggests he has been interrupted.

3 Answers 1, 2, 3, 4, 5, 7, 8 and 10 are appropriate. The following are not: 3 avoid eye contact (this is highly dependent on culture – in some cultures this can help reduce conflict, but in other cultures it may be interpreted quite negatively); 6 don't respond at all; 9 keep your intonation flat (in English, this can be interpreted as aggressive, or bored).

4 Other ways of reducing conflict include apologising and being a supportive listener (through body language and the use of positive words like 'Sure' and 'Absolutely').

Listening 1: Opening the meeting

1

1 false   **2** false   **3** false   **4** true

Listening 2: Disagreements

1

1 no opportunity whatsoever to get any benefit
2 meaningless
3 business sense whatsoever

2 The level of conflict has increased a lot compared to the beginning of the meeting. For instance, they are disagreeing very forcefully with each other, and are using quite emotionally charged language ('stupid', 'ridiculous').

Listening 3: Closing stages

1

1 John's company will pay the legal fees, and David's company will pay the rent.
2 High – the men are very rude to each other.

2 They were not successful at all; the meeting really gets out of control.

Critical analysis

1 The dangers of conflict are that it can cloud people's judgement, and it can have long-term negative effects on the relationship between the speakers and/or their organisations. Many mergers and acquisitions fail because of irreconcilable conflict (see unit 11.1).

2 Making any kind of change will usually involve conflict at some level, and conflict is often seen as an essential part of making and implementing innovations.

Language focus 2: Cooperative and aggressive idioms and metaphors

1

1 h 2 c 3 b 4 d 5 e 6 g 7 a 8 f
2 conflictual 4, 5, 6, 7, 8   not conflictual: 1, 2, 3
3 Suggested answers
1 Well, to be honest, there were discussions about raising it further.
2 We think this proposal needs reconsidering.
3 It's difficult to see how this can be implemented in practice.
4 (As this is a sarcastic comment, it is probably best to say nothing.)

6 Leadership

6.1 Theory: Leadership styles and qualities

Language focus 1: Describing leadership styles

1

1 d 2 f 3 b 4 c 5 a 6 e
2
1 resistant 2 adrift 3 exemplify 4 mastered
5 competencies 6 inhibit 7 hallmark 8 dampens

Reading 1: Leadership styles in practice

1

1 coercive 2 authoritative 3 affiliative 4 democratic
5 pacesetting 6 coaching

2

1 D 2 D 3 A 4 A 5 NG 6 NG 7 NG 8 D 9 A

3

2 Suggested answer
Because different leadership styles are needed for different circumstances and therefore it is important for managers to be able to adapt to the needs of their staff and the circumstances.

Reading 2: Leadership qualities and Emotional Intelligence

1

1 consists 2 composed 3 corresponding

4

1 SS 2 SM 3 SS 4 SM 5 SS 6 SS

Language focus 2: Word partnerships with 'self'

1 c 2 b 3 a 4 c 5 c 6 a

6.2 Practice: Nikki King – a business leader

Introduction

1

1 Nikki King was the first female Managing Director of a truck company in the UK and the first female president of both the Society of Operations Engineers and the Institute of Road Transport Engineers.

3

1 Leadership 2 Management 3 leaders 4 managers
5 manage 6 lead

Listening 1: The qualities of leaders and managers

2

1 Nikki King believes that a good leader has passion, vision and a long-term plan; is consistent and inspirational, and acknowledges that it is the people around him/her who enable him/her to be a good leader.
2 Nikki argues that leaders are born and that good managers can be made.
3 Nikki King says that good leaders are inspirational and lead their followers. Good managers make plans but then delegate someone else to do the job.

Listening 2: Leadership in different sectors

2 Suggested answers
Leader communication: You can tell people what to do in the private sector. In social enterprises you need to be more persuasive.
Staff motivations: People's motivations are more varied in social enterprises.
Level of 'red tape' (bureaucracy): There is a lot more bureaucracy outside of private enterprise.
Commercial mindset: Social enterprises tend to be non-commercial.
Rules: There are many rules and regulations in the local government sector.

Listening 3: Advice for business leaders

1

1 Be honest, be yourself. **2** Practise what you preach.

3 Don't deviate from your vision.

Language focus 1: The language of leadership

1

passion: be passionate about / have a passion for / passions run high

vision: have a vision / have visions / be a visionary

consistent: be consistent / act consistently / lack consistency

inspire: seek divine inspiration / be inspirational / inspire your followers by example

dictator: avoid a dictatorial approach / be a dictatorial ruler / be a real dictator

persuade: be persuasive / have persuasive arguments / lack powers of persuasion

motivate: have the ability to motivate others / be highly motivated / be motivated by greed

2 The inappropriate ones are:

passions run high (= get upset)

have visions (usually associated with unreal mental states)

lack consistency

seek divine inspiration

be a dictatorial ruler / be a real dictator (the term 'dictator' is negative; 'strong leader' is a more positive expression)

lack powers of persuasion

be motivated by greed

3 *Suggested answer*

All of these positive attributes are very important for leaders. Charisma is often cited as very important, as are self-belief and belief in the enterprise. A high degree of energy is also common among leaders.

Language focus 2: Understanding proverbs

1 It means don't be a hypocrite – if you say staff should do something, you should also do it yourself.

2

1 Better late than never – it is better to be late than to not come at all. It suggests that late results are better than no results.

2 A bad workman always blames his tools – employees may blame their tools rather than themselves when something goes wrong. It's important to accept responsibility, even for mistakes.

3 A bird in the hand is worth two in the bush – you should value what you have, rather than value what you might get if conditions favour you. This relates to the importance of concrete results.

4 Give a man a fish, feed him for a day, teach a man to fish, feed him for a lifetime – developing autonomous or empowered employees is of great value. This relates to the importance of training.

5 Too many cooks spoil the broth – too many leaders or managers will lead to problems.

Critical analysis

1 The key issue is that women tend to face far more external (i.e. non-job related) pressures and demands than men – for example, dealing with family problems.

6.3 Skills: Motivating staff

Listening 1: Describing transactional and transformational motivation

1 Transactional: do what the boss says; experience tells us what to expect; telling; pointing

Transformational: need to work in new ways; consulting; togetherness

2 *Suggested answers*

Transactional managers have a very clear idea of what the job involves, because the job doesn't really change, and tell the staff exactly how they should do it. Transformational managers, in contrast, recognise that their work environment is dynamic and changing, and therefore approach their staff more as fellow team members. A transformational manager will encourage the team to understand and solve the problems they face together.

3 The change has come about due to rapid changes driven by technology.

4 Photo A shows a more transactional manager who is directing the player, as opposed to working together with him.

Listening 2: Motivating different types of people

2

a coaster   **b** star   **c** problem child   **d** striver

3 Stars need lots of contact and a manager who praises them. They should be given projects that harness their ability. Problem children mostly need telling what to do. A manager should make a plan of action and help them use and improve their skills.

Listening 3: Team-building meeting in a hotel

It seems unlikely that this manager will motivate this team, due to both his style of speaking and the content of his talk. This group of employees probably will not relate to the football analogy, and his use of very idiomatic expressions like 'singing from the rooftops' and speed of speaking may confuse English speakers of this level.

Language focus: Using transactional and transformational language

1 Transactional: 2, 3, 4, 7, 10   Transformational: 1, 5, 6, 8, 9

2

a A more transactional approach may be good, and the manager may say something direct like 'You need to meet these deadlines, otherwise (the team will suffer / your position may need to be reviewed …)'.

b A more transformational approach here may be good. For instance, the manager can ask what projects the star wants to work on, and what he/she can offer.

c A transactional approach, perhaps with a slight warning. The manager could remind the employee of his/her obligations.

d Perhaps a transformational approach, with the manager exploring how the employee would like to be rewarded (e.g. with more responsibility).

Intercultural analysis

Suggested answers

1 A strongly transactional approach might be best in a workplace where doing the task in exactly the right way is essential. For example, in some factories where safety is an issue.

2 Some people might find the lack of clear direction offered by a transformational manager frustrating, and it may appear that the manager does not know what he/she is doing.

3 In both situations, there is likely to be a lot of friction and misunderstanding. The transactional manager might appear dictatorial to the transformationally minded staff. A transformational manager may seem to lack direction and clarity to transactionally minded staff.

Writing 3: Writing effective emails

Language focus: Features of effective emails

1 *Suggested answers*

The guidelines presented here are general ones relevant for most situations. Some of these rules might not apply, however, depending on the 'house style' and culture of organisations. It might be perfectly acceptable, for example, for internal emails between colleagues within the same organisation to be dry, highly transactional messages that simple convey the necessary information.

3

1 f **2** h **3** b **4** c **5** a **6** g **7** d **8** e

4 *Suggested answers*

1 In reference to [your letter dated 2nd July …]

2 I look forward to hearing from you soon.

3 I'd be happy to help out with …

4 Do you think we could …?

5 Please refer to the documents attached.

6 With regards to [your last email / your idea …]

7 Our view is that …

8 Following on from [the conference call last night, I'd like to emphasise …]

9 Please let me know if this is convenient.

10 We might find that [Option A leads to problems with …]

Writing skill 1: Writing short messages in fast email exchanges

1 E, A, C, B, D

2 b

3 The guidelines are generally followed although there are some punctuation mistakes: the double full stop in the first sentence of email A, the missing apostrophe in 'lets' in email B. The language recognises and builds relationships between the correspondents – this is not simply a dry communication of information.

4

a Hi Marlene, All best

b good job, bit

c – good job – the last bit works very well too – concise

d – concise

e gets across message, All best

f I've, I'll

5

a Dear Marlene, with best wishes

b Well done *or* You've done a good job; bit = part

c Well done. The last part works very well too, as it is concise

d it is concise

e gets across the message, All the best

f I have, I will

6 *Suggested answers*

A Dear Marlene, with best wishes

Well done. The last part works very well too as it is concise and gets across the message that the clients are getting a lot here.

I have put a few comments down with a couple of alternative wordings in a few places (please see the attached document). I will leave it to Sylvie to decide which ones she likes.

With best wishes

Max

B Dear Sylvie,

I think this looks very good. Let's go with this. This is another part of the job that has been done well.

Best wishes

Max

C Dear Max and Sylvie,

Please find my comments attached. The introduction in particular is very nice.

All the best,

Sylvie

Writing skill 2: Writing a longer email

1

Paragraph 1: State purpose of writing

Paragraph 2: Explain issue in detail

Paragraph 3: Request action

2 Months of the year which have more than one syllable have been shortened: 'Nov/Oct/Sept'. Also, the words "at the" have been omitted before the words 'end of Sept'. No other 'informal professional' email features are used, indicating that a more formal and polite style is being used here.

3

1 typically

2 the following

3 are very keen to

4 considerably influence

4 I want to follow up on …

let you know there is a problem with the planned launch dates

we will lose a whole year of sales.

we need to give these customers what they want – it will have a big impact on sales.

Please look at the dates again and see how you can tighten the schedule.

7 International communication

7.1 Theory: Culture in international business

Introduction

1 Culture more relevant to the workplace includes: dress at work, customs of professional groups, punctuality, directness of communication, decision-making, national customs, attitudes to power and of organisation's custom. However traditional aspects of culture such as art and music can be relevant in providing events where business people can socialise and build relationships.

Language focus: Key intercultural words and concepts

1

1 e **2** b **3** h **4** j **5** g **6** i **7** k **8** f **9** c **10** a **11** d

2 Recognition, Respect, Reconciliation, Realisation

3 Respect: 4   Reconciliation: 2   Realisation: 3

Listening 1: International organisations and their cultures

2

1 a **2** c **3** c **4** b **5** a **6** c **7** b **8** c

3 Trans-national organisations

4 *Suggested answer*

They need to be able to work effectively in a diverse environment with people from different cultures and with different ways of doing things, and to enjoy that challenge.

Listening 2: Merging companies with different cultures

1 He argues that culture can sometimes play a very big role in failed M&As, but he also points out that it is sometimes used as an excuse (for example, the mistakes a bad CEO makes).

2

1 false **2** true **3** true **4** false

3 He is arguing that while culture is important, there may be other factors at play as well.

Transferable skill: Avoiding stereotyping others

1 1, 2, 5

3 *Suggested answer*

Stereotypes affect the way we see other people, in that we may not see the reality of the other person, and in fact subconsciously look for behaviour that supports our stereotypes. As many stereotypes are negative, this means we are viewing the 'other' negatively, often unfairly. Given that trust and relationships are so important in business, having such an attitude means that we are less likely to trust the 'other' and develop a good relationship. Furthermore, the 'other' person may pick up on our judgements, which may further damage the relationship.

4 *Suggested answer*

Understanding the culture of the country you are doing business with or in will allow for you to develop better relationships and will be appreciated by your partners.

7.2 Practice: Internationalising a company

Reading 1: Initiating policy

1

1 Very strict; employees will be fired if they do not have the required English level.

2 None

3 The level of staff commitment will dictate the success of this policy.

4 1 in 15 (200 of the 3,000)

Reading 2: Other companies and reactions

1

Uniqlo: English will be the official language, but when the participants are all Japanese, using only Japanese is acceptable.

Nissan: It has no official policy, but when non-Japanese are present, English should be used.

Nomura: No rules, but English is needed for dealing with non-Japanese.

2 Giri Suzuki thinks that the Rakuten policy will fail, but Hiroshi Mikitani seems to see it as essential for the company's success.

Language focus: Linking ideas and information together

1

A adding extra information or explanations: whether, of whom, by, saying it, adding that, as, and thus

B adding contrasting information: while, but none has gone as far as to, though … and, but

2 Apart from 'but' and perhaps 'as', all of the examples are quite formal, and may therefore be unsuitable in less formal spoken situations. The phrases 'of whom', 'adding that' and 'and thus' are very unusual in informal spoken language.

3 *Suggested answers*

2 Whether we are present or not, new markets will want these products.

3 We have 2,000 employees, 700 of whom speak good English.

4 Many companies move their manufacturing plants abroad, but none has gone as far as to move its head office.

5 Staff will receive support, and thus they will be expected to reach a satisfactory English standard.

7.3 Skills: Conducting successful intercultural communication

Language focus: Collaborative turn-taking

1

1 a **2** d **3** f **4** c **5** b **6** e

2

Extract 1: Handing over to another speaker

Extract 2: Reformulating another person's meaning

Extract 3: Repairing misunderstanding about your intended meaning

Extract 4: Summarising the discussion so far

Extract 5: Checking shared viewpoint

Extract 6: Actively supporting the speaker

3
a 5 **b** 1 **c** 3 **d** 6 **e** 4 **f** 2

4 *Suggested answers*
These strategies are commonly used in many types of meetings because they help guarantee successful understanding and the smooth flow of communication. Because of the greater challenges involved in international communication (such as the range of different accents), these strategies are arguably even more important.

Critical analysis

2 *Suggested answer*
The relationship may suffer, as both speakers may develop a negative impression of each other: the former person is likely to think the latter has nothing to say or is in a bad mood, whereas the latter may think the other person is rude. One possible solution is to notice how you tend to communicate, and to adapt your style when you are talking to others who communicate differently.

Listening: Expert advice

1
Speaker 1: Smile sometimes (especially if you are from a culture where people may not smile so much in communication).
Speaker 2: Learn the history of the other culture.
Speaker 3: Use small talk to evaluate the other person's English level.

Intercultural analysis

1 Speaker 3 (use small talk at the beginning of the meeting)
2 Speaker 2 (learn about the culture and a bit of the language first)
3 Speaker 1 (maybe try to do the same yourself) and Speaker 3 (check with your host as small talk.)

8 International outsourcing

8.1 Theory: Avoiding outsourcing pitfalls

Introduction

1 They fear job cuts and deterioration in pay and working conditions for employees.
2 They would be looking for cost benefits and might not have the skills in-house to run these services at the required quality standard.
3 Companies tend to use local outsourcing providers when they need day-to-day control or contact with the providers, such as cleaning companies. Offshore outsourcing is more popular for activities such as data entry, or where face-to-face contact is not needed.

Language focus: The language of outsourcing

1
1 e **2** h **3** f **4** b **5** g **6** c **7** a **8** i **9** j **10** d
2 Answers are within the Reading text.

Reading: Issues facing outsourcing companies

1 The three reasons stated are: cut costs, improve performance, and refocus on the core business.
2 Through a survey of nearly a hundred outsourcing efforts in Europe and the United States.
3 Firms are reluctant to publicise outsourcing failures.

2
1 Writing a poor contract
2 Outsourcing activities that should not be outsourced
3 Overlooking personnel issues
4 Failing to plan an exit strategy
5 Overlooking hidden costs
6 Selecting the wrong outsourcing provider
7 Losing control of the outsourced activity

3
1 The contract was not precise.
2 6–7%
3 Because retiring personnel were not being replaced, which helped to fuel rumours.
4 Because reintegrating the activities back into the company would take longer than switching to another outsourcing provider.
5 The upfront cost of finding the outsourcing provider; the legal costs to negotiate the initial contract and the annual management costs involved in ensuring the outsourcing provider fulfils its contractual obligations.
6 Management at the US HQ thought its subsidiary did not have the expertise to run a just-in-time logistics operation.
7 'A total and dangerous loss of control over IT, inability to cope with the changing environment and command over the future.'
4 The two most deadly sins identified by the author in his research are: 'Writing a poor contract' and 'Losing control over the outsourced activity'.

Transferable skill: Considering the other side of the argument

2 *Suggested answers*
All services could theoretically be outsourced. For example, the possible benefits of outsourcing canteen services include better quality, range of food options and eating experience for diners. One possible option would be to bring in branded food chains to run a franchise on the university campus.

3 *Suggested answers*
Universities have not outsourced academic services as these are core services and the basis of the universities competitive advantage. Outsourcing possibilities include using experts working in the field to teach courses – architects teaching architecture students, business people teaching business students, etc. This would ensure teaching is up to date and relevant to industry needs. Universities could outsource course design to expert management consultancy firms, who can afford to employ the brightest and best in the field to undertake this task.

8.2 Practice: Offshore outsourcing provider's perspective

Listening 1: Benefits of offshore outsourcing

1 2, 3, 5

2 The example (recruiting 2–3,000 accountants) is for illustration purposes.

Critical analysis

3 *Suggested answer*

A number of groups would lose out, including individuals and firms in the outsourcing industry offshore. This would have a wider impact on their national economies. Companies in the industrialised world would also lose out as they would find it difficult to source skilled workers in sufficient quantities in their own countries. Consumers in the industrialised world would lose out as they would inevitably pay more for goods and services that are no longer supported by low-cost back-office operations.

Listening 2: Why companies choose the Philippines

1

1 IT work
2 It does less IT outsourcing than India.
3 They are 'a little bit better than India'. The accent is easier to understand and they are culturally closer to the clients.
4 Hollywood, basketball
5 High customer satisfaction ratings

2

a the population of the Philippines
b the number of graduates every year
c the percentage of graduates who speak English

Intercultural analysis

1 Call centre agents with closer cultural affinity are better able to understand and interpret the subtleties of communication and build better personal rapport with the client.

2 In the case of accounts, there is less direct interaction with client. The communication required will be mainly written, where there is less room for misunderstanding compared to voice communications. Communication for both IT support and accounts will be based on technical competence and knowledge that is far less sensitive to cultural differences.

Listening 3: Challenges facing the industry

1

1 are applying   2 English and computing skills
3 hired immediately   4 intensive English training
5 training process   6 negative perceptions

Language focus: Taking different stances to intensify or tone down the message

1 objective/balanced, tactful/diplomatic. Note that comments favourable to the outsourcing industry in the Philippines are presented objectively: 'Companies tell us ...', so it would be incorrect to say the stance taken is highly subjective / one-sided.

2

1 Our accent <u>seems</u> easier to understand, for Americans ...
2 ... <u>companies tell us</u> that we are <u>a little bit</u> better than India.
3 <u>That can be a challenge</u> [in, for example, a smaller city] ...
Suggested answers for intensified reformulations:
Our accent is <u>far easier</u> to understand for Americans.
Companies tell us that we are <u>significantly</u> better than India.
It is <u>extremely difficult</u> to find in a smaller city.

3 *Suggested answers*

1 I think you might need to look at this report again.
2 I'm not sure that's completely correct. We weren't really responsible for that.

4

A = sort of, kind of, basically, a (little) bit, like
B = very, completely, totally, so, absolutely, such

5

1 such   2 basically   3 <u>kind of</u> / sort of   4 <u>absolutely</u> / totally / completely   5 like / basically / <u>sort of</u> / kind of
(The underlined word *expression* is the one that was actually used in the corpus.)

6

1 softener   2 softener   3 intensifier   4 intensifier   5 intensifier
7 These four words are stressed (emphasised) when the speaker is using them as intensifiers.
8 A describes the use of tone-down softening words. B describes the use of intensifiers.

8.3 Skills: Dealing with Q&A

Listening 1: Managing a Q&A session

1 B

2

1 The two rules are: (i) They can't answer questions which involve confidential information; (ii) They can't deal with personal issues relating to particular shareholders.
2 They should go to the nearest microphone in the aisle and give their name.
3 *Suggested answers*
1 our discussion period / our question and answer period
2 a few ground rules
3 trying to answer all your questions as fully as we can
4 pass on any issues that might involve confidential information
5 to deal with personal issues related to the individual shareholder
6 go to the nearest microphone in the aisle

Language focus 1: Inviting questions from the audience

2

1 proceed   2 happy   3 hand   4 fire   5 start   6 open up
3 Question 1 is more formal and Question 4 is more informal.
4 Questions 1, 2 and 5. These questions would be generally asked during the presentation, not at the end in a Q&A.

Listening 2: Dealing with different question types

1

Non-question – 3
Straightforward question – 1
Difficult question – 4
Hostile question – 5
Multiple question – 2

2

1 a, b   2 a, b, c   3 a, c   4 a, c   5 a, b, d

Language focus 2: Replying to questions

1

1 c 2 a 3 h 4 e 5 f 6 i 7 d 8 b 9 g

Writing 4: Writing follow-up emails

Introduction

1 Transactional: 1, 4, 5   Interpersonal: 2, 3

2 Transactional: 2, 4   Interpersonal: 1, 3

Writing skill: Contrasting transactional and interpersonal emails

1

1 were referred   2 had expressed   3 requested   4 enclosing
5 itemizes   6 provide you   7 participating in

2 The email has a very strong transactional focus, with almost no attention paid to developing the relationship.

3 All of the points suggested would make the email more interpersonal. How interpersonal you make a communication depends on your own preference and how interpersonal you believe the culture of the addressee (the person you are writing to) to be. In general, it is always better to use the recipient's name at the start, if you know it.

4 The email covers all the points in question 3 apart from point 4.

Intercultural analysis

2 *Suggested answer*

While generalisations are useful in helping us understand tendencies across cultures, we cannot expect the next person we meet from the relevant culture to behave in exactly that way. There is often far more variation within cultures than between cultures.

Language focus: Reminding, explaining and requesting in follow-up emails

1 b, c, a

2

a requesting a response: 1, 7, 8, 9
b reminding the reader of the initial discussion or request: 4, 6
c explaining the value of the product or service: 2, 3, 5

3

Requests: we request your comments on / Please let me know your / if you could send us … that would be great

Reminders: we remind you that … continues to be available / if you remember from our previous discussions

The answers are in order of formality (the most formal first).

9 Affordable innovation

9.1 Theory: Affordable innovation through reverse innovation

Introduction

2 The top three drivers in order of importance are: 1f, 2a, 3e

Language focus: Concepts of innovation

1

1 innovation   2 invention

2 patented invention / ingenious invention / license (an) invention
foster innovation / marketing innovation / product innovation / encourage innovation

3

1 f 2 a 3 b 4 d 5 c 6 e

4

1 radical innovation   2 affordable innovations
3 collaborative innovation   4 incremental innovations
5 top-down innovation, bottom-up innovation

Reading: Reverse innovation

1

1 developing   2 adapted   3 local population
4 availability of skilled workers

2

1 PepsiCo   2 Mahindra & Mahindra   3 Deere & Company
4 Renault-Nissan   5 Renault-Nissan

3

1 in a nutshell   2 minor tweaks   3 driver   4 no-frills
5 predominantly   6 mindset   7 frugal   8 on a par
9 came up with   10 know-how   11 unveiled   12 tap into

Output: Debate low-cost innovation solutions

Against: 1, 3, 5   For: 2, 4, 6

9.2 Practice: GE Healthcare – low-cost reverse innovation in practice

Listening 1: GE Healthcare in China

2

1 It costs $15,000 in China compared to $350,000 in the USA for premium models.

2 The first advantage is that it is portable so it can be taken to the patients. This is particularly important in remote villages in rural China, as ultrasound machines are normally located in hospitals and they don't have hospitals in these areas. The second advantage is its ultra low cost, which makes it affordable for customers.

3 $300 million

4 It's used in highway accidents.

Listening 2: GE Healthcare global strategy

1

1 Because global recession has shifted economic growth from developed to developing countries.

2 US, Western Europe, Japan, rest of the world

3 BRIC (Brazil, Russia, India and China), resource-rich countries (Middle East, Canada, Australia), rest of the world

4 The idea that the world population is divided into two parts – 2 billion who can afford to buy products made by companies. and 5 billion who are 'left' to governments, NGOs and charities.

Critical analysis

Turning non-consumers into consumers is desirable as it is a form of inclusion and a moral imperative. The benefits of innovation and technology are multiple and wide-reaching and should be shared by the majority of the world's population who are excluded without addressing issues of affordability. The examples given of Tata and Aakash show that it is realistic. The argument against turning non-consumers into consumers is largely linked to environmental issues. What would happen to the level of carbon emissions, for example, if all the people riding bicycles and mopeds in the developing world started driving cars?

Transferable skill: Keeping the listener's attention

1

1 b **2** a

2 Underlined language: You may wonder how come …
Imagine …   let me just …

Reading: Disrupting international business strategy

1

1 substantially lower costs   **2** emerging economies
3 pioneering new uses   **4** glocalization approach   **5** global scale
6 local customization   **7** rapid development   **8** slowing growth
2
1 false   **2** true   **3** false   **4** false

Language focus: Marketing of innovation – word partnerships

1

1 global, local   **2** global
3
1 wide   **2** initial   **3** multiple   **4** appropriate   **5** price
6 internet   **7** core   **8** enhanced

9.3 Skills: Dealing with criticism

Language focus: Recognising and reacting to criticism

1

1 constructive   **2** indirect   **3** negative   **4** direct
2 Extract A = direct and negative, Extract B = indirect and constructive

3 *Suggested answers*

In Extract A, all of the questions starting with 'why' tell us that the manager is being direct. As he doesn't give the employee a chance to answer the questions we can also sense that he is being negative. He also finishes with an insult, which is clearly negative.

In Extract B, the manager is indirect in that she starts with a question to find out the reason for the problem, rather than a criticism. She also offers advice on how to resolve the problem, which is constructive in that it helps the employee.

4

a 3 **b** 8 **c** 4 **d** 2 **e** 1 **f** 5 **g** 6 **h** 7
6
1 d **2** e **3** g **4** b **5** c

Listening: Discussing the results of an exhibition

1

1 Just over £2,000
2 Because advertising alone doesn't work.
3 Because they haven't had the resources.
4 They also had to send over magazines, which cost £1,000.
5 Because they made some good contacts there.
6 Because it can take between 18 months and 2 years before you see the results.

2 *Suggested answers*

1 The way that she questions Mark is direct, but she frames her criticism in the form of questions that are indirect in order to try and find out what the problem is.
2 It seems to be effective – she gets the information that she wants from Mark and then uses the information constructively.
3 He deals well with the criticism. He does not get defensive; he gives reasons for the lack of results and looks at ways that they can gain positives from the lack of sales.
4 It ends on a positive note, with Sally looking at the positives that can come out of the exhibition.

10 Design and invention

10.1 Theory: Design in business

Listening 1: Design and people

1

1 Designers and engineers   **2** Apple and the iPod
2
1 Designers start with the people who use the product and try to understand their behaviour first. Engineers start with a technical problem and start to solve it.
2 Apple have created a 'delightfulness' through interaction with the product. Users find it delightful but it still has good functionality too.

Listening 2: New ways of thinking

1

1 toaster   **2** toasting   **3** noun   **4** verb   **5** object
6 surrounding, object
2
1 false   **2** true   **3** true

Critical analysis

Suggested answers

1 The quotes suggest that speaking to potential users is a waste of time as they don't know what they want.
2 Innovators like the people Dr Clare Brass talks about are improving on an existing product, so users have an idea of what they want from the product in the future. Inventors are coming up with a completely new product, so people are less likely to know what they want until they see it.
3 They should ask questions about their existing problems and try to solve them rather than ask questions about what they want.

Language focus: Noun-noun partnerships with 'design'

1

1 She is responsible for all types of **design** work for our company.
2 Her main responsibility is (**for designing / to design / designing**) new products. (*or* Her main responsibility is **new product design**.)
3 She is responsible for the **company's** product design department.
4 The shopping malls sell lots of very cheap **designer** clothes.
5 The whole house has used one **overall** design and colour scheme.
6 She will be the core member of the **design** team.
7 The restaurant's **design** reflects aspects of a country's culture.

2

1 design work   2 (new) product design
3 product design / design department   6 design team

3

1 design proposal   2 software design   3 design company
4 design thinking   5 design trick   6 design profession
7 design brief   8 design department

10.2 Practice: Dyson – a design-led company

Reading: The Dyson story

1

1 Against the odds   2 Research and development
3 A cautionary tale

2

1 prototypes   2 determination   3 just around the corner
4 the lifeblood   5 once in a while   6 eclectic pastimes
7 assign the patent ('assigned' in the text)   8 majority shareholders

3

1 determination and hard work
2 eclectic engineering pastimes
3 He lost control of the company and hence his control over his inventions.
4 *Suggested answer*
The writing style is quite an informal, anecdotal style that tells a set of stories of the company's history and founder. Examples of informal language include 'a varied bunch', 'just around the corner', 'James' (not 'James Dyson'). The style communicates a company culture that is the opposite of a 'big hierarchical corporation'.
5 *Suggested answer*
young, dynamic, entrepreneurial, diverse, tolerant, fun, design-focused, creative, determined

Language focus: Describing products using multiple adjectives and analogies

1 a beautiful painted large square eighteenth-century red Chinese wooden box
2 opinion / observation / size / shape / age / colour / origin / material / noun

3

1 a huge range of products
2 beautiful sweet-smelling cosmetic products
3 an inefficient old imported product
4 great American paper products
5 exciting innovative European products.
6 a fantastic innovative product
4 Because it offers an immediately accessible everyday image to demonstrate a complex technical process

5

1 People come in and leave the company all of the time.
2 She feels like she is in the wrong place. / The job doesn't suit her at all.
3 If you talk to her boss you won't get a response.
4 If the product is good, you should have no problem in selling it.

Listening: James Dyson talks about design and invention

1 The original title of this interview was 'Failure'.

2

1 They have one good idea which will make a fortune.
2 Inventors will benefit from understanding why something fails and then think of ways of overcoming this failure.
3 It refers to the number of prototypes and the number of failures before his vacuum cleaner worked.

10.3 Skills: Communicating negative information in a positive light

Language focus 1: Understand how euphemisms provide a more positive alternative

1

1 B   2 A   3 A   4 C   5 C   6 B

2

1 there is an insufficient number of staff in the department
2 we are facing some real difficulties
3 it will be hard to attract these customers (back)

3

1 a really complex set of customers
2 we've got some real challenges
3 focus in on

Listening 1: Talking about the customers

1 1 and 3
2 1 and 3
3 Without teamwork, there is little chance the company can reach these sales targets.

Listening 2: Talking about marketing support

1

1 He hopes that they are going to be more proactive in finding new customers.
2 Some of the marketing workforce have been laid off, so they are now short of staff. The euphemism he uses is 'thin on the ground'.
3 b and c

4 It seems to be in financial difficulty, as he mentions a strange environment, a lack of capital and the fact they have lost staff.

Language focus 2: Making excuses

1

1 f **2** e **3** c **4** a **5** d **6** b

Writing 5: Writing for meetings – notes, minutes and agenda

Introduction

1

1 minutes, are, after **2** agenda, is, before

2 It's not usual practice to include jokes, relationship-building discourse (small talk), private discussions or much background information in minutes and so there is no point in taking notes on these parts of the meeting.

Writing skill 1: Taking meeting notes and interpreting an agenda

1

1 The meeting is at 10 am on 28 May. It will be held in Room S224 in the Stamford Building.

2 The minutes have been circulated to the following people: Dave Sinclair, Peter Chen, Paula Summers, Emile Lahar, Elizabeth Willis. They are all part of the SB Technical Assistance Team.

3 Point 1 refers to apologies received in advance of the meeting from any person invited who knows they will not be able to attend. Point 2 refers to regular minutes from regular meetings (monthly or weekly, for example); it is common to approve (or amend) draft minutes that were circulated after the previous meeting. Point 3 refers to any issues that are arising (coming out) from the previous meeting that still need discussing. Point 9 is a common acronym that stands for 'any other business'. It refers to 'any other issues not on the agenda that people would like to raise or discuss'.

Language focus: Structure and style of meeting minutes

1 All points are covered except point 7. In many organisations it is common practice to highlight agreements in bold and sometimes also in capitals within the minutes, e.g. **AGREED**.

2 The minutes of a meeting are always written as a formal document, even if the meeting was quite informal, as this will be the official record of what was said at the meeting. These minutes can be circulated to people not at the meeting, including bosses, and can be made public.

3 *Suggested answers*

2 **Action**: AG to request Marketing Dept. to provide revised sales figures for last month.

3 **Action**: SK to distribute copies of course outlines for Engineering and Design (the two 'course areas' discussed need to be specified).

4 **Action**: Agreed to do large-scale mailing to all our clients in Spain, Italy and France.

11 The economic environment

11.1 Theory: Government influence on the economic environment

Language focus 1: Financial and economic word partnerships

1 They would have to cut expenses on such things as eating out, and they would need to shop around more for better deals on things like car insurance.

2

1 S **2** SD **3** SD **4** S **5** SD **6** S

4

1 e **2** c **3** b **4** a **5** d

6

1 tax revenue **2** financial crisis **3** economic recovery

4 stable currency **5** government intervention

Listening 1: Government and central bank objectives

1

1 For the welfare of their citizens

2 Poor people want higher taxes and spending, rich people want the opposite.

3 To create a stable financial and economic environment

4 A stable currency that people have trust in

Listening 2: The impact of government spending

1

1 Lower corporation tax collected (business losses), less income tax collected (unemployment) and less VAT collected (people spend less).

2 Governments don't have enough revenue to meet their expenditure programmes

3 Unemployed people need benefits, businesses need government orders and it's a way to stimulate the economy that is slowing down too much.

Listening 3: Taxation

1 Tax rates, tax evasion, tax collection

2

1 **a** 60% – income tax in Scandinavia

   b 0% – income tax in the UAE

   c 13% – income tax in Russia

   d 20% – VAT rate in most of Europe

   e 10% – VAT rate in Korea

2 The UAE has large oil revenues, Scandinavia has good tax discipline, Russia aims to minimise tax evasion.

3 The quote refers to the issue of tax evasion and people inventing numbers when completing their tax returns, i.e. they declare far less than they actually earn.

Critical analysis

Suggested answer

The cartoon shows a very fat man representing an over-inflated economy. In other words, the government has made the mistake of over-stimulating the economy (cutting interest rates too low, cutting taxes too much, spending and borrowing too much) with the result that economic growth is unsustainable and the economy is now moving into recession, as shown by the man falling. 'Uncle Sam', who represents the government of the USA, is attempting to provide a 'soft landing' for the economy by providing a 'stimulus package' as a cushion to soften the inevitable hardships of recession. The small size of the cushion suggests that government action here will have no effect.

Language focus 2: Verb patterns in finance

1

1 cut   **2** fall   **3** move (moving)

2

1 Spending will be reduced in the public sector. / Spending in the public sector will be reduced.

3 Taxes will be cut.

3 intransitive

4

1 intransitive   **2** transitive   **3** intransitive   **4** both

5 both   **6** intransitive

5 *Suggested answers*

1 She was able to raise turnover by 5%.

2 TV sales will rise by 10%.

3 The deficit has disappeared. / The government has made the deficit disappear.

4 The economy has been impacted (on) because of falling exports. / Falling exports have impacted (on) the country's economy.

5 The company's assets will be frozen if he doesn't pay the bill. / They will freeze the company's assets if he doesn't pay the bill.

6 The company had to cut its prices due to the recession.

11.2 Practice: Managing economic and financial risk – Unilever

Introduction

3 Higher levels of economic, political and environmental risk and volatility due to their exposure to developing and emerging markets, where they do over 50% of their business. Foreign exchange rate risk as they earn their money in local currency but will need to pay for supplies in international traded currencies such as the euro or US dollar. The other main risk is to its supply of raw materials, which can change sharply in price.

Language focus: Economic and financial terms and phrases

1 a fluctuate   **b** net cash flow   **c** adverse   **d** viability
e contingency plans   **f** model   **g** exposure   **h** shortfall
i floating rate

2

1 d   **2** e   **3** b   **4** c   **5** f   **6** a

3 *Suggested answer*

2 Customers will increase consumption if Unilever increases brand promotion and it enters new markets. If economic conditions in existing markets improve (e.g. unemployment falls, wages rise), it will give customers more spending power. If commodity prices fall, Unilever may pass the savings on to customers, which will also increase consumption.

If the opposite conditions exist, consumption will decrease.

Reading: Unilever outlook and risks

1

1 a   **2** d   **3** e   **4** f   **5** c   **6** b

2

1 adverse economic conditions

2 It has a broad brand portfolio and geographic reach (in many different countries) so it is not dependent on only one or two brands, or one or two specific local country markets.

3 They have constrained access to credit. (They can no longer get sufficient loans, etc. from the banks to finance their needs.)

4 It has strategies in place to source materials from alternative suppliers or use substitute materials.

5 It gives the company continued access to global debt markets. (It can issue bonds at a reasonable interest rate which will still be attractive to investors who will still want to buy them.)

3 *Suggested answer*

Other risks could include unforeseen risks such as a company being a victim of a cyber attack where it loses key data. Companies operating in parts of the world with unstable governments are exposed to political risk and their operation can be at risk of civil disorder in those countries.

4 *Suggested answer*

Many small businesses are very dependent on their owners – any serious, long-term illness that affects them will seriously affect the company. Also, cash flow problems: if a customer does not pay it may have a bigger impact than it does on a larger company, as smaller companies may find it more difficult to obtain credit.

Language focus 2: Financial terms

1

1 impair   **2** balance sheet value   **3** credit rating

4 intangible assets

2 *Suggested answers*

1 If Unilever sets its credit limits too low, it could discourage its customers from buying from it. These customers might then decide not to stock Unilever products and instead buy more from competitors. If Unilever sets the credit limit for its suppliers too high, the company exposes itself to a higher risk of customer default.

2 If the company's credit rating was cut, it would find it more difficult to raise money (selling its bonds) in the debt market to investors. Investors would view Unilever as a higher risk company and would therefore demand a higher level of interest on the bonds it offers for sale in the debt markets. If the company did not offer higher levels of interest on its bonds, investors would be unlikely to buy them.

11.3 Skills: Presenting charts and statistics

Listening: Analyse a chart in a slide presentation

1

1 Different markets (evolving, emerging, established)

2 The percentage of new car purchasers who give this reason for buying a new car

3 To highlight the most important points (the key data)

4 The present tense is used for describing facts.

5 c

4 Line graphs are best used to show changing numbers (e.g. sales figures) over a period of time. The information presented here is a 'snapshot' in time – it's not a period of time. Pie charts would work well to show figures for <u>one</u> market (established or evolving or emerging) but would not allow people to compare these markets easily. A table of statistics containing a lot of numbers is best used in an Appendix of a written report; in a presentation it is difficult for the audience to understand the data and make comparisons 'at a glance' which is essential in this slide presentation.

Language focus: Structuring and describing a chart

1 *Suggested answers*

1 Now let's look at where people go to find information to buy a new car.

2 So, what is the first source of information people go to when considering buying a new car?

3 As you can see, the Internet is by far the most important source of information for new car purchasers. / When we compare the use of the Internet to other media it's pretty striking.

4 Finally, it's interesting to note how many people in emerging markets use friends and family contacts as a major source of information.

3 b, d, a, c

4

[Part 1] Now, … Where do you go first?//

[Part 2] And it is surprising … it's pretty striking.//

[Part 3] Given the difference … in the auto purchase process.//

[Part 4] Finally, … evolves over time.

5

1 second most   **2** Hardly anyone   **3** twice as many

Transferable skill: Highlighting key data in a chart

3

1 It's very effective. The secondary point is highlighted with a green circle to show clearly that the data refers to emerging markets. Numerical comparison in the form of multiples is clearly shown with red dotted lines, which really emphasises the message the presenter wants to convey.

12 International trade

12.1 Theory: Free trade or protectionism?

Introduction

1 d   **2** a   **3** c   **4** b

Transferable skill: Improving speed-reading techniques

1 pro-free trade = B, D   anti-free trade = A, C, E, F

2

A … support richer countries.

B … help development.

C … does not work.

D … do best.

E … downside of trade liberalisation.

F … less developed countries.

Reading: Making globalisation work

1

1 A   **2** F   **3** B   **4** D   **5** C   **6** E

2

1 Because of the lack of infrastructure and ability to produce goods at right quality levels

2 Because there will be less revenue gained from import tariffs

3 The right measures and policies have to be taken.

4 Specialising in the area in which you excel

5 It would reduce the income gap between Mexico and the USA and reduce illegal immigration.

6 Unskilled workers have been hit the most.

Language focus: Emphasising key points through inversion

1 The text says: Not only does liberalisation require removing tariffs … but to compete, a country may have to lower other taxes as well.

3

1 not only   **2** had we   **3** Under no circumstances can   **4** Were

5 Such   **6** At no time   **7** Only by

4

2 At no time has the reduction of inequality been a more pressing issue.

3 Under no circumstances should the free movement of people between countries be allowed.

4 Such is the power of multinational corporations that fair trade is not possible.

5 Not only do the most powerful countries always win, they also ensure that their corporations have unfair trading advantages.

5

2 Were international trade agreements fairer, the global economy would be more stable.

3 Had the UK adopted the euro 14 months ago, it wouldn't be suffering from a grossly overvalued currency today.

12.2 Practice: NAFTA and Mexico

Introduction

1 Opinions are divided on what effect it has had on the economy. Has it created employment or unemployment and has it increased or decreased wage levels?

Language focus: Terms of economic convergence and divergence

1

1 increased bilateral trade **2** income disparity
3 inward investment **4** regulatory cooperation
5 export-orientated economy **6** duty-free trade
7 removing trade barriers **8** compliance with
9 protectionist trade policies **10** growing polarisation
11 economic integration

2 Economic convergence: economic integration, removing trade barriers, regulatory cooperation, compliance with [an international trade treaty], duty-free trade, inward investment, export-orientated economy, increased bilateral trade

Economic divergence: protectionist trade policies, income disparity, growing polarisation

Listening 1: The role and purpose of NAFTA

1 He mentions: 2, 3, 4, 5 and 6
2

1 **a** harmonised labelling **b** integrated transport
  c procedures, customs
2 Monitoring and compliance of commitments under the NAFTA agreement and promotion of trade and investment between Canada and Mexico.

Listening 2: Benefits of NAFTA to Mexico

1

1 NAFTA makes Mexico attractive for inward investment.
2 NAFTA has forced Mexican companies to be competitive and opened up international markets for them.
3 Five-fold, to $300 billion per annum
4 Auto parts, automotive industry, space sector
5 Oil exports are now a much smaller percentage of total exports (from 70% to 15%). Manufactured goods as a percentage of total exports have increased dramatically (to 60%). Foreign trade is now a much higher percentage of GDP (up from 8% of GDP in 1992 to 60% of GDP now).

Listening 3: Defence of NAFTA

2 Problem: Some segments are not exporting well and are not efficient.
  Defence: He points out that other segments are exporting well and are efficient.
3 Problem: Some segments are not interested in exporting and are having problems adapting to new technologies.
  Defence: These sectors were initially protected under NAFTA ('protected' in terms of import tariffs remaining in place, for a limited period of time).
4 Problem: The USA is a big producer of corn.
  Defence: There was a long period of protection for Mexican farmers up until 2008. Mexican farmers now better off than before NAFTA.
5 Problem: Campaigners say that NAFTA is a threat to local economies and companies.
  Defence: After these campaigners get elected they stop criticising NAFTA.

12.3 Skills: Managing meetings

Listening 1: Starting the meeting

1

1 false **2** false **3** true **4** true **5** true
2

1 *Suggested answer*
  She deals with the start of the meeting in a professional manner and gets to the start of the meeting quickly after checking that everybody is familiar with and happy with the agenda.
2 *Suggested answer*
  The chair may have needed to introduce the other members of the meeting and gone over the agenda in more detail before starting with the first point. It is also sometimes necessary to allocate a person to take minutes.

Listening 2: Discussing a problem colleague

1

1 He thinks that they went very well.
2 She tells her to write down that Jack thinks that he is better than Nick.
3 No
4 That he is very self-important
5 That he only uses PowerPoint and does not provide notes
6 She thinks that participants should be encouraged to fill out evaluation forms of the training sessions.
2 *Suggested answers*
1 It is clear that the group know each other well, so they know when to use humour; it also helps to lighten the mood as it is clear that Jack is going to say something serious. However, using humour can be risky if you don't know the other participants well.
2 The comment is made with good humour, but in general it would be better to hear more of the facts before making a statement.
3 They ignore her. As Stefanie was not warned to turn her phone off at the start of the meeting and finishes the call quickly, this is probably the best tactic.
4 She deals with it well, in that she comes up with a practical solution to get to the bottom of the problem.

Language focus: Negotiating problems in meetings

1

1 e **2** g **3** a **4** d **5** f **6** c **7** b
2

1 refer back **2** absolutely great **3** What I'm saying is
4 wrap it up **5** choices **6** Why don't you
7 I sometimes feel that
3

1 c **2** e **3** a **4** g **5** b **6** f **7** d
4 *Suggested answers*
1 What I'm saying is that you have a fortnight to complete the work, not a week.
2 Can we just refer back to the agenda now? We will have to discuss that another day.

3 I think that you all need to sit down together in the next few days and work out what is going on.

4 I just think there's an element of not all of the information being disclosed.

Writing 6: Describing graphs with financial and economic data

Language focus: Describing financial and economic changes

1

2 ☹↓ **3** ☺↑ **4** ☺↑ **5** ☹↓ **6** ☹↓ **7** ☹↑ **8** ☹↓
9 ☹↓ **10** ☺↓ **11** ☹↑ **12** ☺↑

2

a dip **b** bounce back, rebound **c** plunge, slump, dive
d surge, soar **e** edge forward **f** slide **g** shrink **h** wobble

3

1 a slide **2** a plunge **3** a bounce **4** a rebound **5** a wobble
6 a slump **7** a surge

4 *Suggested answers*

2 The standard of living is set to plunge as inflation is predicted to rise dramatically.

3 Business confidence has bounced back because business leaders see a sharp rise in new orders.

4 There was a strong rebound in retail figures in January as consumers responded to recent government tax cuts.

5 As a result of a surprising slump in export orders, the German economy has shrunk more than expected.

6 After figures released from the government last week showing unemployment soaring to new highs, there has been a dive in consumer confidence.

5 *Suggested answers*

Headline 5: Stock markets fell briefly due to worries about the immediate political situation in the Middle East.

Headline 6: The slump in bank shares over the last six months is a result of non-payment of mortgage loan payments.

Headline 7: The surging household debt in Korea is due to people taking out excessive loans to buy property.

Headline 10: Jobless figures in the USA dipped by 20,000, showing the first positive effects of the government's economic stimulus package.

Headline 11: Plummeting consumer spending over the course of the year has led to soaring levels of corporate bankruptcies.

Headline 12: The strength of the US railroad sector has ensured that FreightCar America's final results have edged forward.

Writing skill 1: Describing a single trend line

1

1 The graph describes the movement of the NASDAQ 100 index over a three-year period from January 2008 to early 2011.

2 in quarters (three-month periods)

2

1 The audience would probably be extremely bored and frustrated. They would also be no wiser as to the real meaning of the graph, which is described with reference to the <u>main</u> trends.

2 See text for question 3

3

1 fluctuated **2** plunged **3** wobble **4** rebounded/recovered
5 dipped **6** bounced **7** soaring/surging

Writing skill 2: Describing multiple trend lines

1

1 changes/movement(s) **2** oil **3** green **4** yellow **5** period

2

1 The stock with the biggest increase in value over the period was Chevron; the lowest increase was BP and Exxon Mobil.

2 BP

3 *Suggested answer*

As the price of other oil company stocks followed a different course, the logical conclusion is that it was not a problem affecting the oil industry or the economy as a whole, but negative news affecting BP in particular. What actually happened was a huge oil leak from one of its drilling platforms in the Gulf of Mexico. BP was hit with a clean-up bill of over $20 billion.

4

1 Shell and Chevron **2** Shell, Chevron and Exxon Mobil
3 Exxon Mobil and BP **4** BP

13 Sustainable development
13.1 Theory: The triple bottom line

Introduction

3 Making profits: connects to all stakeholders (without profits the company will not be able to pay for things that meet the needs of any stakeholder)

Educational visits from nearby schools: local community

Switch to clean energy providers: future generations

Monitor suppliers: wider community (also consumers if they are concerned about this)

Run 'stress management' courses for staff: employees

Ensure honest promotions: consumers

Provide nursery facilities on premises: employees

Language focus: Topic verbs linked to sustainability

1 incorporated **2** accommodate **3** gauge **4** comprise
5 assign **6** secure **7** eliminate **8** advocates **9** driving
10 adapt

Reading 1: Defining and calculating the triple bottom line

1

1 environmental = planet, social = people, financial = profits

2 It measures the impact of an organisation's activities on the world.

3 To measure it – you can't put a monetary value on social capital and the environment.

2

1 They do not have a common unit of measure.
2 They would all have a common unit (dollars).
3 Some critics argue against it on philosophical grounds, while others question the methods needed for finding the right price for non-monetary factors.
4 To calculate the TBC in terms of an index

Reading 2: Creating the index

1 false **2** false **3** false **4** true **5** true **6** false

13.2 Practice: Masdar – the sustainable city

Introduction

1

1 carbon emissions **2** carbon footprint **3** greenhouse gas

Language focus 1: Green vocabulary

1

zero waste   zero carbon   zero emissions
green companies   green knowledge   green markets
energy demand   water demand   reduce demand
consumer waste   waste water

2 *Suggested answer*

The use of renewable energy through solar power and wind towers shows that Masdar City is trying to reduce consumer demand for fossil fuels and may be aiming for zero emissions. It is also trying to reduce waste through its recycling plant.

Listening 1: Masdar City promotion Part 1

1

2 The Vision **3** The Design **4** Transport

2

1 They will build the city's most iconic buildings.
2 The air is clean.
3 The city can be smaller and the streets narrower.
4 They will carry people and freight.

Listening 2: Masdar City promotion Part 2

1 Statements 1–4 refer to 'Water, Waste and Electricity'; statements 6 and 7 refer to 'Source of Wisdom'.

2 1 false **2** false **3** false **4** true **5** true **6** false **7** true

Language focus 2: Using the language of contrasts to persuade

1

1 b **2** d **3** a **4** c

3 *Suggested answers*

1 … the better the air quality.
2 … more renewable sources.
3 … the less time we have to find alternatives.
4 … and less traffic in the city centre.
5 … the best use of existing resources.

13.3 Skills: Problem-solving

Introduction

Critical analysis

Problem b could be the institution's fault if the employee is missing deadlines due to being overworked. Problems e and g could be due to the employee not receiving sufficient training.

Listening 1: Problems and causes

1 a and b
2 b – The team leader expects too much, too soon.

Listening 2: Deadlines and timescales

1

1 c **2** b

2

1 The relationship is a good one: they talk very openly and frankly, and the mood of the conversation is quite calm and friendly.
2 It is important, as otherwise it may be difficult for the team leader to be honest about the problems (because he may worry about the reaction of the boss), and the boss may find it more difficult to offer clear, constructive advice.

Intercultural analysis

Suggested answers

1 There are many factors that could be relevant here, such as are the local staff willing to be managed by a foreigner (their own prejudices may be relevant here), can the manager communicate effectively in the local language, does the manager have negative stereotypes about the local nationality?
2 Advantages would include learning about other countries'/cultures' ways of doing things and improving language skills. Disadvantages could include not understanding colleagues (both language and culture).

Language focus: Suggesting solutions and giving advice

1 a is more direct advice, because of the use of 'can'; b is more indirect because of the use of 'could'

3

1 direct **2** direct/indirect **3** indirect **4** direct

4 The director is more senior than the team leader and can therefore be more direct. If the team leader wanted to suggest something to the director, he would probably use a more indirect form.

5 *Suggested answers*

1 Have you thought about doing it this way?
2 It might be a good idea for you to give the terms.
3 You could think about how you could cater for all these different working styles.
4 You might need to give him a bit more time.
5 You could say, 'Your clothes are not really suitable for work.'

14 Social enterprise

14.1 Theory: Perspectives on social enterprise

Language focus: Common word partnerships linking business and social issues

1

2 social entrepreneurs   **3** social entrepreneurship
4 social responsibility   **5** social housing   **6** social need
7 social change   **8** social problems

2 *Suggested answers*

1 Companies now pay more attention to issues of social responsibility as society as a whole (and customers in particular) care more about these issues.
2 CSR of a private company is one aspect of the company's activities, whereas for a social enterprise the social or environmental dimension is central.

3

1 a, b, c   **2** b, c   **3** a, d, e   **4** a, b

Reading: Comparing social enterprises to profit-making companies

1

A Dr Helen Haugh   **B** Professor Jane Wei-Skillern

2

1 N   **2** HH   **3** N   **4** B   **5** JWS   **6** JWS

Listening 1: Social entrepreneurs

1 No – she says that the stereotypical entrepreneur from the business world can have an adverse effect on mission impact in the social sector, which needs a different kind of entrepreneur.

2

1 charismatic, ego-focused, hard-driving, celebrity type
2 Advancing their organisation and building shareholder value
3 People who are committed to working towards the social mission even at the cost of advancing their own organisation or their own individual interests.

Listening 2: Social enterprise goals

1 No – She says that social and economic goals should be treated equally.

2

1 'Mission drift' is where 'economic goals gradually become more important than the social goals'.
2 It's important not to lose sight of the 'social purpose of the organisation'.

14.2 Practice: Trashy Bags – a social enterprise in action

Reading: About Trashy Bags

1

1 'Life after death' refers to plastic sachets/packaging coming 'back to life' as a fashionable Trashy Bag product after being discarded on the street.
2 'The Problem' refers to the environmental damage caused by discarded plastic litter.
3 'The Solution' refers to increasing the lifespan of plastic packaging by collecting it and turning it into Trashy Bags, thus helping solve the environmental problem.

3

1 Packaging from drinking water, plastic drinking sachets, ice-cream sachets
2 The 22,000 tons of plastic litter per year has risen by 70% in the last 10 years.
3 It blocks drains, causing flooding and disease.
4 It is very environmentally friendly as little energy is used and there is no reprocessing apart from washing the sachets.

Language focus: Using referencing to build cohesion

1

2 plastic packaging   **3** plastic drinks sachets   **4** the sachets
5 waste plastic   **6** people in Africa   **7** sachets
8 people in Ghana   **9** waste produced from plastic packaging
10 waste from plastic packaging   **11** streets in West African countries   **12** discarded plastic   **13** incorporating complete sachets into products

2

2 referring back   **3** adding information   **4** adding information
5 referring back   **6** referring back   **7** referring back
8 outside reference   **9** referring back   **10** referring back
11 referring back   **12** referring back   **13** referring back

4

Trashy Briefcase & Laptop Bag
The Trashy Briefcase or Laptop Bag will really turn heads when you arrive at a business meeting. The difference between the products is that the Laptop Bag has padding stitched between the outer layer and the lining that serves to protect your valuable laptop computer. Inside there are two divisions leaving the central compartment for easy extraction of your laptop; especially useful at airport security! Both products come in two sizes and have a removable shoulder strap and two fixed handles.

14.3 Skills: Conference calls

Listening 1: Opening the call

1

1 a

3 4 and 5

Listening 2: The reputation of the brand

1

1 three

2 She suggests they should 'call on' people (go around and ask them individually).

3 She was on another call.

4 She's not sure, but she also says 'I think it's positive'.

2

1 Mary ignores tip 10.

2 Jane ignores tip 7.

Language focus 1: Managing a conference call

1

1 We ask that you use a mute button … may feed music into the conference.

2 At this time, I would like to turn the conference over to Ms Nancy Meidenburger.

3 Thank you so much, and welcome everyone to the RESNA conference on creating a brand for our financial loan programmes

4 We'd like to have a roll call, so I'd like people to identify themselves and what state … they're from.

5 Why don't you just go on to the next person.

Language focus 2: Interrupting

1

Extract 1 B: Can I interrupt you?

Extract 2 B: Just let me stop you there

Extract 3 B: You might want to shut up

2 The intonation used in example 2 is aggressive. The language used in example 3 appears aggressive when read, but the intonation makes it clear that this is being said in a friendly manner.

Writing 7: Writing a covering letter for a CV

Introduction

1

1 d **2** a **3** b **4** c **5** f **6** h **7** e **8** g

Language focus 1: Correcting common misspellings

1 A misspelling is a spelling mistake where it is clear that the writer is unaware of the correct spelling. A 'typo' is where the writer has pressed the wrong keys on the keyboard and made a mistake – for example, 'follwoing' instead of 'following'.

2

1 accommodation **2** acknowledge **3** definite

4 responsibility **5** disappoint **6** separate **7** liaise

8 occasion (correct) **9** achieve **10** completely (correct)

11 environment **12** truly

Reading: Interpreting the job advertisement and planning the response

2 The following sections of the job advert should be highlighted:

1 devise, develop and deliver new customer relationship strategies

2 your knowledge of call centre technology and industry developments is in-depth and up to the minute

3 constantly improving our customer satisfaction ratings.

4 you'll ensure the smooth running of customer service centre operations at either our Nottingham or Derby sites

5 championing exceptional customer service

3 Missed point: practical experience ('Experience in a similar role is essential'). Accompanying note: I have hands-on experience of doing this kind of job.

Writing skill: Content, structure, format and style of a covering letter

1 Yes

Example of points 1, 2, 5: 'Championed implementation … increased productivity by 2%'.

Example of point 3: Decreased customer waiting times by 4% … waiting times'.

Example of point 4: 'I have three … Endsleigh'. AND 'Cross-trained … training cover'.

2

1 section 2 **2** section 1 **3** section 3

Language focus 2: Correcting errors and writing with confidence

1

1 I'm keen **2** as seen **3** managing **4** incentivising

5 team members **6** which **7** are **8** would **9** commitment

10 assure **11** find **12** look **13** kind regards

2 'I'm keen to …', 'Championed …', 'I would relish …'

3

1 I have the right skills, experience and educational qualifications that make me a strong candidate for the job.

2 I am available for an interview at any time convenient to you over the coming weeks.

3 As part of a team project, I conducted market research to find out customers' perceptions of the brand.

4 I reviewed our contracts with suppliers and managed to save the company over $120,000 last year.

Acknowledgements

Because of confidentiality issues, some of the company names have been changed in the skills lessons.

The authors and publishers acknowledge the following sources of copyright material and are grateful for the permissions granted. While every effort has been made, it has not always been possible to identify the sources of all material used, or to trace all copyright holders. If any omissions are brought to our notice, we will be happy to include the appropriate acknowledgements on reprinting.

Text on p. 12 adapted from *An Introduction to International Marketing* by Keith Lewis and Matthew Housden. Published by Kogan Page. Reproduced with permission;

Thomson Learning for the text on p. 19 adapted from *Principles & Practice of Marketing* by Jim Blythe. Reproduced with permission;

Text on p. 20 adapted from 'Global Marketing: Tailoring Your Strategy to Fit the Culture' by Marieke de Mooij, 2010. *IESE Insight magazine*, IESE Business School, Barcelona. Reproduced with permission;

The estate of Randy Pausch for the listening activity on p. 25 reproduced from a lecture from the University of Virginia by Randy Pausch. Reproduced with permission;

Daily Mail for the text on p. 32 adapted from 'Check out the no-frills hotels' by Frank Barrett, *Mail on Sunday* 22.02.09. Copyright © Daily Mail;

HarperCollins Publishers for the text on p. 40 adapted from *Alibaba* by Liu Shiying and Martha Avery (Excerpt from pp. viii to x "Jack Ma failed the college entrance examination … are substantial"). Copyright © 2009 by Martha Avery. Original Chinese-language edition copyright © China CITIC Press and Liu Shiying. Reprinted by permission of HarperCollins Publishers;

Royal Bank of Canada for the text on p. 45 adapted from 'Business Resources – Starting a Business', www.rbcroyalbank.com/RBC:SP6j471A8cAZWB@CrU/sme/bigidea/kamiko.html. Reproduced with permission of Royal Bank of Canada;

Aon Risk Solutions for the text on p. 47 adapted from 'Keys to Success in Managing a Black Swan Event' by Nancy Green. Reproduced with permission;

Harvard Business Publishing for the text on pp. 55–56 adapted from 'Leadership That Gets Results' by Daniel Goleman, *Harvard Business Review*, March 2000. Reproduced with permission;

The Japan Times for the text on p. 68 adapted from 'Rakuten's all-English edict a bold move, but risky too' by Minoru Matsutani 16.07.10. Reproduced with permission;

Academy of Management for the text on p. 73 adapted from *The Seven Deadly Sins of Outsourcing* by Jérôme Barthélemy, Academy of Management Executive 2003, Vol. 17. No. 2. Reproduced with permission;

Listening activity on pp. 75–76 from an interview with Gillian Virata. Reproduced with permission;

Business Today (India) for the text on p. 84 adapted from 'Made in India, for the world' by N. Madhavan 30.05.10, www.syndicationstoday.com. Reproduced from Business Today © 2012. LMIL. All rights reserved;

Harvard Business Publishing for the text on p. 86 reprinted from "How GE Is Disrupting Itself" by Jeffrey R. Immelt, Vijay Govindarajan, Chris Trimble, Harvard Business Review, September 2009. Reproduced with permission;

Dyson for the text on pp. 93–94 adapted from www.dyson.co.uk/insidedyson. Reproduced with permission;

Unilever for the text on p. 104 adapted from 'Unilever Annual Report and Accounts 2009', www.unilever.com/images/ir_Unilever_AR09_tcm13-208066.pdf. Reproduced with permission;

Listening activity on p. 106 adapted from a webinar presentation by Josh Crandall. Copyright © 2009 Netpop Research, LLC;

Text on p. 109 adapted from *Making Globalization Work* by Joseph E. Stiglitz. Copyright © 2006 by Joseph E. Stiglitz. Used by permission of W.W. Norton & Company, Inc. Reproduced by permission of Penguin Books Ltd;

Indiana Business Review for the text on pp. 119–120 adapted from 'The Triple Bottom Line: What Is It and How Does It Work' by Timothy F. Slaper, Ph.D., and Tanya J. Hall. Reproduced with permission;

Trashy Bags for the text on p. 130 adapted from 'Trashy Background', www.trashybags.org/background.htm. Reproduced with permission;

Trashy Bags for the text on p. 131 adapted from 'Trashy Briefcase & Laptop Bag', www.trashybags.org/laptop.htm. Reproduced with permission;

The publishers are grateful to the following for permission to reproduce copyright photographs and material:

p.3(TC): © Stuart Gold/Trashy Bags; p.3(BR&BC):Bloomberg/Getty Images; p.3(CR): © Clive Green/PA Photos; p.3:© Dr Fons Trompenaars; p.3: © Professor Jane Wei-Skillern; p.3: © Dr Helen Haugh; p.10/11(T): Crestock.com; p.10(B): © Dr Dennis De; p.13(T):© Quintessentially; p.13(B): © Paul Drummond; p.15: © Quintessentially; p.16: © Dimitry Shironosov; p.17(L): Bloomberg/Getty Images; p.17(C): © Ian Dagnall/Alamy; p.17(R): © Lou Linwei/Alamy; p.18: p.21(L): © Rudianto A/Demotix/Corbis; p.21(CR):© Richard Cohen/Corbis; p.21(T): ©Rob Roxton/iStockphoto; p.22(L): ©Constantine Sambuy; p.22(CR&B): Paramount/Kobal; p.24(TR): © Hitoshi Nishimura/Getty Images; p.24:Cartoonstock; p.25: Randy Pausch; p.26(TR): © Peter Dazeley/Getty Images; p.26(L): © Andrew Guy; p.28(R): Westend61/Getty Images; p.28(L): © Dr Alex Muresan; p.31(L): Macana/Alamy; p.31(R): Newscast/Alamy; p.33: Shutterstock; p.34: © Bizantra.com; p.36: Lightspring/Shutterstock; p.37(L): © Dr Shai Vyakarnam; p.37(C): JGI?jamie Grill/Blend Images/Corbis; p.37(B): © Mark Romanelli/Getty Images; p.39(B,T,TR): ChinaFoto Press/Getty Images; p.42: Mediaphotos/iStockphoto; p.44(TR): Coverspot Photography/Alamy; p.44(L): Bloomberg/Getty Images; p.46(T): © Guy Crittenden/Images.com/Corbis; p.46(BL): Bloomberg/Getty Images; p.48: Picsfive/Shutterstock; p.49: CFCL Laboratories; p.50: © Brendan Dow; p.51(T): © Olaf Kowalzick/Alamy; p.51(L): Rynio Productions/Shutterstock; p.51(C): Kurhan/Shutterstock; p.51(B): © Yuri Arcurs/Shutterstock; p.52: © Piotr Marcinski/Shutterstock; p.54(TR): © Rowan Foster/Corbis; p.54(R): © Paul Shoul; p.54(L): © Frank Ward/iStockphoto; p.54(C): © Helen King/Corbis; p.55: © Daniel Goleman; p.57: © Nikki Ward; p.59: © Alashi/iStockphoto; p.60(T): © Alex Livesy/Getty Images; p.60(R): © Roberto Serra/Getty Images; p.60(L): © David Prasher; p.62: ImageZoo/Alamy; p.64: Taxi/Getty Images; p.65: © Fons Trompenaars; p.67: Bloomberg/Getty Images; p.70: Shutterstock; p.71(T): © Hiro Tanaka; p.71(L): © Nikki King; p.71(B): © Charlie Peppiatt; p.72: © John S Dykes/Getty Images; p.75(TL): BPAP; p.75(BL): Getty Images; p.77: © Dondi Tawatao/Getty Images; p.78: © Joe Baker; p.80: ImageZoo/Alamy; p.82: Getty Images; p.85(TL): Bloomberg/Getty Images; p.85(TR): India Today Group/Getty Images; p.85(CR): Gusto Images/Science Photo Library; p.86(CL): © Martial Trezzini/PA Photos; p.86(C): © Gurinder Osan/PA Photos; p.87: ©Victor Savuskin/Alamy; p.88: Fancy/Corbis; p.90: Shutterstock; p.90(R): Getty Images; p.90: © Dr Clare Brass; p.91(BL): Hulton Archive/Getty Images; p.91(BR): © Justin Sullivan/Getty Images; p.92(T): © Feng Zhao/Alamy; p.92(CR): Getty Images; p.92(C): © Jorg Gruel/Getty Images; p.92(BL): © Simon Hindley/Alamy; p.92(BR): © Anneka/Shutterstock; p.93(R): KPA/Zuma/Rex Features; p.93(C&T): Getty Images; p.94(C), Dyson Press Office; p.94(B): © Derek Hudson/Getty Images; p.95: © Clive Green/PA Photos; p.96: © Robert Glusic/Getty Images; p.98: © Dimitry Shironosov; p.100: © Sunisa Botas/Shutterstock; p.101: © Dr Tatiana Damjanovic; p.102: Cartoon Stock; p.103: Imagine China/Corbis;p.108(T): AFP/Getty Images; p.108(B): © Alessandro Della Bella/epa/Corbis; p.111(T): © Jerome Wilson/Alamy; p.113: © Vivianne Moos/Corbis;p.114: Photo Alto/Alamy;p.118(T): AVTG/iStockphoto; p.118(L): © Kyu Oh/iStockphoto; p.118(R): © Nikada/iStockphoto; p.121(T): Getty Images; p.121(C&R): Bloomberg/Getty Images; p.124(L): Fotolia; p.124(R):© Lisa F Young/Shutterstock; p.124(T): Getty Images; p.126(TR): Brians/Shutterstock; p.126(L): © Kirll Livshitsky/Shutterstock; p.126(R):© Kailash K Soni/Shutterstock; p.126(C): Havensen/Shutterstock; p.126(B):© Anneka/Shutterstock; p.127(R): © Professor Jane Wei-Skillern; p.127(L):© Dr Helen Haugh; p.129/130: © Stuart Gold/Trashy Bags; p.132(TL):© Christian Rummel; p.132(TR): Lelu Concepts/iStockphoto; p.132(CR): Stocklite/ Shutterstock; p.134: AgeFotoStock/Getty Images; p.138: © Lauren Hom; p.140: Getty Images; p.142: © Mark Jephcott/Irn Bru; p.144: Everett Kennedy Brown/epa/Corbis.

Coverphoto: istockphoto/Nikada

Photos sourced by: Alison Prior

Proofreader: Marcus Fletcher

The publisher has used its best endeavours to ensure that the URLs for external websites referred to in this book are correct and active at the time of going to press. However, the publisher has no responsibility for the websites and can make no guarantee that a site will remain live or that the content is or will remain appropriate.